Secrets to
Success
for SCIENCE TEACHERS

ELLEN KOTTLER • VICTORIA BROOKHART COSTA

CORWIN
A SAGE Company

For information:

Corwin
A SAGE Company
2455 Teller Road
Thousand Oaks, California 91320
(800) 233-9936
Fax: (800) 417-2466
www.corwinpress.com

SAGE Ltd.
1 Oliver's Yard
55 City Road
London EC1Y 1SP
United Kingdom

SAGE India Pvt. Ltd.
B 1/I 1 Mohan Cooperative
    Industrial Area
Mathura Road,
New Delhi 110 044
India

SAGE Asia-Pacific Pte. Ltd.
33 Pekin Street #02-01
Far East Square
Singapore 048763

Printed in the United States of America.

Library of Congress Cataloging-in-Publication Data

Kottler, Ellen.
Secrets to success for science teachers/Ellen Kottler and Victoria Brookhart Costa.
        p. cm.
Includes bibliographical references and index.
ISBN 978-1-4129-6625-2 (cloth)
ISBN 978-1-4129-6626-9 (pbk.)

    1. Science—Study and teaching. 2. Science teachers. I. Costa, Victoria Brookhart. II. Title.

LB1585.K68 2009
372.35'044—dc22   2008046601

This book is printed on acid-free paper.

09   10   11   12   13   10   9   8   7   6   5   4   3   2   1

Acquisitions Editor:	Jessica Allan
Editorial Assistant:	Joanna Coelho
Production Editor:	Amy Schroller
Copy Editor:	Susan Jarvis
Typesetter:	C&M Digitals (P) Ltd.
Proofreader:	Cheryl Rivard
Indexer:	Judy Hunt
Cover Designer:	Lisa Riley
Graphic Designer:	Anthony Paular

Contents

History of Science Topics

Acknowledgments

The authors would like to thank all the students and teachers who contributed the insights and inspirations of their classroom experiences. They would like to express their gratitude to Helen P. and Glenn Taylor for encouraging and facilitating their many and varied endeavors throughout the years at Cal State Fullerton and to Nancy P. Gallavan for her congeniality, camaraderie, and collegiality.

Ellen would like to thank her family, Jeffrey, Meredith, and Cary Kottler. Victoria would like to thank her family, John and Jesse Costa and Rachael Blasko.

Along with the dedicated professionals at Corwin, the contributions of the following reviewers are gratefully acknowledged:

Regina Brinker
Middle School Science Teacher
Christensen Middle School
Livermore, CA

Lisa Edwards, NBCT
Hickory High School
Science Department
Hickory, NC

Darleen Horton
Science Lab Teacher
Chenoweth Elementary
Presidential Awardee Teacher
    (Science) (K–6)
Louisville, KY

Sally Koczan
Science Specialist
Meramec Elementary School
Clayton, MO

Chris S. Sefcheck
AP Biology/Biology Honors
Coronado High School
Henderson, NV

Sara Sefcheck
Science Teacher
Coronado High School
Henderson, NV

Melissa Wikler
Clark County School District
Las Vegas, NV

About the Authors

 **Ellen Kottler, EdS,** has been a teacher for over thirty years in public and private schools, alternative schools, adult education programs, and universities. She has worked in inner-city schools as well as in suburban and rural settings. She was a curriculum specialist for one of the country's largest school districts. Ellen is the coauthor of *Secrets for Secondary School Teachers: How to Succeed in Your First Year* (2004), *On Being a Teacher* (2005), *Secrets for Beginning Elementary School Teachers* (2007), *Counseling Skills for Teachers* (2007), *Secrets to Success for Social Studies Teachers* (2008), and *English Language Learners in Your Classroom: Strategies That Work* (2008).

Ellen is a Lecturer in the Secondary Education Department at California State University, Fullerton.

 **Victoria Costa, PhD,** is the Director of Science Education at California State University, Fullerton. She has taught chemistry, biology, physics, mathematics, and education at the secondary, community college, and university levels. Her research focuses on the recruitment, development, and support of secondary science teachers and the preparation of all teachers to support twenty-first-century learning in technology-rich environments. She is a consultant for Intel® Education and The JASON Project, and has been the principal investigator for several million-dollar grants to support math and science education, including the Professional Development Resources Online for Mathematics (PD-ROM), Collaborating for Excellence in Middle School Science (CEMSS), and the Math and Science

Teachers Project (MAST). She has published in highly respected journals, including the *Journal of Curriculum Studies*, *Journal of College Science Teaching*, *Science Education*, *International Journal of Science Education*, and *Journal of Research in Science Teaching*.

Introduction

Teaching science—what an awesome responsibility! How do teachers develop relationships with their students and cover the entire required curriculum? Where do they find all the materials and resources to engage students in inquiry learning? What do they do to create communities of learners who become active problem solvers? These are just a few of the many questions most science teachers ask themselves every day.

We have written this book to provide practical ideas, strategies, and insights to help you answer these questions. *Secrets to Success for Science Teachers* includes essential topics that teachers face, from setting up a science classroom and establishing routines to planning meaningful instruction and assessment, building literacy, integrating technology, using a plethora of science resources, establishing relationships with families, and networking with colleagues. With these suggestions, you will be on your way to success in creating an academic environment of collaboration and creativity where differences are honored in a community of learners.

AUDIENCE

We have written this book for all educators who specialize in science education. You include middle-level teachers found in elementary schools and secondary teachers in middle schools or junior high schools and high schools. You teach lessons or courses in general science, or your courses address life science, Earth science, physical science, biology, chemistry, physics, or environmental science exclusively.

This book is also valuable for experienced science teachers, as well as department chairs—especially those teachers seeking

1

guidance and support advancing their professional growth and development. Additionally, we have written this book for preservice teachers enrolled in science methods courses as part of their teacher education programs at universities, colleges, community colleges, or nontraditional licensure programs sponsored by state and county departments of education and school districts.

The concepts and practices presented in this book will benefit every methods instructor in preparing new teachers and help every master teacher, teacher educator, and administrator when mentoring or supervising science teachers.

OVERVIEW

This book provides a detailed overview of effective science education within the diverse context of today's schools and classrooms. Based on research in the field, it contains a multitude of pragmatic guidelines, checklists and resources, and secrets to ensure your immediate success.

Chapter 1 begins with a tour of your school and classroom as you orient yourself for your teaching assignment, setting up your room, establishing policies and procedures, and creating a shared learning environment.

Chapter 2 helps you understand how science standards, state content standards, and district expectations work together to frame your district curriculum.

Chapter 3 focuses on teaching science through an inquiry method that utilizes the scientific method and investigation.

Chapters 4 through 8 address meaningful instruction by knowing your students, identifying objectives, choosing assessments, lesson planning, and selecting purposeful activities accompanied by engaging projects to connect students with their communities.

Chapter 9 describes how to incorporate a variety of resources, including models and specimens, plants and animals, videos, slide presentations, and field trips.

Chapter 10 explores using a variety of technologies in the classroom, working with Web sites, and integrating critical thinking tools.

Chapter 11 suggests a wide range of additional activities to enrich learning, including science programs, science fairs, competitions, guest speakers, service learning, clubs, and community resources.

Chapter 12 suggests ways to collaborate with colleagues through teams and departments, and other school personnel.

Finally, Chapter 13 encourages teachers to reflect on their practices and plan for their future professional development.

FEATURES

A special feature of each chapter is a highlighted section related to the history of science. You will also find Web references and practical examples from all areas of science integrated throughout the book. At the end of each chapter is a list of professional development activities to extend and personalize the content. Finally, you will see suggestions—secrets that experienced teachers have discovered—to organize, simplify, and enrich the learning that takes place inside and outside the classroom. To this we add a sprinkling of voices from students.

A FINAL NOTE

We invite each of you to adapt the tips and strategies offered in this book to your own unique situations. We hope you will customize and extend the information within each chapter for your teaching style and your students. We think you will soon discover that the entire book offers a wealth of ideas that will help you become more competent, confident, and ready as a science teacher.

CHAPTER ONE

Design Your Classroom *to Create Communities of Learners*

Science is a great game. It is inspiring and refreshing. The playing field is the universe itself.

—Isidor Isaac Rabi (1898–1988), 1944 Nobel Laureate in Physics for his resonance method of recording the magnetic properties of atomic nuclei.

How exciting! You have been given your teaching assignment and handed the key to a classroom. Now it is time to use your knowledge, skills, and experience to create a community of learners. Your first task is to set the stage for effective teaching and learning every day in your own science classroom. Your stage, as Isidor Isaac Rabi notes, is the universe itself.

EXPLORE YOUR SCHOOL AND CLASSROOM

Take a tour and see your school in action. As you walk around the building, take note of the layout and activities. Consider these questions: Are classrooms grouped by department or grade level? Do students enter from the outside or from an inside hallway? What types of projects do you see students engaged in, especially in the science classes? How and where do teachers obtain books and supplies? Where is your room located in relation to the other school facilities?

Here are some items you will want to see and discuss in order to be prepared for the first day of school:

District and School Offices and Areas

- Location of the district offices, staff development center, and instructional media center
- Location of the school main office, health office, restrooms, and lunchroom
- Location of the school library, media center, and technology labs
- Location of faculty parking and whether a permit is required
- Directions to the faculty lounge and restrooms

School and District Policies

- Copy of the school district teacher handbook and curriculum guide(s) for each course you are assigned
- Copy of the student handbook
- Copies of the school calendar and schedule
- Web addresses for all district and school programs and resources, including any user IDs and passwords

Science Teaching Assignment and Department

- List of your tentatively assigned grade levels and courses
- Copies of the course textbooks, laboratory manuals, supplements, and syllabi
- List of your assigned students noted with special needs (including learning, social, family, and health) and

information on whether you will have any instructional aides to support these students
- Location of your classroom (or rooms if you will be a traveling teacher)
- Location of laboratory classrooms (if different from your home classroom); portable laboratory equipment; supply cabinets and chemical stockroom; schedules/sign-up process for use of space and resources (if appropriate); safety resources; water, electricity, and gas access and emergency shutoffs
- Types of student desks or tables and chairs assigned to your classroom
- Availability of bulletin boards and display spaces in your classroom and hallway
- Availability of technology resources and storage areas within and near your classroom
- Location of your team/department office or planning room and storage areas

As you become acquainted with each of these items, you will generate more questions and begin to plan for your students. This "preview of coming attractions" will help you get centered and enhance your peace of mind about your career as a science teacher. We will discuss these items in much more detail throughout the upcoming chapters.

MEET YOUR DEPARTMENT AND TEAM

You are going to spend most of your school time outside of your classroom with your department or team members. Although you may have been hired to teach specific science courses, you also were hired to fit into a particular group of people. Most teams want you to be an individual who successfully balances working on your own with working with others. You may be sharing students with other teachers; you may be team teaching with other teachers. You may work together to develop lesson plans and standards-based benchmark assessments to monitor student progress. Each teacher will contribute to both your immediate effectiveness and long-term success in some way. And each teacher will have more or different experiences than you bring to share with you. Our first secret for success is for you to learn from each person's strengths and expertise as you refine your skills and independence.

Many schools are organized into grade levels or academic departments with a group leader known as a department chair. Department chairs usually have been teaching at their schools a long time. They will likely be the ones to help you get your course textbooks, supplementary materials, and classroom supplies. Sometimes department chairs determine course assignments and periods taught. They can usually link you to professional organizations and professional development opportunities. You may also be assigned a mentor who will be able to answer your questions and share information about school policies and procedures.

> *I meet once a week for planning with other science teachers. We share ideas, labs, and lesson plans.*
>
> *—Seventh-grade life science teacher*

INVESTIGATE YOUR SCHOOL'S AND COMMUNITY'S HISTORY AND CUSTOMS

School buildings are frequently named for individuals who may be famous nationally or well known locally. Sometimes the namesake is still living, visits the school, and makes donations. It is exciting when you and your students meet the person for whom your school is named, and learn what contributions this person made to the community to receive this recognition. Or there may be a business or industry that partners with your school, providing mentoring, materials, and professional development for teachers.

Investigate your school's background. Frequently there are trophy cases, wall plaques, and group photographs displayed throughout the building. One secret is to look at the annual yearbooks to explore school traditions and learn the names of teachers. These may be housed in the library. If you ask about your school in the faculty lounge or department planning room, it is likely that someone will be happy to share stories of the school's history. It is both fun and informative to find out more about your school.

Your school also functions around a set of customs and traditions (Cattani, 2002). By watching and listening carefully, you will realize and be able to promote and replicate the accepted ways of doing things at your new school. You will learn who is responsible for various aspects of the school's operations, how teachers and administrators expect you and your students to behave, and so forth. These are excellent topics to discuss with your department chair, team members, and/or a mentor. Current students, alumni, families, and the community look forward to annual and special events.

And don't forget to consider the local culture of the area. See Box 1.1 for examples of science in the local culture of the area. Explore the unique features of your community and region.

BOX 1.1

Examples of Connections
Between Local Culture and Science

- **Oldest Tree in Anaheim**—Science teachers in Anaheim, California, might use the "oldest tree in Anaheim" as a starting point for discussing botany. This Moreton Bay fig is over 150 years old and is situated on the property of the Anaheim Mother Colony house of the original settlement in the area. The tree is one of the largest of the particular species found in the Southern California region.
- **Santa Ana River Bottom**—In Riverside, California, science teachers often take students on field trips to the Santa Ana River Bottom. As is true for much of California, the geology of the Santa Ana River watershed is defined and created by seismic activity. Lessons may focus on the geological features, water demand, or plants and animals of the region.
- **San Diego Kumeyaay**—Ethnobotany is the study of the plant lore and agricultural customs of a group of people. The Kumeyaay were among the earliest inhabitants of the San Diego area, and they took advantage of the food and plants in many different habitats in order to survive.

ACCESS TEXTBOOKS AND EQUIPMENT

Once you've obtained copies of your course textbooks and sample syllabi, you may begin reading them to prepare for the coming school year. Also ask for the teacher's manuals for your text, laboratory manual, and supplementary print and electronic teaching materials that either accompany the books or have been purchased for your courses. Some of these items may be available at the district, so explore thoroughly. The teacher's version of your laboratory manual is very important; it will include all the instructions for setting up the laboratory activities and mixing necessary solutions.

BOX 1.2

Science Materials and Equipment

- **Technology Resources**—including SMART Board; overhead and/or ELMO or other electric imaging projector; document camera; television; DVD, CD, and/or videotape player(s); computers—desktops, laptops; or AlphaSmarts*; printers, scanners, copiers; Internet connections for one or more computers; LCD projector and large screen for projection; cameras, probes, recorders, and other devices to record observations; and audience response systems for interactive slide presentations
- **Permanent Equipment**—including student laboratory stations and storage facilities
- **Visual Aids**—including specimens, models, prepared slides, charts, and posters
- **Portable Laboratory Equipment**—including animal cages; balances, meters, testers, and scales; Bunsen burners and laboratory torches; brushes and sponges; buzzers and bells; ball and ring apparatus; carts and dollies; centrifuges; clamps, ties, rings, hooks, and support stands; electroscopes and calorimeters; dissection equipment; filters; glassware; incubators; hot plates and lamps; microscopes, cameras, and telescopes; motors and generators; magnets; optical filters; stools; timers; tongs, tweezers, and scissors; and wave machines
- **Safety Equipment**—including aprons, disinfectants, eye protection, eye washes, fire protection blankets, first aid, fume hoods, gloves, safety charts and posters, sanitation products, and waste containers
- **Materials and Supplies**—including pH and chromatography papers and materials, specimens, indicators and test solutions, chemicals, lens-cleaning products, lubricants and adhesives, microplate supplies, batteries, bulbs, biological, balance papers, paper towels, and water and soil test kits

Take inventory of the various kinds of available teaching equipment and resources. Inquire whether there is a catalog of your school and/or district video and software collections. The types of equipment you can easily access certainly will impact the ways that you plan and implement your teaching strategies and learning experiences. You will need information on how science supplies are obtained and funded, how to make purchase order requests, whether personal expenses will be reimbursed, and even whether there is a limit on the number of photocopies allowed each semester. Begin a wish list of items you would like to obtain when there is money available in the school budget or a grant-writing opportunity arises. Check to see whether your district has equipment standards for science class-rooms. See Box 1.2 for suggested science materials and equipment.

If you conduct an Internet search on "grants for science teachers," you will find an extensive list. Get ideas at Vernier's Grant Writing Guide at www.vernier.com/grants and the Texas Instruments Funding Sources Grantwriting Site at http://education .ti.com/educationportal/sites/US/sectionHome/grantandfunding .html. You might also consider:

- **Toyota TAPESTRY Grants for Science Teachers:** www.nsta.org/pd/tapestry. Grants up to $10,000 for pro-jects that promote exciting and innovative activities to motivate students in science.
- **Toshiba America Foundation:** www.toshiba.com/tafpub/ jsp/home/default.jsp. Grants for projects in math and sci-ence designed by classroom teachers to improve instruction for students in Grades K–12.

PLAN FOR EXPLORATION AND EXPERIMENTATION

My room is arranged in small pods/groups. I believe it is essential so that students have the opportunity to work together in cooperative groups.

—*Seventh-grade science teacher*

The classroom environment sets the tone for your students (Kottler, Kottler, & Kottler, 2004). You want your room to be both attractive and functional. It should be a place where students feel welcome, safe, and comfortable. Post your name and room number near the door. If possible, place a science-related picture on or beside the door that indicates the subjects taught in your room.

To begin, imagine what your students as well as other visitors will see as they first enter, and display science materials and objects in this space. You may use specimens, equipment, models, timelines, posters, books, and so forth. To stimulate new ideas, periodically change your exhibits to reflect the topics and issues that you are studying in your courses. Display data and reports created by your students. Your goal is to captivate your students' interest and to communicate that engaging, challenging, and rewarding science education is happening in your classroom.

Second, arrange desks and furniture to allow students to move around the room quickly and easily; they need to be able to see you and the boards without any obstructions. Position the desks or tables into groups, semicircles or circles, or a horseshoe shape to offer the most effective learning environments for your activities. Seating arrangements reflect your teaching styles. You want students to interact with one another and to work in collaborative learning groups. Sitting at tables, desks, or laboratory stations grouped in fours can facilitate these activities readily.

I like the classroom arranged with lab partners, so if you don't understand anything, you can get help, and have someone to work with.

—Amy, age fourteen, ninth grade

Third, determine where you will place three-dimensional items, such as specimens and models. For example, your room might have terrariums, fish tanks, skeletons, and/or rock collections. Some objects you will let students handle, while others may be fragile and personal and you will want students to only look at them. Strategically place bookshelves, side tables, and/or display cases within students' view. Then move other furniture, such as filing cabinets, to the walls or corners where students can access them for books, materials, and supplies; this way, you will see all parts of the room. You may have to make accommodations if your classroom is small, the seating is fixed, or other furniture is immovable.

Fourth, consider where to place your desk and your personal cabinets and shelves. You need a place away from students' eyes and fingers to store your computer, grade book, student information cards, and lesson plans. Some teachers want their desks placed near the door; others want them near the front of the classroom, which is usually where the SMART Boards or whiteboards are located. Other teachers want their desks placed near the back of the classroom. Each location has benefits and limitations, and each teacher is unique. We suggest that you walk through other teachers' classrooms and see how they are arranged. You might want to match them since it will be the configuration that the students will expect. Or you might want to be different to capture your students' attention and signal what activities they will engage in while in science class.

Fifth, dedicate distinct portions of your walls to highlight each course that you are teaching. This space may include your national, state, or district content standards as well as a weekly calendar of lessons and activities. Save one area for general information. Use bulletin boards or cork strips to post reference information and related articles from newspapers, magazines, and journals. Set aside a special section to recognize student work. Here are two extremely important secrets. First, find ways to display samples of every student's work from all your courses, and rotate the student work regularly throughout the school year. We also encourage you to display emergency procedures near the door and prepare everyone for all types of emergencies and evacuation from the first day of school. See Box 1.3 for suggested materials and purposes for science bulletin board displays.

BOX 1.3

Materials and Purposes for Science
Bulletin Board Displays

- Visual aids *to build background knowledge*
- Political spectrum *to illustrate varying perspectives on a scientific issue*
- Prompts *to stimulate discussion*
- Quotes by historical and contemporary figures *to inspire student actions and interaction*
- Current event articles from journals, newspapers, and magazines *to connect science to students' daily lives*
- Science-related humor, including jokes and cartoons, *to put a human face on science*
- Examples of professionals in science-related pursuits *to identify science careers*
- Examples, charts, and tables *to provide advance organization for student thinking*
- Timelines *to relate the perspective of time and events in the past or present*
- Rubrics *to show criteria for student work*
- Displays *to recognize students' accomplishments*

COLLECT MATERIALS AND RESOURCES

It is time to brainstorm the kinds of materials and resources you would like to use to make your curriculum and instruction come alive. Look through your textbooks to identify the topics and issues to be covered. Consider what supplies you want for experiments and demonstrations, and what items you will use to illustrate concepts emphasized in your units and lessons, such as charts, tables, photographs, models, and specimens. A subscription to a science trade magazine, such as *Discover* or *National Geographic*, will provide pictures that can quickly be clipped, laminated, and used to create an interesting display on science-related issues. In addition, local utility Web sites often offer free information on energy conservation. Consider using your own photos and videos—this also demonstrates your enthusiasm for science and commitment to lifelong learning. Borrow educational and scientific catalogs from your school's department chair or librarian. We suggest you familiarize yourself with the following scientific catalogs:

- *Flinn Scientific:* www.flinnsci.com
- *Carolina Biological Supply:* www.carolina.com
- *Fisher Science Education:* www.fishersci.com
- *Science Lab:* www.sciencelab.com

Student work is another source of visual aids to introduce and reinforce concepts. One high school–level idea is to assign "element posters" and laminate the best ones for display and to use as a model in the future. At the middle school level, students might complete an oceanography art project with the creation of three-dimensional models of the ocean. Students at any grade level will benefit from creating models of the solar system, plant and animal cells, and molecules, and these models can decorate your classroom in the years to come.

Consider also what specific classroom supplies, such as calculators, graph paper, colored pencils and markers, and construction paper, students will need to use in class. Place these materials in plastic bags on shelves, or in storage bins for easy student access, cleanup, and check-in. Take time to collect materials to keep you organized, such as plastic crates, stackable baskets, or colored file folders. You may store some of these items in your classroom, some in the department or grade-level office, and some at home. You will be amazed at how quickly supplemental materials will accumulate, and in science classrooms they take up a great deal of room. You will also want to talk to your department chair and science colleagues to determine what resources the school already has. Other items may be purchased online or from your local teacher supply store. Schools vary in their budgets and procedures for obtaining resources.

INVESTIGATE LABORATORY SPACE AND EQUIPMENT

We use balances, Bunsen burners, microscopes, and many other scientific instruments in the lab. We have SMART Boards too.

—Robin, age sixteen, eleventh grade

When your students conduct investigations and experiments, they need appropriate space and equipment. An ideal secondary science facility should include the following (Butin, 2000):

- *Laboratory space to conduct investigations.* This space should include flat, durable top surfaces with adequate natural and task lighting. Sinks and electrical/gas outlets should be placed along the perimeter of the room. All science room, preparation room, and storage room doors should lock. Safety equipment and rules should be easily accessible.

- *Preparation room.* The preparation room should be directly accessible from the classroom and may be restricted to teacher preparation for experiments. The room should have the necessary utilities—electricity and water—to prepare for and conduct classroom projects. The room should also have a phone, an acid-resistant sink with hot and cold water, an ice-making refrigerator, and the capacity to handle specialized fixtures such as an autoclave or distiller.

- *Storage room.* This room should be used primarily for the storage of chemicals, specimens, and materials. To prevent sparks and potential explosions, there should be no electrical or gas outlets in this room. A fire-resistant storage cabinet and/or noncorroding acid cabinet (situated below eye level) should used to store hazardous materials. Storage areas should also be earthquake safe.

- *Greenhouse or greenspace.* A greenhouse can greatly enhance the curricular offerings of the science program. The greenhouse should range from 200 to 400 square feet; have separate thermostatic controls, access to ample water, a floor drain, and humidity control;

and be able to function when school is not in session. If a greenhouse is not possible, a greenspace can be established in a large corner of the classroom.

With large classes, teachers often divide students into groups and set up learning centers or stations where they take turns engaging in different activities. Students may either be assigned to or self-select from a list of varied assignments. Or half the students might work on assignments at their seats while the rest perform laboratory experiments. Teachers then have the opportunity to meet with students individually or with small groups to answer questions, monitor progress, and adjust instruction and assessment as needed.

> *I change my room depending on the unit. Sometimes I set up a hands-on station at the back table. Or, to form expert groups, students move their desks into quads.*
>
> —*Third-grade teacher*

SAFELY USE AND STORE SUPPLIES AND EQUIPMENT

Safety is of paramount importance. Bunsen burners, chemicals, and dissection tools are just a few of the multiple hazards lurking in every science classroom. Butin (2000) recommends that all science facilities should have a hands-free eye wash, fire blanket, fire extinguisher, and first-aid kit. A chemical hygiene plan should be revised annually to identify potential health and safety hazards in the classroom and laboratory, precautions and preventive measures that are in place, and required safety rules and procedures. If the space is to be used for chemistry or advanced biology classes, you should consider installing a fume hood and safety shower. A clearly marked master cutoff switch for utilities should be readily accessible, and the classroom area should have easily accessible telephones to summon emergency technicians. Resource A at the end of the book provides a science safety checklist for the classroom.

ESTABLISH YOUR POLICIES AND PROCEDURES

> *One of my favorite expressions is: Don't forget your PANTS (pencil, assignment, notebook, textbook, and smile).*
>
> —*Middle school math teacher*

There are three sources to consult as you establish your classroom policies and procedures. You will need to comply with regulations adopted by the school district (i.e., dress code and weapons), school building (i.e., hall passes and tardies), and your team or department (i.e., interactions and assignments). You want to be firm, fair, consistent, and—most of all—patient as you reflect all three layers of regulations and express your own style. Keep in mind that, for most of you, your students spend only one class session a day with you. They move through many different spaces and must comply with everyone's expectations. Your environment communicates your plans and makes teaching and learning the focus of the school day.

You have several choices when it comes to establishing classroom policies and procedures. Although you could simply tell your students how you expect them to act in your classroom, we encourage you to model effective science by brainstorming possibilities, examining rationale, and reaching consensus. Try accomplishing this during the first few days of class. Divide the class into small cooperative learning groups, and ask each group to construct a list of classroom expectations along with associated consequences (rewards and punishments). Prompt your students to write the list as positive rather than negative statements. You will have to decide whether you want to call them rules or whether you think that term conveys negativity.

I think that the way to make rules is for students to make suggestions. Obviously for science, there are some rules that have to be made, but for everything else, students and teachers can make them together.

—Maggie, age fourteen, ninth grade

You might be amazed at the detailed lists your students will generate. Through consensus, you and your students can determine which expectations to adopt and how they will be managed. You will discover that some items can be grouped together into one overarching expectation, some items have multiple implications, and some items you need to maintain control over. These discoveries are all part of the negotiation and consensus building— excellent models of science processes used in the real world. If you have multiple classes, you will have to decide whether you want one set of expectations for all your classes or whether you want to customize the expectations for each of your classes. Keep in mind the need to revisit and revise both the expectations and the processes from time to time, just as scientists revise theories.

When you talk with your colleagues, you may find that most of them follow similar procedures. This approach makes it much easier for your students and for you, if you are comfortable with the procedures. Then you can discuss the outcome with your team to make changes as a group or individually.

> *All of my rules are stated positively. For instance, treat others as you would like to be treated, help keep our classroom a neat and orderly place to learn, and be accountable for your actions.*
>
> —*Eighth-grade science teacher*

CREATE A SHARED LEARNING ENVIRONMENT

Your goal is to make your classroom a shared learning environment. Therefore, you need to refer to it as "our classroom" rather than "my classroom." The same advice applies to your classroom management. By setting expectations together, you and your students have a sense of ownership and responsibility relative to how everyone will participate in the shared learning community.

Some student expectations from the school and/or district include:

1. Wear clothing in compliance with the dress code.
2. Respect all people and the school campus.
3. Avoid gum, tobacco products, cell phones, and music players on campus.

Some student expectations from teachers include:

1. Arrive to class on time ready to participate.
2. Bring supplies and assignments to class every day.
3. Do your best on every assignment.

Some student expectations from the students include:

1. Talk only at appropriate times and in consideration of other speakers.
2. Use polite language and speaking tones.
3. Take responsibility for your actions.

There will be several opportunities to review these expectations and share them with your students' parents and families. Most schools require them to be posted on classroom walls, and included in the information sent home with letters of introduction at the beginning of the school year, and at "Back to School" night. Parents/guardians will also appreciate information on how to contact you (school telephone number, time to call, and school e-mail address).

ENSURE EQUITY AND FAIRNESS

You want to be fair (Danielson, 1996), you want your students to understand fairness and act fairly, you want to ensure fairness among your students, and you want your students to appreciate fairness in the classroom and in the world. Fairness entails a significant concept of science that assures that everyone is provided equity and justice. Think of this as providing everyone equal information, access, and opportunity (Gallavan, in press) for effective learning and living.

Equity and fairness do not mean you treat all students exactly the same. Some students will require more time and attention; some students will need less energy. You need to be aware of each of your students' individual needs and interests so you can provide for them appropriately. And not all students will need the same amount of attention at the same time. Equity and fairness should be considered in terms of what you think or believe is a student's past performance, what you see is a student's immediate progress, and what you predict is a student's long-term potential. These conditions are all important aspects of equity and fairness. The triad of performance, progress, and potential can guide you in working with your students throughout the school year. See Box 1.4 for suggestions for establishing equity and fairness in the classroom.

BOX 1.4

Suggestions for Establishing Equity and Fairness

1. Establish and maintain high academic and social expectations for all of your students at all times.

2. Share expectations with students and parents in writing.

3. Model and reinforce respect and politeness with everyone at all times.

4. Apologize sincerely when you make a mistake.

5. Provide specific feedback and show genuine appreciation. If you applaud for one presentation, you must applaud for all.

6. Allow students to finish speaking and redirect interruptions, although you may have to ask students to keep their comments to a limited amount of time.

7. Select students equitably, using name cards, sticks, or tokens (for questions, comments, activities, errands, and so forth). All students need to know that they should be prepared at all times and that you have both the right and responsibility to call on them at any time.

8. Delve fairly; this means that you probe and follow up with all students using higher-order and critical thinking.

9. Use a stopwatch or clock to monitor ample wait time when asking students questions or giving them instructions to demonstrate an action. Your students will appreciate the consistency.

10. Establish clear consequences for students who cannot show respect and fairness for others.

USE APPROPRIATE AND NEUTRAL LANGUAGE

Your students and their families look to you as a positive role model. For some of your students, you are one of the few educated individuals who will help prepare them for their future studies and career success. And for some of your students, English is a language they are learning. They need to hear, speak, write, and read proper English in both formal and informal conversations and written communications.

Using gender-neutral language is important for both modeling and inclusion. Be aware of your word choices so your female students feel valued and all your students experience the power of language. When addressing your students collectively, call them "ladies and gentlemen," rather than "girls and boys" or "guys" for everyone. When referencing professions, use words such as "firefighter" and "police officer," rather than "fireman" and "policeman." Use the term "humankind," rather than "mankind," when talking about all people. You might want to ask a colleague to listen to your word choices to be sure you are using appropriate and gender-neutral language.

The same guidelines apply to using culturally sensitive language. You want to be aware if you use any inappropriate cultural references or imply bias. Sometimes teachers make comments that communicate prejudice, such as stereotyping or making negative comments about the nutrition or health practices of a particular people as a whole. All educators must be cognizant of their word choices. And as science teachers, we should lead others in this effort. You should emphasize that science is and has been done by men and women of all cultures. Textbooks often emphasize the contributions of Western Europeans. You will want to make sure that you included examples of scientific discoveries from all over the world. Our History of Science examples, used throughout this book, are provided to demonstrate this diversity of discovery. See Box 1.5, which provides a summary of how multiple scientists were involved in the development of an understanding of germs and the cause of disease. In addition, Chapter 10 includes a list of Web resources for information on women and minority scientists.

BOX 1.5

History of Science

Microbes or Miasmas?

Dutch lens maker Antoni van Leeuwenhoek (1632–1723), playing with a newly invented microscope, scraped some plaque off his own teeth and looked at it through a microscope. To his horror, he observed tiny organisms or "wee animalcules," invisible to the naked eye.

About two centuries later, knowledge of this invisible universe led Hungarian Ignaz Semmelweis (1818–1865) to reconsider the causes of diseases. In 1840, Semmelweis theorized that doctors and medical students were killing large numbers of new mothers by working with festering wounds in surgery (or worse, cadavers) and then immediately assisting with births without even washing their hands. He conducted an experiment to demonstrate that childbed fever could be prevented by making doctors wash their hands between patients.

The theory that diseases are caused by invisible microorganisms, rather than by "miasmas" (poisonous vapors mistakenly believed to cause disease), spontaneous generation, or supernatural causes, is the foundation of modern medicine and public health, and a major contributor to the welfare of people all over the world. Other scientists also built upon van Leeuwenhoek's work. Frenchman Louis Pasteur (1822–1895) proved that spoilage and disease occurred only by contamination or infection (1860s). Joseph Lister, an Englishman (1827–1912), developed aseptic surgery. In the 1870s, Robert Koch (1843–1910) proposed his Postulates, which are still used to demonstrate the connection between a specific microbe and a specific disease. Koch, a German Nobel Prize winner, is also famous for isolating *Bacillus anthracis* (1877), the *tuberculosis bacillus* (1882), and the *cholera vibrio* (1883).

Final note: Semmelweis's theory was initially dismissed by the medical community and he spent his final years in a mental institution.

For more information on Semmelweis and his colleagues, consider the following resources:

- **Childbed Fever: A Nineteenth-Century Mystery:** www.science cases.org/childbed_fever/childbed_fever.asp. The context, steps, and results of Semmelweis's experiment are detailed in this case study provided by the National Center for Case Study Teaching in Science at the University of Buffalo (State University of New York).
- **What are Koch's Postulates?** www.cps-scp.ca/kochpostulates .htm. This site of the Canadian Phytopathological Society reviews Koch's Postulates as the scientific method for proving that a particular organism was the cause of a plant disease.

INVOLVE PARENTS AND FAMILIES

You have many different avenues for inviting your students' parents into your classroom. They are a wonderful resource, and the more you include them, the more effective you will be as a teacher. Parents and family members will understand your purposes and situation more clearly when they visit; they are more likely to listen and support you if you encounter difficulties with their children; and they will contribute their expertise to your classroom.

You can ask for parent volunteers to either work with you in the classroom and with individual students and/or assist you with clerical work and special events. With large classes in particular, having additional adults in the classroom will offer supplementary supervision. Talk with your department chair and colleagues to investigate how other teachers involve parents. If you want to have parents help in your classroom, think carefully about their roles and their interactions with students. This would be a great topic to discuss at a classroom meeting with your students, too.

Another way to involve parents and family members is to invite them to discuss their professions, hobbies, special interests, collections, and personal life experiences as they relate to your curriculum. Send home a survey at the beginning of the school year with specific topics and issues to solicit potential speakers. You may discover that your students' parents have much to share on topics relevant to your standards.

> *I had a parent come speak to my classes. He was passionate about astronomy. He set up his personal telescopes that allowed my students to look at the sun and see its spots.*
>
> *—Seventh-grade science teacher*

Your school will sponsor all kinds of special events that you can relate to science, such as holiday festivals, unit culminations, science fair competitions, science Olympiad events, career days, and so forth. You will want to invite parents and family members to be in the audience and to participate in many different capacities. You might need help with handing out programs, decorations, sales, judging, scorekeeping, and/or prizes. These are ideal opportunities to connect with parents, strengthen relationships with students, and extend your classroom. We provide you with more ideas and guidance in Chapter 11.

Also, we recommend that you look at *Secrets to Success for Beginning Elementary School Teachers* (Kottler & Gallavan, 2007) or *Secrets for Secondary School Teachers: How to Succeed in Your First Year* (Kottler et al., 2004) for specific suggestions on organizing your room and creating communities of learners.

BEGIN EACH DAY ANEW

Be ready for each class and greet students with a smile every day. This means having all of your teaching materials arranged in advance so you are free to welcome students into your room. Find a spot where you will stand and welcome students as they enter the classroom. This may be the same spot where you stand after you close the learning as you dismiss the students. Following these routines will let your students know you are approachable and help you stay organized.

Include a moment at the beginning of each class for everyone to get settled. This is the perfect time for you to discuss some current events and help your students take a breath to focus on science before you launch into your agenda. The more you can model and reinforce a positive and productive manner, the more your students will participate and achieve.

ESTABLISH A SENSE OF PLACE . . .

You've dreamed of this day, and now it is here. You want this classroom to be an inviting, exciting, and rewarding space where everyone engages in and contributes to the learning experience. You want to engage students in the game of scientific discovery, with the entire universe as the playing field. The secret is creating a safe and welcoming sense of place. Help the students feel comfortable around you and with science. When students walk in the door, they will experience immediately that this is a science classroom. Now you are ready to think about your curriculum.

Suggested Activities

1. Design your ideal classroom. Consider placement and movement, investigations and experiments, information and displays, resources and references, materials and supplies, presentations and demonstrations, and equipment and storage.

2. Develop one display—preferably interactive—that will attract your students' attention and motivate their interests in a selected science topic or issue.

3. Brainstorm and share ways to connect science concepts to the contemporary world of your students throughout the week. These may include pictures of students' activities and articles of interest to them.

4. On a bulletin board, feature a small group of scientists each week. Include a photo and their accomplishments.

CHAPTER TWO

Understand Standards *to Develop Your Curriculum*

The challenge for all of us who want to improve education is to create an educational system that exploits the natural curiosity of children, so that they maintain their motivation for learning not only through their school years but throughout life.

—National Research Council, *Inquiry and the National Science Education Standards*, 2000

Science has always been seen as a critical content area to include in education. Since Sputnik, however, it has become contested as scientists, educators, and policy makers argue over whether the purpose of secondary education should be to educate future scientists or to prepare all citizens to be scientifically literate. Such differences of opinion have prompted significant rhetoric and the development of various curricula. For purposes of this text, we want to review three major reform efforts in the last sixty years.

CONSIDER THE HISTORY OF SCIENCE EDUCATION

In 1957, the Soviets successfully launched a satellite into orbit, resulting in significant concern that the Soviets had beaten Americans into space and sparking a revolution in scientific education in the United States. Scientists and educators felt we were slipping behind in our preparation of future scientists and called for curriculum reform. What resulted was the National Science Foundation's (NSF) development of the "alphabet-soup" science curricula of the 1960s and 1970s, including PSSC (Physical Science Curriculum Study), BSCS (Biological Sciences Curriculum Study), Chem Study, and many more (Abramson, 2007). These curricula focused on three themes: the discovery learning emphasis on inquiry, process skills, and inductive approaches; the structure of the discipline; and the notion of students as miniature scientists. For example, PSCS materials in eighth-grade science classes in the 1970s featured experiments involving battery-operated carts, ticker tape timers, and meter sticks. Basically, students were given the science materials and told to come up with some ideas about motion, friction, and force. Many of these course guides are still utilized, such as the biology curricular materials. (Read more at www.bscs.org.) As a result of these curricular reforms, many scientists, engineers, technologists, and mathematicians were educated via an inquiry approach. The investments in science education paid high dividends because the United States reclaimed its technological leadership for decades (Colwell, 2008).

In the early 1980s, reform efforts expanded the inquiry focus to include increased attention on content (Marx & Harris, 2006). The National Commission on Excellence in Education released *A Nation at Risk* (see the full text at www.ed.gov/pubs/NatAtRisk/index.html) in 1983. With its dramatic rhetoric ("If an unfriendly power had attempted to impose on America the mediocre educational performance that exists today, we might well have viewed it as an act of war." [*A Nation at Risk,* 1983]), this report set off a focus on standards-based science education and prompted two major organizations (the American Association for Advancement of Science and the National Academy of Science National Research Council) to identify standards that are still in place today. We'll cover more on these standards a little later in this chapter.

Most recently, the emphasis has turned to recruitment of scientists, engineers, and science teachers. Authored by the Committee on Prospering in the Global Economy of the 21st Century, *Rising Above the Gathering Storm* (2007) argues that the advantages enjoyed by the United States in science and technology have begun to erode, and calls for four major recommendations:

1. Increase America's talent pool by vastly improving K–12 mathematics and science education.

2. Sustain and strengthen the nation's commitment to long-term basic research.

3. Develop, recruit, and retain top students, scientists, and engineers from both the United States and abroad.

4. Ensure that the United States is the premier place in the world for innovation.

Specific actions related to science education call for annual recruitment of 10,000 science and math teachers, strengthening the skills of 250,000 teachers through training and education programs, and creating opportunities and incentives for middle school and high school students to pursue advanced work in science and mathematics.

UNDERSTAND THE NATURE OF SCIENCE

There are many professional organizations that concern themselves with the definition of science and the purposes and goals of science education. In what follows, we will focus on the American Association for the Advancement of Science (AAAS) and the National Academy of Science National Research Council (NRC). However, many content-specific organizations, such as the American Chemical Society, have also identified what they deem is important for students to know and be able to do.

In 1985, the American Association for the Advancement of Science (AAAS) initiated a new educational reform, Project 2061. The goal was to raise the quality, increase the relevance, and broaden the availability of science, math, and technology for American students. Comet Halley was in the Earth's vicinity in 1985, and that coincidence prompted the project's name because the children who would see the return of the comet in 2061 would soon be starting their school years. With the publication of *Science for All Americans* in 1989, Project 2061 defined science literacy and outlined what all students should know and be able to do by the time they graduated from high school.

A critical part of scientific literacy is the definition of science. AAAS outlines three components of the nature of science in the first chapter of *Science for All Americans* (1989):

1. *The scientific world view.* Scientists share certain basic beliefs and attitudes about what they do and how they view their work. These have to do with the nature of the world and what can be learned about it. Four major tenets underlie the scientific world view: the world is understandable; scientific ideas are subject to change; scientific knowledge is durable; and science cannot provide answers to all questions.

2. *Scientific inquiry.* Scientific disciplines rely on the demonstration of evidence, the use of hypothesis and theories, the kinds of logic used, and much more. Science depends on reason and imagination. It explains and predicts. Scientists try to identify and avoid bias. Science is not authoritarian.

3. *The scientific enterprise.* The enterprise of science has individual, social, and institutional dimensions. Scientific activity distinguishes our times from earlier centuries. It is a complex, social activity that is organized into disciplines and conducted by institutions, and there are generally accepted ethical principles of conducting science, including consideration of the harmful effects of research and treatment of experimental subjects. Finally, it is important to acknowledge that scientists participate in public affairs as specialists and as citizens.

ACCOMPLISH PROJECT 2061 BENCHMARKS FOR SCIENTIFIC LITERACY

In the early 1990s, AAAS transformed the Project 2061 goals into K–12 Benchmarks for Science Literacy. Table 2.1 provides a summary of the Project 2061 benchmarks, but you will also want to review the details of each benchmark for your grade levels at www.sciencenetlinks.com/benchmark_index.cfm. This site also includes lessons and activities organized by benchmark.

Table 2.1   Project 2061 Benchmarks for Scientific Literacy

Chapter	Benchmark
1. The Nature of Science How science works	A. The Scientific World View B. Scientific Inquiry C. The Scientific Enterprise
2. The Nature of Mathematics Mathematics as part of the scientific endeavor	A. Patterns and Relationships B. Mathematics, Science, and Technology C. Mathematical Inquiry
3. The Nature of Technology General principles of technology and engineering	A. Technology and Science B. Design and Systems C. Issues in Technology
4. The Physical Setting The makeup and structure of the universe	A. The Universe B. The Earth C. Processes That Shape the Earth D. The Structure of Matter E. Energy Transformations F. Motion G. Forces of Nature
5. The Living Environment How living things function and interact	A. Diversity of Life B. Heredity C. Cells D. Interdependence of Life E. Flow of Matter and Energy F. Evolution of Life
6. The Human Organism The biology of humans	A. Human Identity B. Human Development C. Basic Functions D. Learning E. Physical Health F. Mental Health
7. Human Society Social behavior of individuals and groups	A. Cultural Effects on Behavior B. Group Behavior C. Social Change D. Social Tradeoffs E. Political and Economic Systems F. Social Conflict G. Global Interdependence

Chapter	Benchmark
8. The Designed World Key technologies that shape our world	A. Agriculture B. Materials and Manufacturing C. Energy Sources and Use D. Communication E. Information Processing F. Health Technology
9. The Mathematical World Basic mathematical ideas	A. Numbers B. Symbolic Relationships C. Shapes D. Uncertainty E. Reasoning
10. Historical Perspectives Key episodes in the history of science	A. Displacing the Earth From the Center of the Universe B. Uniting the Heavens and Earth C. Extending Time D. Moving the Continents E. Understanding Fire F. Splitting the Atom G. Explaining the Diversity of Life
11. Common Themes Crosscutting themes and ideas	A. Systems B. Models C. Constancy and Change D. Scale
12. Habits of Mind Values, skills, and attitudes	A. Values and Attitudes B. Computation and Estimation C. Manipulation and Observation D. Communication Skills

Source: Adapted from AAAS (1993, 2008).

ADDRESS NATIONAL SCIENCE EDUCATION STANDARDS FOR STUDENTS

Developed by the National Research Council, the National Science Education Content Standards outline what students should know, understand, and be able to do in the natural sciences over the course of their K–12 education. The standards refer to broad areas of content, such as objects in the sky, the interdependence of organisms, or the nature of scientific knowledge. They are divided into eight categories.

Table 2.2   National Science Education Content Standards

National Science Education Content Standards		
Unifying Concepts and Processes	As a result of activities in Grades K–12, all students should develop understanding and abilities aligned with the following concepts and processes: systems, order, and organization; evidence, models, and explanation; constancy, change, and measurement; evolution and equilibrium; form and function	
	As a result of activities in Grades K–4, all students should develop understanding of:	*As a result of activities in Grades 5–8, all students should develop understanding of:*	*As a result of activities in Grades 9–12, all students should develop understanding of:*
Science as Inquiry	Abilities necessary to do scientific inquiry Understanding about scientific inquiry		
Physical Science	Properties of objects and materials Position and motion of objects Light, heat, electricity, and magnetism	Properties and changes of properties in matter Motions and forces Transfer of energy	Structure of atoms Structure and properties of matter Chemical reactions Motions and forces Conservation of energy and increase in disorder Interactions of energy and matter
Life Science	The characteristics of organisms Life cycles of organisms Organisms and environments	Structure and function in living systems Reproduction and heredity Regulation and behavior Populations and ecosystems Diversity and adaptations of organisms	The cell Molecular basis of heredity Biological evolution Interdependence of organisms Matter, energy, and organization in living systems Behavior of organisms

National Science Education Content Standards

Earth and Space Science	Properties of earth materials Objects in the sky Changes in earth and sky	Structure of the earth system Earth's history Earth in the solar system	Energy in the earth system Geochemical cycles Origin and evolution of the earth system Origin and evolution of the universe
Science and Technology	Abilities of technological design Understanding about science and technology Abilities to distinguish between natural objects and objects made by humans	Abilities of technological design Understandings about science and technology	Abilities of technological design Understandings about science and technology
Science in Personal and Social Perspective	Personal health Characteristics and changes in populations Types of resources Changes in environments Science and technology in local challenges	Personal health Populations, resources, and environments Natural hazards Risks and benefits Science and technology in society	Personal and community health Population growth Natural resources Environmental quality Natural and human-induced hazards Science and technology in local, national, and global challenges
History and Nature of Science	Science as a human endeavor	Science as a human endeavor Nature of science History of science	Science as a human endeavor Nature of scientific knowledge Historical perspectives

Source: Adapted from *NSES* (1995).

Although distinct sets of standards and developed by different organizations, Benchmarks for Science Literacy (developed by AAAS) and the National Science Education Standards (developed by NRC) share about 90 percent of the same content recommendations.

MEET NATIONAL SCIENCE EDUCATION TEACHING STANDARDS FOR TEACHERS

In addition to standards for student learning, the National Research Council (2000) has also developed a set of six standards for teaching science. These describe what teachers of science at all grade levels should understand and be able to do. Based on the goal of effective teachers of science creating an environment in which they and students work together as active learners, the teaching standards begin with a focus on the long-term planning that teachers do; move to facilitating learning, assessment, and the classroom environment; and culminate in addressing the teacher's role in the school community. They are grounded in five assumptions: that effective science education requires change throughout the entire system; that what students learn is greatly influenced by how they are taught; that the actions of teachers are deeply influenced by their perceptions of science as an enterprise and as a subject to be taught and learned; that student understanding is actively constructed through individual and social processes; and that actions of teachers are deeply influenced by their understanding of and relationships with students. These six standards are reflected throughout this text, but most explicitly in the chapters identified with the standards below:

1. Teachers of science plan an inquiry-based science program for their students (Chapters 2, 3, and 8). In doing this, teachers:
   a. Develop a framework of yearlong and short-term goals for students.
   b. Select science content and adapt and design curricula to meet the interests, knowledge, understanding, abilities, and experiences of students.
   c. Determine teaching and assessment strategies that support the development of student understanding and nurture a community of science learners.
   d. Work together as colleagues within and across disciplines and grade levels.

2. Teachers of science guide and facilitate learning (Chapters 4 and 7). In doing this, teachers:

   a. Focus and support inquiries while interacting with students.
   b. Orchestrate discourse among students about scientific ideas.
   c. Challenge students to accept and share responsibility for their own learning.
   d. Recognize and respond to student diversity and encourage all students to participate fully in science learning.
   e. Encourage and model the skills of scientific inquiry, as well as the curiosity, openness to new ideas and data, and skepticism that characterize science.

3. Teachers of science engage in ongoing assessment of their teaching and of student learning (Chapters 5, 12, and 13). In doing this, teachers:

   a. Use multiple methods and systematically gather data about student understanding and ability.
   b. Analyze assessment data to guide teaching.
   c. Guide students in self-assessment.
   d. Use student data, observations of teaching, and inter-actions with colleagues to reflect on and improve teaching practice.
   e. Use student data, observations of teaching, and inter-actions with colleagues to report student achievement and opportunities to learn to students and teachers.

4. Teachers of science design and manage learning environments that provide students with the time, space, and resources needed for learning science (Chapters 1, 9, and 10). In doing this, teachers:

   a. Structure the time available so that students are able to engage in extended investigations.
   b. Create a setting for student work that is flexible and supportive of science inquiry.
   c. Ensure a safe working environment.
   d. Make the available science tools, materials, media, and technological resources accessible to students.
   e. Identify and use resources outside the school.
   f. Engage students in designing the learning environment.

5. Teachers of science develop communities of science learners that reflect the intellectual rigor of scientific inquiry and the attitudes and social values conducive to science learning (Chapters 4, 6, and 11). In doing this, teachers:

   a. Display and demand respect for the diverse ideas, skills, and experiences of all students.
   b. Enable students to have a significant voice in decisions about the content and context of their work and require students to take responsibility for the learning of all members of the community.
   c. Nurture collaboration among students.
   d. Structure and facilitate ongoing formal and informal discussion based on a shared understanding of rules of scientific discourse.
   e. Model and emphasize the skills, attitudes, and values of scientific inquiry.

6. Teachers of science actively participate in the ongoing planning and development of the school science program (Chapters 12 and 13). In doing this, teachers:

   a. Plan and develop the school science program.
   b. Participate in decisions concerning the allocation of time and other resources to the science program.
   c. Participate fully in planning and implementing professional growth and development strategies for themselves and their colleagues.

DRAW FROM THE ACADEMIC DISCIPLINES

At times, your teaching will emphasize primarily one discipline, yet you will draw from all of them throughout the year. For example, if you are teaching about acids and bases in chemistry, students will learn aqueous acid-base reactions, properties of acids and bases, and pH as a measure of acidity and basicity (chemistry); they may also explore how acid-base reactions may result in energy transfers and store potential energy (physics) and how pH can influence the rate of biochemical reactions in the human body (biology), as well as how industrial waste can result in acid rain, which negatively impacts ecosystems (biology) and the chemical erosion of landforms (geological sciences).

The four main academic disciplines and their primary processes are identified and described as follows:

1. *Chemistry*—includes chemistry, organic chemistry, biochemistry, quantitative analysis/qualitative analysis, nuclear chemistry, and physical science-chemistry. The discipline of chemistry is the study of matter and the transformations it undergoes. Chemistry considers both the macroscopic properties of matter and the microscopic properties of matter's constituent particles.

2. *Biology*—includes life sciences, anatomy, botany, genetics, physiology, zoology, microbiology, biochemistry/molecular biology, biotechnology, marine biology, ecology, and environmental science. Biology includes the study of life at all levels. Topics include the chemistry of living systems, principles of cellular biology, molecular and Mendelian genetics, population genetics, diversity of form and physiology, and ecology.

3. *Geological sciences*—includes Earth sciences, astronomy, geology, oceanography, conservation, geophysics, and marine science. The geological sciences include analysis of Earth's place in the universe, dynamic Earth processes, energy in the Earth system, structure and composition of the atmosphere, and biochemical cycles, and U.S. and world geology.

4. *Physics*—includes physics and physical science-physics. The discipline of physics covers the study of motion, forces, energy, heat, waves, light, electricity, and magnetism. Physics focuses on the development of mathematical models to describe and predict natural phenomena and to express principles and theories.

It is important to consider the disciplines for which you will be primarily responsible, and review state and national standards on those disciplines. In addition to the Project 2061 and National Science Education Standards, determine whether your discipline associations have developed voluntary content standards. A list of those organizations is found in Chapter 13.

TEACH SKILLS IN EXPERIMENTATION AND INVESTIGATION

In addition to these academic disciplines, the skills and knowledge that students use to perform investigations and experiments are taught throughout all grade levels and content areas. Students learn to make concrete associations between science and the study of nature, and to take measurements and use basic and complex mathematics. They need to be able to use scientific tools and equipment (from Bunsen burners and beakers to graphing calculators) to perform experiments and collect, analyze, and present data. They need to be able to formulate hypotheses, interpret findings, and formulate explanations. They need to be able to solve complex problems that require combining and applying concepts from more than one area of science. And they need to understand that when an observation does not agree with an accepted scientific theory, the observation is sometimes mistaken or fraudulent and that the theory is sometimes wrong. Read more about how discrepancies between accepted theory and observations regarding the transmission of yellow fever and malaria were dealt with by Carlos Finlay and Robert Ross in Box 2.1.

BOX 2.1

History of Science

Malaria, Mosquitoes, and Yellow Fever

Malaria is a mosquito-borne disease caused by a parasite. People with malaria often experience fever, chills, and flulike illness. Left untreated, they may develop severe complications and die. Each year, 350–500 million cases of malaria occur worldwide, and over one million people die—most of them young children in sub-Saharan Africa. The etiology of yellow fever—its causes and origins—puzzled medical practitioners since the earliest recorded cases of the disease in the fifteenth and sixteenth centuries.

In 1881, Carlos Finlay (1833–1915), a Cuban doctor treating patients with yellow fever in Havana, suggested that mosquitoes were transmitting disease to and from humans. Finlay's earlier research on cholera—the result of a severe outbreak of the disease in Havana in 1867—led him to conclude that the disease was waterborne. Although this theory was initially rejected, it was later verified, and Finlay hoped to have similar results with his yellow fever mosquito transmission theory. However, it was Ronald Ross, a British medical officer stationed in India, who was credited with the discovery.

On August 20, 1897, Ross demonstrated that malaria parasites could be transmitted from infected patients to mosquitoes. He later also showed that mosquitoes could transmit malaria parasites from bird to bird. Ross received the 1902 Nobel Prize for Physiology or Medicine for "his work on malaria, by which he has shown how it enters the organism and thereby has laid the foundation for successful research on this disease and methods of combating it" (Nobel Prize, 1902).

Finally, in 1900, the U.S. Army Yellow Fever Commission confirmed the findings of Finlay and Ross and demonstrated irrefutably that the mosquito was the vector of transmission for yellow fever. The team made its discovery while part of the American occupation force in Cuba in the wake of the Spanish-American War of 1898. During the war, yellow fever, malaria, and dysentery accounted for far more army casualties than bullets, and the postwar occupation seemed to be the perfect opportunity to study the disease at its source.

Recommendations from the Yellow Fever Commission were implemented by William C. Gorgas in the health measures undertaken during construction of the Panama Canal in 1905–1910. This resulted in a significant drop in the number of deaths due to yellow fever and malaria among workers in the area.

- **History: Ross and the Discovery That Mosquitoes Transmit Malaria Parasites:** www.cdc.gov/malaria/history/ross.htm. The Center for Disease Control's Web site provides a thorough history of yellow fever and malaria.
- **Yellow Fever and the Reed Commission:** www.healthsystem.virginia.edu/internet/library/wdc-lib/historical/medical_history/yellow_fever and **Yellow Fever Collection** yellowfever.lib.virginia.edu/reed/story.html. These two sites of the University of Virginia provide extensive information on the history of yellow fever.

REFERENCE YOUR STATE STANDARDS

States have written science standards or academic frameworks that can be found on their state Department of Education Web sites. They are frequently based on national standards as well as local concerns, such as landforms and weather. It is vital that you know how to locate the standards and have a copy of these documents at your fingertips when developing your curriculum and planning your lessons. Many school administrations require their teachers to note the specific state standard(s) they are teaching in the written plans they turn in to their administrators weekly, and to post them daily for all to see.

In many states, the standards or frameworks also are presented by grade level and/or course syllabi. You can go directly to a specific grade level or course where you will find many of the following:

- Essential understandings—that is, the big ideas supported by specific knowledge and skills
- Learning expectations
- Grade-level benchmarks
- Aligned assessments
- Teaching strategies for each standard

In addition, many state documents include glossaries, sample learning scenarios, ideas for cross-curricular integration, suggested assessments, and Internet references. These resources provide you with a solid foundation necessary for constructing your own curriculum.

While state standards for science are numerous, states and/or districts may formally differentiate the standards for teachers. For example, one state we know categorized the standards as *Worth Being Familiar With, Important to Know,* or *Enduring Understandings,* based on the work of Wiggins and McTighe (1998). In other places, teachers work together to distinguish "power" standards— those they feel are most essential—from standards that are "nice to know" and those that will best prepare students for the next level of work based on the work of Ainsworth (2003). In this way, the science standards are prioritized. Check with your district and state regarding requirements on covering the standards.

INCORPORATE YOUR DISTRICT'S EXPECTATIONS

Next, it is important to become acquainted with your school district's academic expectations. Most likely you will be given a copy (print or digital) of the district's Scope and Sequence Guide, or be told where to find it on the Web. This guide allows you to see what courses are taught at each grade level, along with what is expected of your particular grade level and courses (scope) within the context of other grade levels and courses (sequence).

School district expectations are built upon state standards or frameworks. Some school districts have identified topics and issues, sample lesson plans, activities, suggested forms of assessment with rubrics for each grade level, and/or course syllabi. These resources were created to enhance your effectiveness and success based on state expectations and the students in your district. The secret is they will also help you pace your instruction.

Keep in mind that all students need to have mastered all of the knowledge and skills for the previous grade levels, regardless of what is expected at their current grade level. That means that teachers and students in tenth grade are responsible for all standards in Grades K–9, in addition to the standards for tenth grade. We would like to think that all of the previous standards have been taught and learned. Yet teachers understand that their students come with varying learning experiences and achievement levels, so they revisit and incorporate the standards set for earlier grades throughout the school year.

FEATURE YOUR SCHOOL'S ORGANIZATION AND MISSION

Finally, it is important to look at your school's organization and mission. Some schools are neighborhood schools, some are magnet schools, some are technical or vocational schools, and others are partners with community colleges. Some schools are divided into houses or academies. Your school may have a special emphasis, such as environmental education, international relations, and so forth. Your school may host a particular event or participate in a special competition annually that is related to the science education. We know of one school that requires all of its seventh graders to complete a Science Fair project. Another elementary school involves all of its students (Grades K–6) in the Science Olympiad. These events are part of the school's organization and culture.

Usually, you can find the school's mission statement published in the school handbook, posted on the school Web site, and/or displayed in the school entranceway. Many schools have crafted mission statements that sound something like this: "At our school, we are a community formed of students, families, faculty, and staff committed to developing responsibility, building self-confidence, fostering lifelong learning, and providing essential experiences for daily success."

Find your school's mission statement and post it on your wall. This is an important school document to highlight in your classroom and with your students. Mission statements support science education completely. Refer to your school's organization and mission statement as a way to connect your classroom, your students, and the school.

LINK REFERENCES TO DEVELOP CURRICULUM

Now that you have a clear definition of science and are increasing your awareness of the purposes of science with their supporting concepts, you can start developing your curriculum or what you are going to teach. During this process, you rely upon many different sources, including the national, state, and school district standards and expectations/syllabi. Reflect on and apply your own prior experiences as a science student and teacher candidate during your teacher education program. Then delve into the current curriculum in place at your school and collaborate with your colleagues. Table 2.3 provides an example of how curriculum planning relies on all these references.

PLAN YOUR YEAR WITH A CURRICULUM BLUEPRINT

We suggest that you construct a basic blueprint for the entire school year at the beginning of the year. Take a calendar and divide sections into grading periods. Next, block out vacation days and staff development days. Note the school events, such as Open House, Back-to-School Night, Parent Conferences, and Homecoming. Also, indicate your district or school assessment dates (benchmark tests, if any, as well as standardized testing) on your calendar. Then, using your district curriculum guide, determine the number of units you will need to cover. Estimate the length of time for each unit and space the units throughout the year. List

Table 2.3   Sample Curriculum Planning

Grade Level/Subject	*Grades 9–12, Earth Science*
Project 2061 Benchmark	*The Physical Setting (C. Processes that Shape the Earth)* By the end of twelfth grade, students should know that: • Plants alter the Earth's atmosphere by removing carbon dioxide from it, using the carbon to make sugars and releasing oxygen. • The formation, weathering, sedimentation, and reformation of rock constitute a continuing "rock cycle," in which the total amount of material stays the same as its forms change. • The slow movement of material within the Earth results from heat flowing out from the deep interior and the action of gravitational forces on regions of different density. • The solid crust of the Earth, including both the continents and the ocean basins, consists of separate plates that ride on a denser, hot, gradually deformable layer of the Earth. • Earthquakes often occur along the boundaries between colliding plates, and molten rock from below creates pressure that is released by volcanic eruptions, helping to build up mountains.
NSES Standard	*Earth and Space Science* As a result of their activities in Grades 9–12, all students should develop an understanding of: • Energy in the Earth system. • Geochemical cycles. • Origin and evolution of the Earth system. • Origin and evolution of the universe.
State Standards	Students know that plate tectonics accounts for important features of Earth's surface and major geologic events. (California, Grades 9–12). Students can explain the processes that move and shape Earth's surface. (Ohio, Grades 9–10).
School District Mission	To create and preserve an intellectually challenging and holistic learning experience that empowers learners with the knowledge, skills, and dispositions to find satisfaction as a participating member of a global society and to compete successfully in the international workplace of the future.

(Continued)

Table 2.3 (Continued)

Grade Level/Subject	Grades 9–12, Earth Science
Course Overview	Focus on Earth Science includes the foundations of geology and geophysics, including plate tectonics and Earth structure, topography, and energy.
Subject Standard	Students know evidence of plate tectonics is derived from the fit of the continents; the location of earthquakes, volcanoes, and midocean ridges; and the distribution of fossils, rock types, and ancient climatic zones.
Essential Understanding or Big Idea/Topic	Characteristics of Earth
Learning Experience	Draw and label a map of the seven continents and four oceans from memory using paper and pencil (label location of major volcanoes, mountain ridges, earthquakes, ring of fire, and oceanic ridges).
Current Events	Research the results of a current earthquake or volcanic activity and how the United States has provided aid.
Integration	Literacy—Read cultural myths of why earthquakes occurred. Math—Compare data on the most dangerous areas to live due to earthquakes and volcanoes. Social Studies—Investigate how cultures responded to earthquake and volcanic activity and dangers. Arts—Examine the cartographers' details included in ancient maps.

the major topics for each unit. Though you will make changes, this guide will serve you well.

This blueprint will help you:

- ensure that all themes, topics, concepts, activities, and assessments are on the calendar;
- allocate and adjust the time for each unit as you want;
- teach in the moment and plan for the future;
- communicate with students, parents, and colleagues; and
- satisfy a department or school accountability requirement to submit a yearlong plan.

Once you have an overview, you can begin planning units and lessons for your students. We will share a wealth of instructional practices and assessment techniques later in the book.

CONNECT SCIENCE WITH YOUR STUDENTS . . .

Science is about us—all of us, here and now. It combines our individual and collective stories. Not only do new discoveries occur daily; simultaneously, we grow, develop, and modify our understanding related to discoveries of the past, how they influence the present, and the possibilities they offer the future. We continually adapt our thoughts, words, and actions as we socially construct and reconstruct meanings gained from both our learned and shared experiences. Teaching science gives you a process by which to engage all your students. The secret to success is that by identifying the meaning and purpose, students will enjoy learning science as students and live science as citizens in their communities. In the next chapter, we look at strategies to engage students in inquiry.

Suggested Activities

1. Reflect upon your own science experiences. Identify one experience that helped you increase your knowledge, one experience that helped you develop your skills, and one experience that helped you expand your dispositions.

2. Examine the National Science Education Standards. Identify those teaching areas in which you feel particularly strong and those areas you would like to strengthen.

3. Compare the Project 2061 Benchmarks and National Science Education Content Standards with your state science content standards. How closely are they aligned? What are the major differences?

4. Ask one or more of your science team members if you can read through their curriculum plans for a unit or the year. Note how they pace their instruction. See whether and when benchmark assessments are given.

CHAPTER THREE

Emphasize Inquiry Science to Deepen Understanding

Believe me, my young friend, there is nothing—absolutely nothing—half so much worth doing as simply messing about in boats. Simply messing.

—Spoken by Ratty to Mole in *Wind in the Willows*
(1992 [1913]), a children's book by
Kenneth Grahame (1859–1932)

In 1974, David Hawkins wrote an essay, "Messing About in Science," in which he maintained that students needed unstructured time to explore their natural world (Hawkins, 1974). This phrase has since been used to describe the early phases of inquiry. Hawkins felt strongly that a significant amount of time involved in learning science should be spent in free and unguided exploratory work.

The idea of allowing your students time to "mess about in science" is a powerful one. Sometimes, science exploration should be messy, exploratory, and unpredictable. However, inquiry should be structured effectively so that students utilize accurate science content as they construct meaning of their investigations. There should be a balance of informal messing about and structured experimentation. Which approach you choose should be based on the content to be learned.

As a science teacher, you will give students opportunities to engage their imaginations. Inquiry is such a powerful approach to teaching and learning science—it enables the teacher to assess and meet the needs of a wide range of learners, it taps children's natural curiosity, and it deepens their understanding of science.

USE THE INQUIRY CONTINUUM

Teaching using inquiry can be seen as a continuum, with three key points (Hinrichsen & Jarrett, 1999):

- *Structured inquiry.* In this very controlled approach, you would give the students a problem to solve, the materials needed to solve the problem, and the specific instructions that should be followed. You would provide detailed steps on how to proceed with the investigation.
  - *Example:* Physics/physical science students are given bulbs, wires, batteries, and switches and step-by-step instructions to construct two different electrical circuits, where lights are connected in series and in parallel. Questions prompt students to remove bulbs and record what they see. Students are asked where these two types of circuits are used in society.

- *Guided inquiry.* In this modified structure, you would again give the students a problem to solve, and you would also provide the materials for solving it. However, you would not provide detailed steps on how to proceed with the investigation. Instead, your students would have to develop their own methods to solve the problem.
  - *Example:* Physics/physical science students are shown two different sets of decorating lights—one in which if you remove a light, the others stay lit (parallel circuit), and the other in which if you remove a light, the others go out as well (series circuit). They are asked to form a hypothesis about what could make the difference. Students are then given bulbs, wire, batteries, and switches and instructed to test their hypotheses by creating the two types of circuits.

- *Open inquiry.* In this nonstructured approach, you would not give the students a problem to solve. You would still, however, provide the materials and resources students might need to solve whatever problems they formulate. Students would then formulate their own problems to investigate, design appropriate methods of investigation, and determine solutions to their problems.
  - *Example:* Physics/physical science students are given bulbs, wire, and batteries, and instructed to investigate how bulbs light in electrical circuits. They are asked to report what they have learned.

Students need time to develop the skills necessary for open inquiry. Science lessons should be scaffolded, with students being helped a lot at first. As they become better and more confident at using inquiry, this help can gradually be removed.

INVOLVE STUDENTS IN DOING SCIENCE

Research shows that lab activities are more likely to help students reach important goals of science education, including cultivating an interest in science, developing scientific reasoning skills, and mastering science subjects. Unfortunately, lab experiences are sometimes disconnected from the flow of science lessons.

What can be done to ensure these connections? The National Academies (2005) have identified four key principles of effective instruction that improve these experiences:

- Design science lab experiences with clear learning outcomes in mind.
- Thoughtfully sequence lab experiences into science instruction.
- Integrate learning science content and learning about the processes of science.
- Incorporate ongoing student reflection and discussion.

Students should participate in a range of lab activities to verify known scientific concepts, pose research questions, conceive their own investigations, and create models of natural phenomena, the report says. Further, students need to do science—and they also need to talk and write about the science they are doing. Requiring the use of science notebooks, the writing of formal laboratory reports, collaborative group work, oral reports, and writing fiction are all ways to help students think about what they are observing.

> *Genetics is very real to students—they can relate to it and see examples of it in their own family. They also think it is so cool that they can transform bacteria or do a DNA forensics lab just like they see on TV.*
>
> *—Eleventh-grade biology teacher*

Communicating can be enhanced with the use of technology. Requiring students to use presentation software to deliver oral reports, blog their scientific notebook online, and collaborate in the development of a Wiki-based laboratory report are all ways to use technology effectively. You can then extend the learning by asking other students to review and report on what they are learning from their peers. Read more about how to use technology as a communication tool in Chapter 10.

ENGAGE IN HYPOTHESIS TESTING

In this book, we will provide a look at the nine research-based strategies identified in improving student achievement by Marzano, Pickering, and Pollock (2001), one of which is the generation and testing of hypotheses. When students generate and test hypotheses, they are applying knowledge. In fact, we naturally generate and test hypotheses all the time. If I do this, what might happen? If that thing acts in this particular way, how will it act if I do this?

A hypothesis is a precisely worded, tentative statement about the relationships between two or more variables.

To generate a hypothesis, we might:

- identify two or more variables about the situation;
- think about how the variables work together;
- create an "if–then" statement involving two of the variables; and
- make sure that the hypothesis created is testable.

To test a hypothesis, we might collect data that support or refute the hypothesis. If data support the hypothesis, the hypothesis may be accepted as a possible truth. If data do not support the hypothesis, the hypothesis may be rejected. Data may also be inclusive, and students should be given the option of making statements to that effect.

Research shows that we generate and test hypotheses in two ways: either inductively or deductively. Here's how they are broken down:

- *Inductive.* When hypothesizing inductively, students must generate hypotheses to discover the principles. Inductive thinking uses prior knowledge and assumptions to formulate hypotheses. It begins with specific observations to detect patterns and irregularities. Students then formulate a tentative hypothesis that can, after much testing, be turned into an overall theory.
  - *Example:* To study acids and bases inductively, chemistry/ physical science students would first be invited to observe the color changes of the three indicators when interacting with various substances (OBSERVATION). They would look for commonalties among the substances and the color changes (PATTERN). They would then formulate various hypotheses about these color changes—for example, that "Litmus paper always changes to red when it interacts with a sour substance" or "Cabbage juice color changes vary from pink to green" (TENTATIVE HYPOTHESIS). Students would then engage in further experimentation with known substances to determine whether their hypothesis will be able to explain and predict the results (THEORY).

- *Deductive.* A teacher using a deductive approach would present students with a formula and then ask them to test their hypotheses regarding the formula. Deductive instructional techniques require students to generate and test hypotheses based on specific principles they have been taught. Deductive reasoning requires that students take information from a general theory and create a hypothesis on how that theory will apply in a new situation.

Observations are made to determine and to confirm their hypothesis.

○ *Example:* To study acids and bases deductively, chemistry/ physical science students might be informed that acid/ base indicators are weak acids or bases that change color in the presence of an acid or base. They would be told the specific pH levels and color changes for phenolphthalein, cabbage juice, and litmus paper (THEORY). Based on their knowledge of the pH of a set of substances, they would hypothesize what the color change will be, and then accept or reject their hypothesis based on testing (HYPOTHESIS). They would then use these three indicators to determine whether the unknown substance they are testing is an acid, a base, or a neutral substance (OBSERVATION). Finally, they would compare their observations to the theory and confirm their hypothesis (CONFIRMATION).

It isn't enough that students predict, accept or reject, and reformulate their hypotheses, however. Research also shows that asking students to explain their hypotheses and conclusions enhances their learning (Marzano et al., 2001). So be sure to include quick writes, pair shares, and other ways to get students to talk and write about what they are thinking. Read more about these ideas in Chapter 6.

PROMOTE THE USE OF THE SCIENTIFIC METHOD

The scientific method is a process for predicting, on the basis of a handful of scientific principles, what will happen next in a natural sequence of events, testing, and theorizing natural phenomena. Because of its success, this invention of the human mind is used in many fields of study. The scientific method is a flexible, highly creative process built on three broad assumptions (*Science Framework,* 2004):

1. Change occurs in observable patterns that can be extended by logic to predict what will happen next.

2. Anyone can observe something and apply logic.

3. Scientific discoveries are replicable.

The scientific method may be presented at any grade level. Typically, the method consists of between four and six steps. The basis of the scientific method is asking questions and then trying to come up with the answers.

1. OBSERVE: View some aspect of the universe.

2. QUESTION: Post questions based on observations.

3. HYPOTHESIZE: Invent a tentative description, called a *hypothesis*, that is consistent with what you have observed.

4. PREDICT: Use the hypothesis to make predictions.

5. TEST: Perform an experiment to test those predictions or further observe, modifying the hypothesis in the light of your results.

6. THEORIZE: Accept or reject your hypothesis. Repeat steps until there are no discrepancies between theory and experiment and/or observation.

The scientific method has been utilized for investigations and experiments throughout history. The scientific method is an inductive approach to scientific investigations of nature. The development of this method by Galileo Galilei in Italy, Francis Bacon in England, and Tycho Brahe in Denmark (among others) provided an alternative to Aristotle's deductive method. See Box 3.1, History of Science—Galileo's Feather.

BOX 3.1

History of Science

Galileo's Feather

Galileo Galilei (1571–1630) was an Italian astronomer, mathematician, and physicist. He used the scientific method to disprove a popular theory of the late 1500s. It was generally believed that an object would fall at a speed proportional to its weight—the bigger an object, the faster it would fall. Galileo believed that the forces acting on a falling object were independent of the object's weight. In 1590, Galileo planned an experiment. He dropped several different-sized weights off the top of the Leaning Tower of Pisa and had colleagues watch the weights as they fell and record observations. Galileo found that two objects with different weights fell at exactly the same speed. This experiment disproved the previously held belief that objects with different weights fall at different rates.

Galileo is credited with anticipating Isaac Newton's laws of motion, and constructed the first astronomical telescope, which he used to discover the composition of the Milky Way. In 1632, Galileo published *Dialogue Concerning the Two Chief World Systems*, a work that upheld the Copernican system rather than the Ptolematic system. The following year, he was brought before the Inquisition in Rome and forced to renounce all his beliefs and writings supporting the Copernican theory.

Hundreds of years later, astronaut Commander David Scott repeated Galileo's gravity experiment on the moon using a falcon feather and a hammer. Because they were essentially in a vacuum, there was no air resistance and the feather fell at the same rate as the hammer, as Galileo had concluded hundreds of years earlier. You may view a video of this famous experiment at the following links:

- **Leaning Tower of Pisa Experiment Simulation:** www.visionlearning .com/library/module_viewer.php?mid=45. This site includes a reenactment of Galileo's experiment. The site is part of Visionlearning, an educational resource for faculty and students funded by the National Science Foundation.
- **Apollo 15 Hammer-Feather Drop:** http://nssdc.gsfc.nasa.gov/ planetary/lunar/apollo_15_feather_drop.html. This provides video footage of the Apollo 15 version of Galileo's experiment. This site is part of the National Space Science Data Center, NASA's permanent archive for space science mission data.

INTEGRATE SCIENTIFIC PROCESS SKILLS INTO ALL ACTIVITIES

When scientists study their world, they use specific skills. Science process skills were developed originally by the American Association for the Advancement of Science (AAAS) in the 1960s. See Box 3.2 for a summary. For more than four decades, they have been widely accepted throughout education, often described as the building blocks of inquiry and investigation. The skills may be divided into basic and integrated categories and are often delineated by grade level.

BOX 3.2

Scientific Process Skills

Basic Science Skills

Observing

- Using the five senses (sight, hearing, touch, smell, taste) to find out about objects and events, their characteristics, properties, differences, similarities, and changes
- Identifying properties of an object—that is, shape, color, size, and texture
- Using indirect methods—such as hand lenses, microscopes, thermometers—to observe objects and events
- Observing objects or events by counting, comparing, estimating, and measuring

Classifying

- Grouping or ordering objects or events according to similarities or differences to identify properties useful for classifying objects
- Constructing and using classification systems

Measuring

- Comparing an unknown quantity with a known (metric units, time, student-generated frames of reference)
- Quantifying observations by using proper measuring devices and techniques
- Ordering objects by length, area, weight, volume, etc.
- Measuring volume, mass, weight, temperature, area, length, and time using appropriate units and appropriate measuring instruments

Inferring

- Interpreting or explaining observations; suggesting explanations for events based on observations
- Distinguishing between an observation and an inference

Predicting

- Forming an idea of an expected result—not a guess, but a belief about what will occur based upon present knowledge and understandings, observations, and inferences; forecasting a future event based on prior experience—that is, observations, inferences, or experiments

Communicating

- Using the written and spoken work, graphs, demonstrations, drawings, diagrams, or tables to transmit information and ideas to others; constructing and using written reports, drawings, diagrams, graphs, or charts to transmit information learned from science experiments

- Asking questions about, discussing, explaining, or reporting observations
- After an investigation, reporting the question tested, the experimental design used, results, and conclusions drawn, using tables and graphs where appropriate

Using Number Relationships

- Applying numbers and their mathematical relationships to make decisions

Using Space/Time Relations

- Describing an object's position—for example, above, below, beside, etc.—in relation to other objects
- Describing the motion, direction, spatial arrangement, symmetry, and shape of an object compared with another object

Integrated Science Skills

Making Models

- Constructing mental, verbal, or physical representations of ideas, objects, or events to clarify explanations or demonstrate relationships
- Creating mental, physical, or verbal representation of an idea, object, or event
- Using models to describe and explain interrelationships of ideas, objects, or events

Defining Operationally

- Creating a definition by describing what is done and observed; stating definitions of objects or events in terms of what the object is doing or what is occurring in the event
- Stating definitions of objects or events based on observable characteristics

Collecting Data

- Gathering and recording information about observations and measurements in a systematic way

Interpreting Data

- Organizing, analyzing, and synthesizing data using tables, graphs, and diagrams to locate patterns that lead to the construction of inferences, predictions, or hypotheses; organizing and stating in the student's own words information derived from a science investigation
- Revising interpretations of data based on new information or revised data

(Continued)

(Continued)

Identifying and Controlling Variables

- Manipulating one factor to investigate the outcome of an event while other factors are held constant
- Identifying the manipulated (independent) variable, responding (dependent) variable, and variables held constant in an experiment
- Controlling the variables in an investigation

Formulating Hypotheses (Hypothesizing)

- Making educated guesses based on evidence that can be tested through experimentation
- Differentiating between questions and statements that can and cannot be tested

Experimenting

- Designing one's own experiment to test a hypothesis using procedures to obtain reliable data
- Designing an investigation to test a hypothesis
- Conducting simple experiments
- Recognizing limitations of methods and tools used in experiments and accounting for experimental error
- Utilizing safe procedures while conducting investigations

Source: Adapted from American Association for the Advancement of Science (1990).

WEAVE INQUIRY-BASED LABORATORY INVESTIGATIONS INTO EVERY LESSON

> *My favorite unit is Moon Phases because the students develop their science vocabulary by keeping a monthly moon calendar. It's simple and enjoyable.*
>
> —*Third-grade teacher*

The National Science Teachers Association (NSTA, 2007) recommends that inquiry-based laboratory investigations be at the core of the science program and woven into every lesson and concept strand. According to the NSTA:

A hallmark of science is that it generates theories and laws that must be consistent with observations. Much of the evidence from these observations is collected during laboratory investigations. A school laboratory investigation is defined as an experience in the laboratory, classroom, or the field that provides students with opportunities to interact directly with natural phenomena or with data collected by others using tools, materials, data collection techniques, and models. Throughout the process, students should have opportunities to design investigations, engage in scientific reasoning, manipulate equipment, record data, analyze results, and discuss their findings. These skills and knowledge, fostered by laboratory investigations, are an important part of inquiry—the process of asking questions and conducting experiments as a way to understand the natural world. While reading about science, using computer simulations, and observing teacher demonstrations may be valuable, they are not a substitute for laboratory investigations by students. For science to be taught properly and effectively, labs must be an integral part of the science curriculum. (NSTA, 2007)

The NSTA recommends that middle and high school–level students have *multiple* opportunities *every week* to be in the science lab or field. Further, as students progress through middle and high school, they should improve their ability to collaborate effectively with others in carrying out complex tasks, share the work of the task, assume different roles at different times, and contribute and respond to ideas.

Some science experiments and investigations may be conducted in one class period, but others take more time. They may also require data collection outside of class. Science teachers sometimes avoid the inclusion of such experiments and observations because students do not always do their homework. The best way to approach these investigations is to reduce the dependence on a single set of data. Instead, use whole-class or small-group data sets to make it possible for all students to participate and learn.

One example of a long-term investigation is the FOSS *Phases of the Moon Investigation.* As part of a larger module on Planetary Science, this investigation helps students gain a better understanding of the motions of Earth and the moon in relation to the sun, which result in the phases of the moon we observe on Earth.

Among other activities, students track the phases of the moon over a twenty-eight-day period in their Moon Logs to determine the sequence of changes and study moonrise in an effort to understand the reasons for phases. An elementary version (based on the third-grade California Science Standards) is also available. See details of this investigation at the FOSS Web site.

HEAD FOR THE OUTDOORS

"Earth and sky, woods and fields, lakes and rivers, the mountain and the sea, are excellent schoolmasters, and teach us more than we can ever learn from books." So spoke Sir John Lubbock (1834–1913), an English naturalist—and we think he made a lot of sense! Investigating and understanding science, especially biology and the life sciences, can be enhanced greatly when students have access to the outdoors. It is commonly accepted that teachers bring examples into the classroom; however, many go beyond to take their students outdoors. Some examples include creating a nature trail, a flower or vegetable garden, a weather station, a wetland area with a stream, or an outdoor classroom or greenhouse.

Outdoor activities allow students another opportunity to experience science as a relevant, hands-on aspect of their daily lives. They enhance overall achievement in science while promoting deeper knowledge of environmental concepts for local and global environmental stewardship. Creation of outdoor science spaces can also enhance the school settings. There are even grants available for outdoor classrooms.

> When I talk about plants, we all go outside and walk around the campus. We just look at plants on the first day of the unit. I ask questions like, "Do you see any leaves similar to this one?" or "Does it look like the strips of bark on this trunk used to fit together?" This sets up some questions, or dissonance in their minds that I tap as we go through the unit.
>
> —Ninth-grade biology teacher

Outdoor science activities provide the opportunity for short- and long-term investigations. Students face situations of genuine inquiry where they have to make collaborative decisions at the right time about different elements of inquiry, including posing researchable questions and using proper equipment, as well as collecting and analyzing data. Students have opportunities to think like scientists, and it is important to allow students to formulate their own questions or devise experiments. Topics include the following:

- *Biology*—effects of soil, water, and hormones on plant growth, bird attraction and migration, animal signs, insect capture/recapture, soil dwellers, adopt an insect, pond water survey, butterfly attraction
- *Earth science*—weather patterns, litter, cloud cover, surface temperature, erosion
- *Chemistry*—air quality, water quality, biodegradability, effects of acid rain on plants
- *Physics*—solar energy, flight of kite flying, swing set pendulums, launching a rocket

SUPPORT SCIENTIFIC INVESTIGATIONS WITH RESOURCES

There are many publisher resources that can be used to support scientific investigations and experimentation. Publishers of science texts usually provide accompanying laboratory manuals or include directions for experiments and investigations throughout the textbook. Some of these investigations may be conducted at home, but most require the supervision of a teacher within a safe learning environment. The teachers' edition of the textbook provides additional ideas for activities as well as directions for preparing materials for these activities. Finally, most publishers are now providing enrichment activities on their Web sites.

In addition to publisher materials, there are many packaged investigations. Some companies include free teacher development when these materials are purchased.

- **FOSS:** http://lhsfoss.org. FOSS is a research-based inquiry science program for Grades K–8, developed at the Lawrence Hall of Science with support from the National Science Foundation and published by Delta Education.
  - ○ *Example:* See the *Phases of the Moon* example presented earlier in this chapter.
- **AIMS:** www.aimsedu.org. The AIMS Education Foundation was established as a nonprofit, independent organization

that creates and distributes curricula that integrate math and science. Its science activities are inquiry based.

○ *Example: Dropping In on a Protozoa,* students in Grades 5–9 investigate what organisms can be observed in a drop of pond water. Preview parts of this investigation at wwws.aimsedu.org/previews/DA1529.html.

- **GEMS:** www.lawrencehallofscience.org/gems/aboutgems .html. GEMS is a program of the Lawrence Hall of Science, the public science education center at the University of California at Berkeley. GEMS publishes science and math curricula, offers specialized workshops, and maintains an international support network.

○ *Example:* Students explore acids and bases using the special indicator properties of red cabbage juice in *Of Cabbages and Chemistry,* Grades 4–8: www.lawrence-hallofscience.org/gems/GEM195.html.

USE DEMONSTRATIONS TO PROMOTE LEARNING

It is great to involve students in actual experiments, but sometimes equipment and materials can be too expensive, or the experiments are too dangerous for students to do on their own. Demonstrations may be used in a variety of ways. They can be stand-alone examples of concepts presented during lectures; they can be treated as the experiment for student analysis; or they can be utilized as discrepant events when presented by the teacher.

Where can you find ideas and directions for demonstrations? Your textbooks will have many suggestions, and there are also books and Web resources available. A simple Google search by topic will result in many ideas. Be sure to practice the demonstration in advance to make sure it works properly before you do it in front of students!

I enjoy teaching physics in eighth grade because there are so many practical, everyday examples that can be integrated. For example, to teach students about friction and forces, we play tug of war. We also have friction scooters that they love to race. Students can learn about air resistance and Bernoulli's principle by making paper airplanes.

—Eighth-grade life and physical science teacher

TEACH THROUGH DISCREPANT EVENTS

A discrepant event is a "puzzling" happening, a surprising phenomenon, an unexpected and unanticipated incident (Fensham & Kass, 1988). It causes the observer to wonder why the event occurred as it did. It leaves the observer at a momentary, or longer, loss to explain what has taken place—and allows for the opportunity to "mess about in science."

An Earth science teacher, for example, can demonstrate the power of vapor pressure when imploding a soda can by flipping it upside down into a shallow tray of water. To begin, heat a small amount of water in the can until the class can hear it boiling inside. Then quickly flip the can and position it open, tab-down, in a pan of room-temperature water. The can will implode with a satisfying bang and crumple.

Prompt the students to explain what they have seen: What happened? How could I make it happen again? How could I make it happen even quicker, with different results? What caused it to happen? Students might call out suggestions: Fill it halfway! Fill it all the way! Keep it empty! Don't heat the water! Perform these suggestions and have a helpful student post the results on the board for all to see. With all of the students fully engaged and leaning forward in their seats, the teacher can tease out hypotheses implied in these suggestions, and lead students to the correct conclusion.

Cognitive research has established a strong connection between motivation and learning for students of all ages. Using discrepant events in science instruction results in cognitive conflict that enhances student's conceptual understanding and their attitudes toward critical thinking activities (Fensham & Kass, 1988). Not only does this cognitive conflict "activate" motivation, it also drives inquiry. What is critical, though, is that students have time to think about, discuss, and try to explain the discrepant event. Discrepant events are fun to use at all grade levels, and there are many examples available on the Web.

> *One of my favorite discrepant events uses baking yeast sprinkled on a cup of hydrogen peroxide. When stirred, bubbles quickly form. Then, I light a splint of wood and blow gently on the flame to reduce it to a glowing tip. I use this glowing tip to pop a bubble and the splint quickly bursts into a flame. Why? The yeast acts as a catalyst to speed up the decomposition of hydrogen peroxide (H_2O_2) to water (H_2O) and oxygen (O_2). The pure oxygen bubbles support burning. The splint*

sparks into a full flame in the enriched oxygen environment. I've used this demonstration to talk about decomposition reactions, catalysts, or even the properties of oxygen.

—Tenth-grade chemistry teacher

TEACH SAFETY TO STUDENTS

Students come from diverse backgrounds, and most will have had no previous experience in handling chemicals or equipment. The school science laboratory provides an opportunity to instill good attitudes and habits by allowing students to observe and select appropriate practices and perform laboratory operations safely. Safety and health training lays the foundation for acquiring these skills. The students should think through implications and risks of experiments that they observe or conduct in order to learn that safe procedures are part of the way science must be done.

Most science textbooks and laboratory manuals include a section on laboratory safety. It is a good idea to plan for several days of instruction on safety issues at the beginning of each semester. This should be followed with a review of the related safety issues prior to each experiment or unit. You may even want to require students to pass a safety quiz and sign (along with their parent or guardian) a safety contract prior to allowing them to complete science investigations and experiments. See examples of safety quizzes and contracts at the following links:

- **Science Aware:** www.scienceaware.com
- **Dupont Science Safety Zone:** www.sciencenewsforkids .org/pages/safetyzone.asp
- **Science Education Safely, Council of State Science Supervisors:** www.csss-science.org/safety.shtml
- **Flinn Scientific Safety:** www.flinnsci.com/Sections/Safety/ safety.asp

You play the most important role in ensuring a safe learning environment for your students. You are responsible for creating and maintaining a safe environment, choosing safe experiments and investigations for students, and instructing students in basic safety practices in science laboratories. A science safety checklist for the high school laboratory is included in Resource A at the end of the book.

EQUIP YOUR STUDENTS TO UNDERSTAND THEIR WORLD . . .

The big idea from this chapter is to help students understand their world by using inquiry methods. The secret is giving your students the opportunity to mess about in science every day—through investigations, experiments, discrepant events, meaningful content, and rich activities. They will be able to apply the scientific process skills learned in your classroom in every area of their personal, academic, and future professional lives. In the chapters that follow, we will explore further methods to help students understand their world.

Suggested Activities

1. Identify the topic for an experiment and delineate the steps for both an inductive and a deductive approach. Which approach would be most appropriate for elementary students? For middle school students? For high school students? Do you prefer one approach over the other? If so, why?

2. Think about some of the demonstrations that were presented by your high school and college science teachers. What made these demonstrations effective? How did they help you understand the scientific method and/or the science content?

3. Examine the instructional resources available through FOSS, GEMS, AIMS, or another source. Which would be appropriate for your curriculum? Find out if any are being used at your school or in your district and if your site has any funding to support the purchase of these inquiry-based instructional materials.

4. Determine how you might make sure that your students have *multiple* opportunities *every week* to be in the science lab or field, as recommended by NSTA.

CHAPTER FOUR

Know Your Students *to Support Science Achievement*

We especially need imagination in science. Question everything.

—Maria Mitchell (1818–1889), first
professional woman astronomer and
discoverer of Mitchell's Comet in 1847

Athis point you have developed a curriculum plan or blueprint for the entire school year. You have accounted for all
the major topics and issues identified in the state standards and
academic frameworks along with the school district curricular
guidelines. You have met with your colleagues and organized
yourself around the grading periods and testing dates. You have
checked the school calendar to include major school events so
that your plan fits into your students' schedules. You have pre-
viewed the textbooks and supplementary teaching materials. Now
it is time to consider who your students are, how you will get to
know them, and how you can best support their learning.

BEGIN FROM THE PERSPECTIVE OF THE LEARNERS

We know you are anxious to be the teacher and start teaching, so we share this important secret to ensure your success. Reflect on *the perspective of the learners*. In other words, imagine that you are enrolled in your own class. Ask yourself some key questions that all students wonder, such as:

- Why do I have to learn this?
- What does it have to do with me?
- What do I have to do for this class?
- How much will I have to read every day?
- Will I have to (or can I) work on my own or with a partner?
- Will I make presentations in front of the class?
- What kind of experiments and investigations will I get to do?
- Do we get to take any field trips in this class?
- Will there be any guest speakers?

The answers to these questions can help steer you as you begin to focus on instruction. You want your students to enjoy the class, to be actively involved in learning, and to be able to show you what they have learned. Think for a moment about your most and least favorite classes. Your memories can guide you to success.

My favorite science teacher was really nice. She balanced the class between lecture, labs, and group activities.

—Lily, age sixteen, tenth grade

SEE STUDENTS AS INDIVIDUALS

With the diversity of today's society, you will likely have students representing different heritages, different customs, different countries, and different languages. They bring a variety of past school experiences with them along with different learning abilities—some more successful than others. You will need to get to know your students on an individual basis.

Science teachers show they care for you by acknowledging you and paying attention. Also, at the beginning of the year, learning names quickly shows that you care about students.

—Meredith, age fifteen, tenth grade

The relationships you establish with your students will motivate them to achieve and to continue to achieve (Tomlinson & McTighe, 2006). When students perceive that teachers care about them and their levels of achievement, they are more likely to engage in the classroom. Take time to get to know your students. Use surveys and interest inventories, talk to them individually and in small groups, use dialogue journals, solicit their opinions, have them share their perspectives. For example, many teachers have students mark a place on a laminated map indicating where they were born or where they have lived or traveled. They ask students to write autobiographies and share special talents or hobbies. Science classes provide great opportunities for social interaction.

Science teachers show that they care for you by going around the classroom while people are working and working with each person for a little bit individually.

—Zachary, age fourteen, eighth grade

Feedback from students is the most compelling evidence and provides clear guidelines for teachers. In prioritizing their comments about teachers, students say they want teachers who like their students and care about them as individuals, control the class so that students have a chance to learn what they need and want to learn, demonstrate fairness in their classroom interactions and assignment assessment, know how to teach and help students succeed, and know their content and make it interesting (Gallavan, in press).

I show students I care by giving them one-on-one time, flexing assignments/due dates for personal issues, and just checking in— students really appreciate when you remember something about them or their family.

—Eighth-grade physical science teacher

UNDERSTAND CHANGES IN TODAY'S STUDENTS

One of the most important points to remember when reflecting is the changes in today's students. Keep in mind that you are no longer the student, you are no longer the age of your students, and your students are different from you (Wallis & Steptoe, 2006).

Today's students can think broadly and holistically, yet they prefer to concentrate on minutiae. They can operate in an interdisciplinary manner in both form and function while focused on a single event, but they are more concrete than abstract thinkers. They approach problem solving and decision making eagerly as a personal challenge, utilizing resources and creating solutions. They like the responsibility and productivity of their own advancement; however, some of today's students exhibit a limited attention span and perseverance.

Many of today's students are smarter and more adept with technology than you were—or maybe you are now (Prensky, 2001a, 2001b). They embrace technology as a way of thinking, acting, and communicating. Some say today's students are technology natives, since they grew up with much of the technology we take for granted today. Today's students can be a bit impatient if and when technology is unavailable or fails to operate as expected.

Today's students like to work cooperatively and in teams. They like the group spirit and a feeling of helping others succeed . . . as long as they also succeed individually. They think of themselves as rather special; they have been overly organized and extremely sheltered (Howe & Strauss, 2000). Many of them have been involved in all kinds of team sports, and been given all kinds of awards. However, today's students tend to be extremely competitive, feel pressured to produce and achieve, and see winning as a way to be financially comfortable. Schools have gravitated away from cooperative learning and teamwork, thereby placing today's students at a disadvantage. Science can help develop these skills.

Today's students may know more about the world than you knew when you were their age, or maybe more than you know now. (Some of them know that information is power, and like having that power.) Many more of them seem to know isolated pieces of information and need help connecting the dots. They may not always see the world on a global scale, and don't understand the interplay among nations, governments, and economies.

Today's teachers do their best to stay ahead of their students, and view and represent the world from multiple perspectives. In general, today's students value diversity and avoid prejudice, bias, and stereotyping. Many of today's students are or have multiracial and multilingual family members, divide their lives between many different family members, and accept aspects of many different faiths and beliefs. Sometimes their cultural knowledge is challenged by scientific theories, and you will need to be respectful and sensitive, even as you also have the responsibility to teach the content.

I am a good listener. I make myself available outside of their class time.

—Middle school life and physical science teacher

CONSIDER THE CONTEXTS OF STUDENTS' FAMILIES AND PEERS

Science students may be categorized according to the ease with which they succeed in school science, an ease related to the similarity between the culture of their worlds of family and peers and the culture of school science (Aikenhead, 1996, 2001; Costa, 1995). There are distinctive patterns among the relationships between students' worlds of family and friends and their success in school and in science classrooms that influence how students approach science in the classroom. These patterns may be described in five categories (Costa, 1995):

1. *Potential Scientists.* Worlds of family and friends are congruent with the worlds of both school and science. Potential scientists have professional career aspirations for which their science classes play a significant role.

2. *Other Smart Kids.* Worlds of family and friends are congruent with the world of school but inconsistent with the world of science. Other smart kids (a phrase borrowed from Tobias, 1990) do well at school, even in science, although science is not particularly personally meaningful or useful.

3. *"I Don't Know" Students.* Worlds of family and friends are inconsistent with the worlds of both school and science. The "I don't know" students were labeled for their ubiquitous responses to questions about science and about school, and for their noncommittal overall attitude toward school science. Generally, science classes were no different than other classes at school. Many of

these students have learned to play the school game of passing a course without necessarily understanding the content.

4. *Outsiders.* Worlds of family and friends are discordant with the worlds of both school and science. For outsiders, all school work is busy work and emphasizes compliance with directions from authorities. Even when science content makes sense to them, they may not care enough to hand in homework or pass examinations.

5. *Inside Outsiders.* Worlds of family and friends are irreconcilable with the world of school, but are potentially compatible with the world of science. These students are interested in science, but they are inhibited because of the marginalization they experience at school and a consistent lack of support from peers and family.

When teachers consider the ease with which students cross cultural borders into school science, they will be able to differentiate instruction and provide individualized support that increases student motivation to learn science. In addition, a curriculum rich in STS (science, technology, and society) allows students to enrich their own life-worlds as they draw upon scientific knowledge and skills in appropriate situations, such as employment decisions, forming defensible positions on a science-related personal or social issue, and making sense of their personal world and communities (Aikenhead, 1996, 2001; Costa, 1995). Read more about the STS approach in Chapter 6.

SHOWCASE POWERFUL TEACHING AND LEARNING

Because your time and energy are limited, you will want to get the most out of every teachable moment. To do this, powerful teaching and learning must take place. The American Association for the Advancement of Science (AAAS) identifies five core principles of science teaching (AAAS, 1990):

1. *Teaching Should Be Consistent With the Nature of Scientific Inquiry.* Because science is a way of thinking and doing, as well as a body of knowledge, students should have experience with the kinds of thought and action that are typical of scientific fields. Thus, AAAS recommends that teachers start with questions about nature, engage

students actively, concentrate on the collection and use of evidence, provide historical perspectives, insist on clear expression, use a team approach, do not separate knowing from finding out, and de-emphasize the memorization of technical vocabulary.

2. *Science Teaching Should Reflect Scientific Values.* Because science is a social activity that incorporates certain human values, AAAS recommends that science teachers welcome curiosity, reward creativity, encourage a spirit of healthy questioning, avoid dogmatism, and promote aesthetic responses.

3. *Science Teaching Should Aim to Counteract Learning Anxieties.* Because the learning of science may involve feelings of severe anxiety and fear of failure, AAAS recommends that science teachers build on success, provide abundant experience in using tools, support the roles of girls and minorities in science, and emphasize group learning.

4. *Science Teaching Should Extend Beyond the School.* Because children learn from a range of individuals at many different events in a variety of settings, AAAS recommends that science teachers should exploit the rich resources of the larger community and involve parents and other concerned adults in useful ways.

5. *Teaching Should Take Its Time.* AAAS recommends that students be given time for exploring, constructing physical and mathematical models for testing ideas, and wrestling with unfamiliar and counterintuitive ideas.

FEATURE ACTIONS AND VERBS FROM BLOOM'S TAXONOMY

Effective instruction develops all levels of cognitive processes. Bloom's Taxonomy presents a framework that features six levels of cognitive processes: Knowledge, Comprehension, Application, Analysis, Synthesis, and Evaluation. With this taxonomy, you can develop your content objectives and assessments strategically. See Table 4.1 for a description and examples of verbs associated with each level.

FORM HABITS OF MIND

Art Costa (no relation to author) and Bena Kallick (Costa & Kallick, 2000) describe Habits of Mind as the "dispositions toward behaving intelligently when confronted with problems, the answers to which are not immediately known: dichotomies, dilemmas, enigmas and

Table 4.1   Suggested Verbs to Accompany Bloom's Taxonomy

Bloom's Taxonomy Relating to the Cognitive Domain *Key verbs to guide activities and assignments or to start questions during conversations*	
Evaluation: Determining the value of something	Appraise, argue, assess, choose, compare, conclude, contrast, critique, debate, decide, defend, dispute, estimate, evaluate, grade, interpret, judge, justify, measure, opinionate, prioritize, prove, rank, rate, recommend, state opinion, select, solve, support, validate, value, verify
Synthesis: Putting something together in a new way	Arrange, change, combine, compile, compose, construct, create, derive, design, find an unusual way, forecast, formulate, generalize, generate, group, hypothesize, imagine, improve, integrate, invent, modify, organize, originate, plan, predict, pretend, produce, rearrange, reconstruct, relate, reorganize, revise, suggest, summarize, suppose, visualize, write
Analysis: Taking something apart	Analyze, arrange, break down, calculate, categorize, chart, classify, compare, contrast, debate, deduct, detect, determine the factors, diagnose, diagram, differentiate, discriminate, dissect, distinguish, examine, infer, investigate, outline, relate, research, separate, show alike and different, solve, specify, subdivide, survey, test
Application: Using what you know in a new situation	Act out, apply, change, collect, compute, conclude, construct, demonstrate, determine, draw, employ, exemplify, find out, give examples, illustrate, make, operate, paint, practice, predict, prepare, put in order, record, relate, report, show, solve, state a rule or principle, use
Comprehension: Understanding	Classify, compare, convert, contrast, describe, discuss, distinguish, estimate, explain, find, generalize, give examples, give main idea, infer, interpret, paraphrase, put in order, reason, restate, retell in your own words, review, rewrite, show, summarize, trace, translate, "why"
Knowledge: Remembering	Choose, count, define, describe, fill in the blank, identify, label, list, locate, match, memorize, name, outline, point out, quote, recall, recite, recognize, relate, remember, repeat, report, reproduce, select, spell, state, tell, trace, underline, "who, what, when, where"

Source: Adapted from Bloom (1984).

uncertainties" (p. 1). They explain that Habits of Mind are a composite of many skills, attitudes, and proclivities, including the following:

- *Value*—choosing to employ a pattern of intellectual behaviors rather than other, less productive patterns
- *Inclination*—feeling the tendency toward employing a pattern of intellectual behaviors
- *Sensitivity*—perceiving opportunities for, and appropriateness of, employing the pattern of behavior
- *Capability*—possessing the basic skills and capacities to carry through with the behaviors
- *Commitment*—constantly striving to reflect on and improve performance of the pattern of intellectual behavior

The Habits of Mind identified by Costa and Kallick are characteristics of what intelligent people do when they solve problems that have no readily apparent solutions. These attitudes include the following:[1]

- *Persisting*—sticking with a task until it is completed
- *Thinking and communicating with clarity and precision*—supporting statements, avoiding overgeneralizations, using specific language
- *Managing impulsivity*—thinking through the consequences of behavior before acting
- *Gathering data through all senses*—using sight, touch, hearing, seeing, and smelling as well as every available strategy and opportunity
- *Listening with understanding and empathy*—close attention to what is said and what is indicated between the words
- *Creating, imagining, innovating*—generating novel, clever, and unique ideas and products
- *Thinking flexibly*—approaching problems from new angles and perspectives
- *Responding with wonderment and awe*—communing with the world around us, like Rat does with the River in *The Wind in the Willows* (see Chapter 1)
- *Thinking about thinking (metacognition)*—evaluating the quality of your own thinking and refining plans and ideas
- *Taking responsible risks*—going beyond established limits
- *Striving for accuracy*—managing to hit the center of the target (accuracy and clarity) every time (precision)

---

1. Although Costa and Kallick identify sixteen Habits of Mind, they emphasize that this list is not exhaustive and encourage others to continue the search for additional Habits of Mind.

- *Finding humor*—laughing to liberate creativity
- *Questioning and posing problems*—discovering a problem, formulating questions, and posing hypotheses
- *Thinking interdependently*—collaborating to solve a problem
- *Applying past knowledge to new situations*—learning from experience
- *Remaining open to continuous learning*—being in a learning mode

These Habits of Mind are well utilized in science education, especially in inquiry-based learning, where students need to be able to solve complex problems and think critically in either inductive or deductive situations. The American Association for the Advancement of Science (1990) also offers recommendations about promoting four specific aspects of values and attitudes: the values inherent in science, mathematics, and technology; the social value of science and technology; the reinforcement of general social values; and people's attitudes toward their own ability to understand science and mathematics. Science education is in a particularly strong position to foster three of these attitudes and values—curiosity, openness to new ideas, and informed skepticism. Also recommended is a focus on a set of skills related to computation and estimation, to manipulation and observation, to communication, and to critical response to arguments. These attitudes and values correlate with Costa and Kallick's Habits of Mind. You may read more about AAAS recommendations in *Science for All Americans* (AAAS, 1990).

When you examine the lives of most scientists, you will see that they employ these Habits of Mind throughout their studies—with curiosity, openness, and skepticism foremost in their routines. Consider how Charles Darwin employed these Habits of Mind (see Box 4.1).

BOX 4.1

History of Science

The Dynamic Nature of Life on Earth

People used to think that every life form now on Earth was here from the start, and that none had ever changed. Charles Darwin's theory of evolution revealed the dynamic nature of life on Earth. But Darwin, an English naturalist, was not the first person to propose evolution. It was widely discussed in scientific circles long before he published his theories and Alfred

(Continued)

(Continued)

Wallace, another naturalist, had basically arrived at the same theory. Darwin's contribution was that he proposed a viable mechanism for evolution—natural selection—which he backed with numerous examples from his observations while on the HMS *Beagle* voyage in the 1830s.

Darwin's theory is based on five key observations:

- *Offspring.* Organisms produce more offspring than can survive.
- *Genetics.* Organisms pass genetic traits on to their offspring.
- *Variation.* There is variation in every population.
- *Competition.* Organisms compete for limited resources.
- *Natural selection.* Those organisms with the most beneficial traits are more likely to survive, reproduce, and pass these traits on to their offspring.

Here's how natural selection works: In any population, there will be variations. The individual organisms must compete for limited resources, and those born with certain characteristics, such as speed or a keen sense of smell, will enjoy an advantage over their peers. They will be more likely to live to adulthood and pass these traits on to their offspring. If the surrounding environment gradually changes, it may come to pass that new characteristics are more advantageous than old ones. As the environment changes, individuals with these new characteristics live longer and produce more viable offspring until the population eventually looks very different.

An example of this is the evolution of the peppered moth. Originally, those peppered moths with light coloration were effectively camouflaged against the light-colored trees and lichens on which they lived. This coloration made it difficult for their predators to see them. Over time, however, widespread pollution during the Industrial Revolution in England killed many of the lichens, and the trees became blackened by soot, making the light-colored moths visible to predators. At the same time, the initially few dark-colored moths flourished because of their ability to hide on the darkened trees. The result was a dramatic change in the peppered moth population.

Read more about early theories of evolution on the following Web sites:

- **AboutDarwin.com:** www.aboutdarwin.com. This site is dedicated to the life and contributions of Charles Darwin. The link's database has many resources for teachers and students.
- **Darwin and Natural Selection:** http://anthro.palomar.edu/ evolve/evolve_2.htm. Maintained by the Department of Biological Sciences at Palomar College, this site reviews seventeenth- to nineteenth-century discoveries that led to the acceptance of biological evolution. It also includes teaching and learning resources.

CAPITALIZE UPON THE MULTIPLE INTELLIGENCES

You enrich your science instruction when you incorporate Gardner's (1983) eight multiple intelligences to examine science concepts, practices, and contexts. Gardner tells us that people learn and express their learning in eight different ways. Each of us has a preferred way of learning and expressing ourselves. Teachers need to be aware of their students' strengths and capitalize upon them to help their students learn science and show optimum achievement. See Table 4.2 for examples and science applications in each intelligence area.

Over time, strategic teachers include all eight of the multiple intelligences as students grow and learn from opportunities to build upon their weaker areas. As teachers design their learning experiences, they balance times when students have choice with times when students must try new avenues of learning and expression. Ultimately, all students need to increase competency and confidence in learning and expressing themselves in all eight multiple intelligences.

As you plan your units, you will want to make sure you are including activities that give students the chance to learn with all intelligences. For example, *Project Learning Tree* and *Project WILD*, environmental education programs for K–12 educators and their students, include activities that allow students to demonstrate and develop the different multiple intelligences. In *Oh Deer!* a *Project WILD* activity that illustrates how wildlife populations naturally fluctuate, students engage in a kinesthetic activity by assuming roles of deer and habitat elements (water, food, shelter, and space). Both these programs provide extensive free professional development for teachers.

- **Project Wild:** www.projectwild.org. The *Project WILD K–12 Curriculum and Activity Guide* focuses on wildlife and habitat. The *Project WILD Aquatic K–12 Curriculum and Activity Guide* emphasizes aquatic wildlife and aquatic ecosystems. *Project WILD's* new high school curriculum, *Science and Civics: Sustaining Wildlife*, is designed to serve as a guide for involving students in environmental action projects aimed at benefitting the local wildlife found in a community. It involves young people in decisions affecting people, wildlife, and their shared habitat in the community.

- **Project Learning Tree:** www.plt.org. Sponsored by the American Forest Foundation, *Project Learning Tree* is a multidisciplinary environmental education program for educators and

Table 4.2   Gardner's Multiple Intelligences Connected to Science
Applications

Gardner's Multiple Intelligences		
Type of Multiple Intelligence	*Examples*	*Science Applications*
Verbal linguistic/word smart: Ability to understand order, multiple meanings, and messages of words	Reading, writing, speaking, listening: accounts, books, diaries, journals, plays, presentations, readers' theatre, research, speeches, stories	Books, signs, posters, newspapers, notes in diaries, reference materials, laboratory and research reports and presentations
Visual spatial/picture smart: Ability to perceive the world accurately and to manipulate the nature of space	Art, charts, color, graphs, graphic organizers, illustrations, patterns, photographs, pictures, symbols, visualizing	Maps, charts of experiment results, diagrams, models, graphs of data, graphic organizers of concepts, photographs of events, illustrations, art, multimedia presentations, and animations
Logical mathematical/logic smart: Ability to reason with numbers and to recognize patterns and orders	Attributes, data, logic, manipulatives, maps, measuring, money, numbers, problems, puzzles, reasoning, time, tools	Timelines, lengths of time; measurements, statistics, percentages, data, stoichiometry, algebra, amounts, quantities, and totals
Bodily kinesthetic/body smart: Ability to use the body and to handle objects skillfully	Activities, body awareness, creative movement, crafts, dance, experiments, field trips, drama, dance, investigations	Tours of museums and industrial plants, outdoor education and investigations; laboratory experiments, simulations
Musical rhythmic/ music smart: Ability to replicate and appreciate pitch, melody, rhythm, and tone	Background music, form, instruments, moods, patterns, poetry, rhythms, songs	Study of sound, mnemonic tricks, science poetry and humor

Type of Multiple Intelligence	Examples	Science Applications
Interpersonal/ people smart: Ability to understand people and relationships	Brainstorming, clubs, conflict resolution, consensus, cooperative learning, discussions, group work, peer editing, sharing, social awareness	Problem identification and problem solving, decision making and democratic process, group lab reports, service-learning projects
Intrapersonal/self smart: Ability to assess one's emotions as a means to understand and appreciate oneself, others, and society	Goal setting, choice, individual expression, individual reading, responses, reflections, self-efficacy, self-esteem, self-sufficiency	Personal connections and reflections; opinions, perspectives, and points of view; autobiographies, individual research and experimentation
Naturalist/nature smart: Ability to recognize and appreciate flora and fauna	Awareness of nature and natural living, balance of nature and human, community, movement, sensory experiences	Connections with outdoors, study of ecosystems, care of surroundings, environmental topics and issues

Source: Adapted from Gardner (1983).

students in PreK–Grade 12. Be sure to check out *GreenWorks!* which offers educators the opportunity to apply for grants to implement community action and service-learning projects. Additional resources include an *Earth and Sky* radio show and an annotated *Webliography of Urban and Community Forestry Education Resources.*

All *Project WILD* and *Project Learning Tree* materials are correlated to state and national standards, and grounded in scientifically proven instructional approaches. Activities are inquiry based and emphasize cooperative learning.

We also want to point out that teachers need to be aware of their own strengths, and which multiple intelligences they tend to rely on and use most frequently. Teachers may be surprised to discover that they tend to teach through the same multiple intelligences, thus limiting their students' learning opportunities and choices. Armstrong (1994) suggests that we should each make a "Multiple Intelligence Pizza." Draw a large circle and divide it into eight pieces like the slices of a pizza. Label each pizza slice as: self smart, word smart, logic smart, people smart, music smart, body smart, picture smart, and nature smart. Describe a way you are smart that matches each pizza slice. For example, for self smart you may know that you have a good and clear sense of yourself. Then assemble your pizza for a total view of your intelligences or strengths.

Making this pizza incorporates your own words and meanings to describe concepts you understand and value. This exercise allows you to evaluate yourself to see the whole picture of your personality and become aware of areas that you may want to fortify so that you can teach holistically to meet the needs and interests of all your students. Your students will enjoy doing this activity too, in order to become aware of their own multiple intelligences.

DIFFERENTIATE INSTRUCTION

Teachers must be uniquely aware of the students in their classrooms as well as the content they are delivering (Tomlinson & McTighe, 2006). By taking time to get to know students, teachers become aware of their strengths, their dreams, and how to support their learning. With the diversity of learners in today's classrooms, teachers must find ways to identify not only what will be taught and assessed but also the processes and procedures that will facilitate learning by all. It is especially important to recognize that while goals will be addressed by everyone, students may complete different tasks with different materials under different time constraints. Differentiated learning hinges on asking students the big essential questions that can be answered by everyone in different ways. Everyone gains not only new information but new ways of learning through individual expression of ideas and opinions (Tomlinson, 1999).

Differentiated instruction involves responsive environments and flexible grouping for all students as well as interest-based instruction, instructional strategies targeted to varied learning abilities, and varied assessment. Teachers set up routines where students move in and out of learning activities in a quiet, orderly fashion, selecting materials and partners as appropriate. In particular, self-directed learning benefits classes with large numbers of students, gifted and talented students, struggling readers, English learners, students with preferred learning styles, and students with disabilities. The teacher preferably determines the assessment with the student. Effective instructional strategies meet the needs of multiple groups of learners at the same time. These include graphic organizers, learning centers, and student groupings by addressing multiple intelligences, providing a variety of materials (print and digital), and giving different homework assignments.

Science teachers may differentiate instruction by assigning different students different reading assignments to share in various ways; letting students work together during experiments and projects; generating lists of ways from which students select a method to demonstrate their learning; and using complex cooperative learning strategies, such as a jigsaw. In a jigsaw activity, students are placed into home groups and then divide again to become experts in special areas. After expert learning occurs, the students return to their original groups to share their knowledge. For example, biology/life science students might start out in groups of five to plan a poster promoting what they feel is the most important of the major body systems (i.e., musculoskeletal, circulatory, immune, digestive, respiratory, and nervous). They would then jigsaw out to become experts on one of the systems. Finally, they would rejoin their original group and reach consensus on which system to promote on their poster/brochure.

The keys to differentiated learning include working collaboratively with students to plan the learning experiences so that many different experiences are available, letting students select ways that fit them best, and expressing your understanding and appreciation of the various forms of expression. It is essential that teachers who promote differentiated learning reflect sincere acceptance of the learning demonstrations and their students' efforts.

We do geology as an inquiry unit in which students select projects they would like to work on with their partners. This keeps interest levels high. The unit is set up on a board with categories at the top: Reading, Activities, Labs, and "Questions I Have." Students have an occasional "must do" in a category but generally they are directed to pick one or two of interest to them. Every day before we start our partner work, students gather to share information they learned in class the day before. We then keep a fact wall where students can post interesting information they have learned. Examples of activities that the students can do include doing a skit, song, or poem about a book they have read; doing a poster on a pet rock; growing beans, covering them with plaster of Paris, and seeing whether plants really are strong enough to wear away rock; growing a crystal garden; doing Internet research on a site such as Nettrekker; or doing mineral tests on a group of minerals.

—Third-grade science teacher

SUPPORT ALL STUDENTS

When teaching English learners, the notion of "comprehensible input" is a critical component of instruction to develop students' content knowledge as they learn a new language. Students need access to the knowledge they need in language that is slightly beyond what they can easily understand (Krashen, 1996). Therefore, teachers must selectively choose what they present to students.

Teachers can adjust their communication with students by speaking in natural but slower speech, using shorter sentences, pausing frequently to allow students to process information, including and discussing the language as well as the content objectives in each lesson, targeting academic vocabulary, writing and orally emphasizing key phrases on the board and in handouts, using visuals and demonstrations, and reviewing *all* objectives at the end of each lesson (Short & Echevarria, 2004/2005). By frequently checking for understanding, facilitating classroom discussions and incorporating a variety of writing tools, English learners will further be supported (Dong, 2004/2005).

With respect to written communication, teachers are advised to print (which students learn to read first) rather than use cursive writing. Whether providing notes or directions on a board, giving feedback or encouragement on an assignment, or sending a letter home, simple and legible writing will be appreciated by all.

Assistive technologies, in the form of software and hardware, may greatly assist students with special needs. Software for improving writing includes word processing with spell check and thesaurus, speech recognition, and even story-starter programs. Students with physical disabilities may benefit from AlphaSmart™ keyboards; alternative keyboards, such as IntelliKeys; assisted keyboard features such as sticky or slow keys; and mouse alternatives, such as trackballs and track pads. Students who need reading accommodations may benefit from digitizing text so that it can be read by a computer, page turners, or a talking dictionary. Some of these resources may be available at your school site. See Chapter 10 for additional ideas for using technology to address the needs of all learners.

INCORPORATE INSTRUCTION THAT WORKS

Marzano, Pickering, and Pollock (2001) have identified nine research-based strategies that will help you maximize your science instruction. The nine strategies include:

1. *Setting Objectives and Providing Feedback.* Objectives should be focused and specific with clear expectations, conditions, and criteria, yet flexible to allow learners to make personal connections. Feedback should be specific, positive, and helpful.

2. *Generating and Testing Hypotheses.* Hypotheses may be approached inductively or deductively, must be explained thoroughly, and should show conclusions clearly.

3. *Providing Cues, Questions, and Advance Organizers.* Cues and questions must focus on key ideas, emphasize higher-level thinking, and allow time for students to think and respond; graphic organizers help learners manage large quantities of information in their own ways.

4. *Summarizing and Note Taking.* Summarizing requires learners to select the information that is worth knowing, analyze information deeply, and be aware of the explicit context for meaning and understanding the text. Note taking enables students to record new concepts and use new terms.

5. *Identifying Similarities and Differences.* Students benefit from explicit modeling, guided assistance, and direct applications to graphic organizers for comparisons and contrasts.

6. *Using Nonlinguistic Representations.* Nonlinguistic representations, such as pictures, symbols, and objects, extend many different topics and issues, activate learners' prior knowledge and experiences, and introduce new concepts and practices that are mental, physical, and kinesthetic.

7. *Facilitating Cooperative Learning.* Cooperative learning groups of diverse learners should be small and short term; members should be provided with clear guidelines (Slavin, 1995).

8. *Designing Homework and Practice.* Homework should increase as learners age, be completed independently from parents, have clear purposes and guidelines, and be assessed; teachers must establish a clear homework policy for increasing student understanding and application as students master a particular skill or outcome.

9. *Reinforcing Effort and Providing Recognition.* Effort must be reinforced specifically, positively, and authentically; rewards should bolster intrinsic motivation, relate to a standard of performance, and be tangible.

These nine strategies can be used throughout your units and lesson plans in every part of your science curriculum and instruction. It is up to you to determine when and how you will integrate them.

LET YOUR STUDENTS TEACH ONE ANOTHER . . .

The most valuable secret we can offer in planning and facilitating your instruction is to stop doing all the work and let your students teach one another. You want to create classroom environments that are thoughtful and caring (Newmann, 1990). Adopting this approach allows your students to talk with one another using concepts and vocabulary that are their own. When they have to teach one another, they must take ownership of the learning. This is called *reciprocal teaching and learning.* One student summarizes and shares what is learned; other students ask questions and clarify the main ideas. Together, students (and teacher) can then predict future events. Reciprocal teaching and learning helps solidify your learning communities and make your science exciting. It will allow students to employ their imagination and, as Maria Mitchell recommends, question everything. In the next chapter, we present ways to develop authentic and alternative assessments that align with your curriculum objectives and instruction.

Suggested Activities

1. You have now reviewed a number of taxonomies regarding the capacities, skills, values, beliefs, and characteristics to develop in students. From these, create your own taxonomy of thinking and learning. What is most important for your students to learn in your science classroom?

2. Think of your favorite science unit and design one instructional strategy featuring each of the eight multiple intelligences.

3. Find out where *Project WILD* and *Project Learning Tree* professional development opportunities are available in your community.

4. Identify one application for each of the nine instructional strategies that work and decide and how you will make that strategy come alive in one of your units of instruction.

CHAPTER FIVE

Design Assessments *To Align With Objectives*

My goal is simple. It is complete understanding of the universe, why it is as it is and why it exists at all.

—Stephen Hawking (1942–)

What is your goal for your students? What do you want them to be able to know and do once the lessons have ended? One of the most important factors of successful teaching and learning is to align your assessments with the objectives of your instruction and outcomes. As you plan your units of learning, you will select various types of assessments to evaluate your students' growth and achievement. Your assessments will give your students, their families, and you a clear sense of progress, accounting for both the learning and the teaching. Assessments should be positive and productive experiences that demonstrate and document how well your students have learned and how effectively you have taught.

SET GOALS, OBJECTIVES, AND EXPECTATIONS

The first task in developing units and lessons is to identify goals and objectives. Goals are the long-range outcomes, big ideas, or concepts you want your students to understand, apply, and appreciate in relationship to both learning and living. Goals are often found in your state standards and district expectations. For example, the goal may be for students to conduct scientific investigations and experiments. This goal fits with almost every theme, topic, and issue within the subject areas of biology, chemistry, geology, and physics. Goals are brought to life through unlimited kinds of learning experiences, showcasing all kinds of important science knowledge, skills, and dispositions. Progress toward achieving goals is checked or measured with the accumulation of many different learning experiences and assessments during a unit of learning or grading period.

Goal: Students will perform scientific investigations and experiments.

You choose how to make the goal come alive in your classroom through an instructional plan. You begin your lesson plan for the learning experience by identifying an objective or series of objectives, for each goal. Objectives are grade-appropriate, short-range statements of narrowly defined outcomes that you can immediately observe or measure. Objectives may be listed as part of the school district's scope and sequence chart or in an established course syllabus.

As you introduce individual lessons, you should explain to students what they are going to learn, provide them with a purpose or reason for learning (just as you do prior to reading), and identify how they will demonstrate their learning. Objectives address learning that is cognitive (about content), psychomotor (about skills), or affective (about feelings and dispositions). It is easiest to write objectives using sentences that begin with, "The student will . . ." and follow with a verb that indicates performance, such as "define," "identify," "compare," or "solve." See Chapter 3 for a list of action verbs to consider when composing objectives.

Some administrators expect you to write the objective(s) on the board and align them with state content standards. We suggest that this expectation become a daily routine. By posting the objective and content standard, you and the students will have a visual reference during the lesson. This enables everyone to stay focused.

As mentioned earlier, objectives should align with your students' grade levels. Continuing our earlier example, possible objectives might include:

Goal: Students will perform scientific investigations and experiments.	
Grades	Sample Objective
2–4	Students will make predictions based on observed patterns.
6–8	Students will communicate the steps and results from an investigation in a written report.
9–12	Students will identify and communicate sources of unavoidable experimental error.

Next, you need to determine how you will monitor students' progress in achieving the objective(s). You have many questions to answer and communicate to your students prior to the learning experience, such as:

- What are students going to do for their assessments?
- Why have you chosen these forms of assessment?
- How will they demonstrate learning (both the process and outcomes)?
- How will learning be assessed?
- What are the assessment criteria?
- Who will assess outcomes?
- Will assessments apply to individuals or groups or both?
- How will these assessments fit into students' overall grades for the course?

Clarify why you have chosen selected forms of assessment and how they align with objective(s), then determine an instructional plan that will enable students to be successful. Additionally, consider whether you are using a balanced variety of assessments throughout the unit, semester, and year. In the following sample, assessments and activities are differentiated by content areas. In this example, only one assessment is identified for each objective.

Goal: Students will perform scientific investigations.			
Grades	Sample Objectives	Sample Assessment	Sample Activity
2–4 Life Science	Students will make predictions based on observed patterns.	Students will observe the contents of an owl pellet and make predictions on what the owl eats.	Students will dissect an owl pellet and reconstruct the bones of the animals eaten.
6–8 Earth Science	Students will communicate the steps and results from an investigation in a written report.	Students will delineate the steps to make a model of a tornado in a glass jar.	Students will create a tornado in a glass jar.
9–12 Chemistry	Students will identify and communicate sources of unavoidable experimental error.	Students will identify two actual sources of experimental error for their experiment.	Students will burn magnesium ribbon in a crucible and calculate the theoretical and experimental yield.

START WITH THE END IN MIND

When you have your assessments in mind, you will be able to select instructional strategies to ensure student success. Wiggins and McTighe (2005) promote this concept of "backward design" in planning:

1. Identify your objectives, the exact science knowledge, skills, and dispositions that you want your students to demonstrate at the completion of the learning experience.

2. Select how students will demonstrate their outcomes, modifying expectations for various kinds of learners.

3. Decide the assessment criteria or levels of proficiency that are anticipated as satisfactory and unsatisfactory, combining criteria into a rubric or scoring guide as appropriate.

4. Organize the instruction that needs to precede the assessment.

See *Understanding by Design* (expanded 2nd edition, 2005), by Grant Wiggins and Jay McTighe, for more on learning design.

Assessment is more than a test score to record in your grade book and send home on a report card. During a unit of learning, science assessments should incorporate four significant areas that include:

- higher-order thinking;
- deep knowledge;
- substantive conversations; and
- meaningful connections to the world beyond the classroom.

Reflecting Stephen Hawking's goal at the start of the chapter, let's look at another example.

Goal: Students will understand the structure and composition of the universe. (Grades 6–9)

Working backwards, you design the teaching and learning so that students can demonstrate successful achievement. You decide to ask students what they think are the differences between planets, planetary satellites, comets, and asteroids via a K-W-L chart (what is *k*nown, what is *w*ondered about, and what is *l*earned); to form investigative cooperative learning groups via a jigsaw approach to look at the materials you have made available; to answer key questions about an object in the solar system, including its appearance, general composition, relative size and position, and motion; and to ask for reports in thirty minutes. You then regroup students so that each new group includes "experts" for each category. Each group is given an overhead transparency and colored transparency pens to create a solar system that must include a wide range of objects.

You also inform the students that they will prepare an oral presentation on their solar system, which must answer a series of provided questions. The questions should cover all levels of knowledge as identified in Bloom's Taxonomy. Two key questions are evaluative and must be decided by group consensus: What is the most important type of object in a solar system? What is important to learn about the structure and composition of the universe? Finally, students will return to the K-W-L chart and fill in what they have learned. In addition, students complete an evaluation of their own and peer participation in the group learning experience.

> *Objective:* Students will describe the appearance, general composition, relative size and position, and motion of five different objects in the solar system.

> *Assessments:* K-W-L chart of what is known, wondered, and learned about planets, comets, and asteroids; drawing of a solar system; oral presentations that addresses six key questions about solar system objects; evaluation of group participation.

This combination of assessments measures higher-order thinking, deep knowledge, substantive conversations, and meaningful connections to the world beyond the classrooms. Your assessment is organized, offers alternatives, draws content and processes from disciplines, and is elaborated through written communications. By sending work home to be shared with parents, you have reached an audience beyond the school.

FEATURE ALL THREE TYPES OF ASSESSMENT

Assessment can be divided into three categories based on when it takes place and its purpose: entry level, formative, and summative.

Entry level takes place before or at the beginning of a unit to see whether students have mastered the prerequisite knowledge and skills. Checking prior learning and experiences lets you know whether it will be necessary to integrate any background content or skill development. It also tells you whether your students already have specific knowledge and skills so that you do not have to teach in depth. Entry-level assessment can be written or oral, or a combination of both.

> *Entry-level assessment* might take place by the teacher asking students what they think are the differences among planets, planetary satellites, comets, and asteroids via a K-W-L chart (what is known, what is wondered about, and what is learned).

Formative assessment takes place during instruction and informs you of the degree to which students are progressing. Examples of formative assessment include checking for understanding by monitoring student work as it is completed in class or as homework. One way is to ask questions as you present new material or demonstrate a new skill to make sure students comprehend what you are talking about or modeling. Student responses might also be in the form of showing you answers on individual whiteboards, writing a summary at the end of a lesson for you to read, completing a graphic organizer to submit for your review, or taking a quiz.

> *Formative assessment* takes place as the teacher monitors the progress of the research on the solar system. In addition, the teacher checks the solar system drawings the students are creating.

Summative assessment takes place at the end of a unit. Examples of summative assessment include a unit test or an alternative assessment, such as a poster, report, or performance. You will not be able to use all the various types of assessments for any given unit, but over the course of a semester or year, you can offer students a variety of assessment experiences. Remember, the more types you employ, the more different opportunities you give the students to demonstrate their achievements.

> *Summative assessment* takes place as the teacher evaluates the drawings, oral presentations, and the completed K-W-L chart.

On a given day, you may use one, two, or all three types of assessment (entry level, formative or progress monitoring, and summative). During a unit of instruction, you will use all three. While there may be assessments based on group or whole-class responses, ultimately there should be some individual summative assessment (Bol & Strange, 1996).

DETERMINE THE FUNCTIONS AND PURPOSES

Assessment is the process by which students demonstrate five functions of, and purposes for, learning (Stiggins, 2005):

1. *Knowledge and understanding function.* Answers the questions of who, what, and where.

2. *Logic and reasoning function.* Answers the questions of why, why not, and how do you know.

3. *Skills and demonstration function.* Answers the questions of how do you do it and can you show me.

4. *Productivity and creativity function.* Answers the questions of what else and how might you do this, or do it differently.

5. *Outlooks and dispositions function.* Answers the questions of what do you think is important, how do you feel, and how might someone else think or feel.

You want to include assessments that provide feedback on all five functions, either independently of one another or in combination with other functions. For example, you may want your students to demonstrate knowledge only. Or you may want your students to demonstrate a combination of knowledge and skill. It is essential that you are clear about your expectations before you determine what you want your students to demonstrate. Then you need to select the structure or format as described in the next section.

VARY THE STRUCTURES AND FORMATS

Assessment is not as overwhelming as many teachers might believe. Let's look at four general structures and formats that you want to incorporate into your assignments and assessments (Stiggins, 2005): *selected responses, constructed essays, demonstrated performances,* and *personal communications.* Again, you will want to create outcomes that use all four types of structures either independently or in combination with the other structures. For example, you can develop an assessment with only selected responses, such as multiple-choice items, or you can create an assessment with both selected responses, such as true/false, and constructed essays, such as short answers.

I always use a variety of assessments for every unit. For example, in a unit on properties of matter and the periodic table, I ask students to quick write everything they know about an element of their choice on the periodic table. Students are assessed throughout the unit through in-class assignments and homework, a laboratory experiment on separating a mixture, and a dichotomous key activity involving the physical and chemical properties of a selection of elements and compounds. The unit exam includes multiple choice, short answer, problems, a table on the three states of matter, and at least one essay question. For the essay question, I provide a scoring guide so students know how the points will be distributed. Finally, I use a checklist and a rubric to guide student completion of element posters.

—Tenth-grade chemistry teacher

The more important aspects of designing assessments are (1) to align the assessment with the curriculum and instruction so the objective matches the assessment, and (2) to be sure the assessment measures what you want to measure—for example, if you want to know if your students can produce a reasoned argument, then ask your students to write a constructed essay to a question they can prepare for and answer intelligently. And (3), you want your assessments to be developmentally appropriate. Your assessments should be an opportunity for your students to showcase their learning. The assessments must allow them chances to do well and for students to feel good about their accomplishments. Assessments are not a time to surprise students or to make them feel inadequate.

USE SELECTED RESPONSES

Selected responses sounds just like the name: students pick the answer from a prepared written group (usually a list) of items. Selected responses include multiple choice, matching, true/false, fill in the blanks, or checklists. Selected responses are the most liked assessment by most students because the answers are given to them. Students simply have to choose one of the responses; they do not have to think or remember or analyze or connect. Through a process of elimination, students can narrow their choices to a few items and make their best guess. There is no reason for a student to not complete this form of assessment because the student can always take a chance on getting the right answer.

Selected responses also are the most liked by most teachers because they are quick and easy to grade. You can make an answer key or template; often you use a Scantron machine to do the checking. You can give a selected response exam one day and return it the next day, even when you assess five or six sections of the same course in one day. Plus, you can mix up the order of questions quite easily to create five or six different versions of the same test, giving a different version of the same exam to each section of the same course. This prevents students from memorizing the order of answers by their initials and sharing the answers with friends throughout the day.

However, writing a selected response assessment is not as easy as it might appear to be. You must craft the wording of the statements carefully to avoid ambiguity and confusion. You may find yourself writing selected response statements identical to phrases you have spoken in class, written on overheads, and/or distributed in notes and assignments. You may want to consider whether your selected response assessment is just asking for recognition of vocabulary and concepts, or whether students have to think about application.

Many of the assessments that accompany your textbooks rely primarily upon various forms of selected responses. The questions usually contain the same vocabulary as presented in the textbook, and frequently in much the same way. However, make sure the language of the test bank is the same as the language of the text, as sometimes they are written by different authors.

INCLUDE CONSTRUCTED ESSAYS

Constructed essays include written words, sentences, and paragraphs originating from the student's memory. They can vary in format from a traditional essay to a creative exercise, such as a newspaper article, editorial, or letter. They are probably the least liked form of assessment by most students and most teachers. These assessments take time to write, time to complete, and time to check. You must prepare your students thoroughly to not only know the main ideas and supportive examples but also to be able to connect the main ideas and communicate their thoughts coherently.

The following question can be used repeatedly to focus student attention: "How does science (or, more specifically, chemistry or biology) impact your personal life and society?" (Costa, 1993b). Students can periodically respond with how what they learned during a unit contributed to their understanding of science.

Sometimes these essays might be written collaboratively, sometimes individually. In fact, it can be used as part of a final exam.

Students will want to know exactly how they are going to be graded on their writing; therefore, detailed rubrics accounting for inclusion of information and presentation of ideas need to be developed in advance. Rubrics also enable you to give your students credit if your students' answers are not complete. You also must be prepared to give a student credit if the answer is different from the usual or anticipated response. Finally, you need to decide whether you will assess the English language development as well as the science development.

HIGHLIGHT DEMONSTRATED PERFORMANCES AND LABORATORY SKILLS

Demonstrated performances, such as laboratory skills and scientific processes, include actions and presentations shown to an individual or to a group (either spontaneously or prepared). They can be quick and easy, or much longer and more involved. For example, asking a student to prepare a cheek cell slide for a microscope, measure a quantity of liquid with a graduated cylinder, or defend their position on the dangers of global warming are all performances. Other examples are more extensive, such as determining an unknown substance or specimens, dissecting a frog, or setting up a working circuit. Performance of these skills may be also accompanied by student explanations or recitations. Formal presentation of data and the findings of an investigation are also important performances.

Teachers must provide students with plenty of direction and support so they will understand and be able to achieve the performance assessment successfully. A detailed rubric or checklist informs students of the content and processes related to science. For example, Figure 5.1 provides a sample checklist for using a microscope. This checklist can be used by the student to learn the skill, and then by the teacher to assess the skill. Showing a sample video or modeling your expectation will also help guide students. You must take time to guide your students with intellectual and emotional reassurance. Students will need time to practice, and your encouragement is vital.

Figure 5.1   Checklist for Using a Microscope

❑   Wipes slide with lens paper

❑   Places drop or two of culture on slide

❑   Adds few drops of water

❑   Applies cover

❑   Places slide on stage

❑   Turns to low power

❑   Looks through eyepiece with one eye

❑   Adjusts mirror

❑   Turns to high power

❑   Adjusts for maximum enlargement and resolution

Demonstrated performances allow students to showcase their knowledge, understanding, logic, reasoning, productivity, and creativity with skills that the teacher and other students may not be aware of. You may be surprised to discover the public speaking and intellectual demonstration talents of some of your quieter students. These are important skills to promote, as many students will need these skills when attending universities and in their careers.

Teachers frequently ask their students to assess other students during demonstrated performances. This approach to assessment expands the audience and helps students to direct their products toward their peers. Guide students to measure peers against realistic expectations while providing positive and constructive feedback.

REMEMBER PERSONAL COMMUNICATIONS

Personal communications are overlooked as a viable form of assessment, yet they are the most frequently used types of assessment. Personal communications include short oral answers or responses to questions or lengthier verbal explanations conducted through both formal and informal conversations. When you ask a student any kind of question and expect a verbal response, it becomes a personal communication. Your question may be related to your lesson or to the student. Conversations may be highly structured and organized, in a panel discussion format, or a prepared list of questions related to information in the textbook; or your conversations may be more spontaneous, such as when you use the Socratic Method. This form of assessment may be particularly useful during group work and laboratory activities.

You probably are not formally grading your students during personal communications; however, you are assessing their responses in the moment to confirm understanding. You decide whether a student or a group of students—perhaps the entire class—comprehends an idea, allowing you to move to the next idea, or whether you need to revisit and reteach the idea. Every teacher does this every day. This is a form of progress monitoring, or the formative assessment mentioned above. If you are grading during personal communications, let the students know.

OFFER AUTHENTIC AND ALTERNATIVE ASSESSMENTS

Many teachers tend to use the same types of assessments over and over. Like teaching methods, however, assessment techniques are unlimited. The secret to success is to select a variety of alternative assessments that serve the purpose of the objective, fit assignments authentically, and help connect learning to the real world. For example, to learn the definitions and spelling of scientific terminology, consider these different possibilities: your students can spell the words aloud to a partner; they can write or draw the words on paper, or with markers on the board, or on an overhead transparency; you can organize a spelling bee; the students can write the words on the computer and use spell check for feedback; they could teach another student how to spell and use the new words; students might be given a list of words and be asked to compose sentences using the word in a scientific context and also in a nonscience context (i.e., "A base can neutralize an acid." versus "The baseball player ran to first base."); or they could select which word is spelled either correctly or incorrectly in a sentence or story. The students could even write the sentence or story themselves or in small groups and then exchange papers with one another. One version of collaborative writing is a "write-around," where a group of four students must write four paragraphs using four predetermined words in each paragraph. As each paragraph is completed, the paper is passed to a different writer. The content is collaborative, and the write-around format ensures that all students participate. Be thoughtful and creative. Another authentic assessment would be for students to write articles for a student magazine. Consider the topic of plate tectonics featured in Box 5.1.

Authentic assessments are based on work that is produced for a real audience or is carried out in a real-world context. Tomlinson and McTighe (2006) suggest having students perform real-world tasks and solve problems with real-world applications. Students will enjoy activities that involve writing, photography, audio- or videotaping, and interviewing. Another example of authentic work and authentic assessment is to have students engage in service-learning projects, which have many applications in science (see Chapter 11). This is also a great place for students to incorporate the use of technology to create Wikis, blogs, Web sites, multimedia presentations, and animations (see Chapter 10).

BOX 5.1

History of Science

Pangaea and Plate Tectonics

Plate tectonic theory had its beginnings in 1915 when Alfred Wegener (1880–1930) proposed his theory of "continental drift." Wegener, a German astronomer, meteorologist, and explorer, observed that the continents seem to fit together like a puzzle. For example, the West African coastline fits nicely into the east coast of South America and the Caribbean Sea, and a similar fit appears across the Pacific. Wagner theorized that the continents were once compressed into a single protocontinent, which he called Pangaea (meaning "all lands"), and over time they have drifted apart into their current distribution. Wegener's ideas were very controversial because he was not able to explain why the continents moved, only that there was observational evidence that they had.

Although Wegener's "continental drift" theory was later disproved, it was one of the first introductions of the idea of crustal movement. His theorizing laid the groundwork for the development of modern plate tectonics. As the years passed, more and more evidence was uncovered to support the idea that the plates move constantly over geological time. In 1929, Arthur Holmes, a British geologist, elaborated on one of Wegener's many hypotheses—that the mantle undergoes thermal convection.

Convection occurs because when a substance is heated, its density decreases and it rises to the surface until it is cooled and sinks again. Holmes argued that this repeated heating and cooling results in a current that may be enough to cause continents to move.

Holmes's ideas were largely ignored until the 1960s, when greater understanding of the sea floor led scientists to theorize that mantle convection currents result in sea floor spreading. Also occurring about the same time, a worldwide array of seismometers were installed to monitor nuclear testing, and these instruments revealed that earthquakes, volcanoes, and other active geologic features for the most part aligned along distinct belts around the world, and those belts defined the edges of tectonic plates. These were some of the final pieces of the puzzle that led to the development of modern plate tectonic theory.

Since its emergence in the 1960s, plate tectonic theory has gained widespread acceptance as the model of Earth processes. More information is available on the following Web sites:

- **History of Plate Tectonics:** http://scign.jpl.nasa.gov/learn/plate2.htm. This link is part of the Southern California Integrated GPS Network (SCIGN) Education Module, designed to assist high school and college students understand the concepts of plate tectonics, earthquakes, GPS, and space technology at work.
- **Plate Tectonics: The Rocky History of an Idea:** www.ucmp.berkeley.edu/geology/techist.html. This link is part of the University of California Museum of Paleontology. The UCMP Web site contains thousands of pages of content about the history of life on Earth.
- **On the Move: Continental Drift and Plate Tectonics:** http://kids.earth.nasa.gov/archive/pangaea/evidence.html. This link is part of the NASA Kids Only Web site, which provides great information and resources, including teacher guides, for topics related to air, natural hazards, land, water, and people.
- **Plate Tectonics Animations:** http://www2.nature.nps.gov/GEOLOGY/usgsnps/animate/pltecan.html. Animations were created by the U.S. Geological Survey; see also its Web site at www.usgs.gov for many more resources.

INCORPORATE PORTFOLIOS

Portfolio assessments have students demonstrate what they have learned, and provide teachers (and other viewers, such as parents) with a fuller picture of students' progress, attitudes, and interests.

They may be electronic or printed. With portfolios, students select the best examples of their work. Often, they are asked to evaluate their selections and write a brief reflection on the significance of each piece that is included. Selections may include the following:

- laboratory reports, written observations, and results;
- charts, graphs, and drawings;
- written reports and evaluations of science videos, field trips, and activities;
- media/digitized projects such as photographs, audio- or videotape, presentations, concept maps and timelines, Web sites, blogs, and Wikis; and
- problem-solving worksheets, texts and examinations, and other scored work samples.

Portfolio documents should represent a variety of the following: thorough description, valid interpretation, balanced research, rigorous investigation, structured analysis, productive problem solving, reasoned persuasion, and critical implications. Portfolio rubrics should address:

- content evidence, description, and support;
- skills and processes relevant to the content;
- conceptual understanding connecting content and processes to life; and
- articulation, communication, and presentation of portfolio.

Portfolio assessment allows you to delve into your students' thinking, understanding, logic, and reasoning, plus outlooks and dispositions, extremely well. When you ask for strongly developed constructed essays, you can assess your students' abilities to give a clear and succinct explanation, contextualization, or connection that reflects your best teaching.

PREPARE RUBRICS AND SCORING GUIDES

With selected responses, the scoring is straightforward. Answers are correct or incorrect. With constructed essays, demonstrated performances, and personal communications, however, scoring is more complicated. You will find that rubrics or scoring guides facilitate the assessment process.

Rubrics, or scoring guides, identify the criteria for the characteristics of the product or skills that will be evaluated and how the grade will be determined. Rubrics include the knowledge and skills, the degree of proficiency or whether a behavior is observed or not, use of required procedures, demonstrations of dispositions, and exhibition of social skills (Borich & Tombari, 2004). Scoring can be holistic and give an overall evaluation of student work, or it can be analytic based on specific identified behaviors and traits of students' skills, knowledge, and dispositions. Both students and parents appreciate such detailed information. The mystery is taken out of grading as it becomes more objective. Students can be involved in creating the rubrics and can self-evaluate their work based on what has been developed. You will also find that rubrics enable you to grade student work more quickly and return it in a timely way.

In particular, using a rubric greatly facilitates assessing students' ability to problem solve. Science is full of problems to solve—both mathematical and nonmathematical. It is critical to help students learn to reflect on how they solved the problem, and a rubric can assist in this process. Below is a sample rubric.

Problem-Solving Rubric			
4	*3*	*2*	*1*
Student demonstrates excellent understanding of the problem to be solved.\n\nSolution has no errors in computation. All work was shown. Problem was correctly solved.	Student demonstrates solid understanding of the problem to be solved. Not all work was shown but problem was correctly solved.\nOR\nProblem was incorrectly solved with only one error in computation.	Student demonstrates some understanding of the problem to be solved. Problem was solved incorrectly and there are substantial errors in computation and content. There was some progress toward a solution.	Student demonstrates little or no understanding of the problem to be solved. Problem was started but there are significant errors in computation and content. There was little progress toward a solution.

UNDERSTAND THE RESULTS OF STANDARDIZED TESTING

Standardized testing, a form of summative assessment, is the focus of many discussions both in schools and throughout society. You may have mixed feelings about standardized testing. We all need to know that what is being taught is indeed being learned. We all need to know that the majority of students have achieved the goals of a particular grade level and/or subject area and are ready for the next level. As teachers, we want to know whether our methods of teaching are effective and help our students to succeed. As the data from standardized testing become available, the results will be given to you to make improvements in your teaching and your students' learning.

Criterion-referenced tests are designed to measure what students have learned against a set of standards (criteria), such as the district objectives. They are locally developed. The tests you give at the end of a semester, for example, will likely be criterion-referenced tests. Your district may have benchmark and/or quarterly exams or high school exit exams. This type of test tells you whether or not your students have mastered identified objectives. You receive specific feedback from this kind of evaluation. You will see how well your students did, and whether any learning gaps exist that you will need to address. This information will enable you to identify areas for reteaching.

Some schools participate in international tests, such as the Trends in International Mathematics and Science Study (TIMMS) or Program for the International Student Assessment (PISA). However, these assessments do not give individual results.

Norm-referenced tests measure students against like students, usually across the nation. For example, the achievement of a second-semester "x grade" student in your school is compared to all second-semester "x grade" students who took the test. These are the tests that are being used as the basis for school accountability today. You will receive information on how students did on various tasks included in the test; however, information from the task analysis tends to be general rather than specific. Also, these tests are highly dependent on reading ability, which can be a problem for many students. Unfortunately, there is often a lag time of weeks or months between the date the test is submitted for scoring and the date the received results are shared with teachers. Check your district and school calendars for dates of mandated standardized testing.

DEVELOP AN ASSESSMENT BLUEPRINT

As you develope a yearlong plan to cover your standards as suggested in Chapter 2, another secret is to develop an assessment plan. Plot your summative assessments over the course of the unit and entire year so that students have the opportunity to experience many different kinds of assessments, including tests, projects, and performances. Incorporate your students' learning styles and multiple intelligences. Explore with students which types of assessments they think are the most fun and engaging. A list of additional alternative and authentic assessments is found in Box 5.2.

BOX 5.2

A to Z of Authentic and Alternative Assessments

Advertisement, animated story, animation modeling

Blog, brochure, bulletin board

Cartoon, children's or young people's book, collage, contest

Dance, database or data analysis, debate, demonstration, dichotomous key, diorama, display, drawing

Editorial, e-pen pal, e-mail, experiment

Finger puppets, fishbowl discussion

Game, graphic organizer

Historical portrayal of person or event

Illustrated timeline, illustrations, interview

Journal entry

K-W-L chart

Laboratory report, learning log, letter

Map, microscope slide, mobile, mock trial, model, museum

Newscast, newsletter

Obituary, oral history

Performance, photographic essay, play, podcast, poem, poster, presentation, problem solving

Questionnaire and results analysis, quilt

Reenactments, role play

Science fair project, Science Olympiad participation, simulation, slide show, song, specimen, speech, storyboard, survey

Television program, thinking aloud, tiered timeline

Unit summary with illustrations

Video documentary, virtual field trip

Web site, Wiki, word wall

Xylograph-wood engraving or other artistic rendering

Yearbook or similar-type documentary

Z to A or A to Z alphabet-type presentation

Source: Adapted from Kottler, Kottler, & Kottler (2004).

Then, within each unit, identify what type of entry-level assessment you will use to find out what content and skills the students already possess. Throughout the unit, plan formative assessment activities and conclude with summative activities that align with your objectives. Consider the goals and purpose for each assessment, the type of assessment utilized, the timing and implementation of the assessment, how you will provide feedback to students regarding their achievement, and how your assessment data will inform future teaching.

MAKE SURE THE PROCESS MAKES SENSE FOR EVERYONE . . .

Align your curriculum and assessments so they make sense to you and your students. We recommend that you approach your planning holistically so these components are well developed long in advance of your actual teaching. Be sure that you have included all structures of assessment to accomplish all the functions. With the assessments in mind, you'll be ready to take on the role of instructional leader.

Here's an important secret. As you begin teaching, remember how you felt as a student. You wanted to know how you were doing in class and the grade you were earning. You liked feedback and to be updated with each assignment. Today's students and their parents feel the same way. Announce assessments in advance and provide feedback—oral and written—on a regular basis to students as quickly as possible.

In the next chapter, we look at how to connect the learning to your students' lives. Your students will be engaged in meaningful skills they will use throughout their lives.

Suggested Activities

1. Reflect on your own science classes. Identify the type of assessment that was used most often, and the type of assessment that you preferred.

2. Think of one science objective and describe how you would assess mastery learning of that objective through selected responses, constructed essays, demonstrated performance, and personal communication.

3. From your curriculum, select one topic and make a connection between the topic and the five functions of assessment.

4. Make a list of natural and supportive ways in which you can prepare your students for standardized testing.

CHAPTER SIX

Connect the Learning to Reach Students' Lives

The scientist is not a person who gives the right answers, he's one who asks the right questions.

—Claude Lévi-Strauss, *Le Cru et le cuit*, 1964

What are some of the essential questions of science? What questions have been adequately answered, and what questions have yet to be answered? We suggest that you concentrate on science content and skills that students need to connect the learning quickly and easily to their lives. This is a two-part secret. First, the more you can engage your students in actively participating in their learning, the more they will learn and the more they will enjoy the learning. Second, as you advance their learning and your students become more motivated, they will make more connections, personalize the learning, and take ownership of the outcomes.

Levi-Strauss's observation that a scientist is the one who "asks the right questions" demonstrates the importance of teaching students to ask their own questions. Consider the story of Lord

Ernest Rutherford. Challenging the accepted model of the atom in his day, Rutherford constructed an experiment to disprove the theory. Although he did not expect the results, his posing the question, "What's wrong with this model?" led to a revolution in our understanding of atomic structure. Read more about Rutherford's Gold Foil Experiment in Box 6.1.

CREATE CONSTRUCTIVIST CLASSROOMS

Through constructivism, teachers and students are continuously checking and revising their thoughts, words, actions, and interactions as they compare and contrast the known with the unknown in the process of acquiring new knowledge, skills, and dispositions. Teachers help students negotiate dissonance and conflict, an aspect of essential development to support middle-level, middle school, and high school students.

Constructivist teachers advocate the following approach:

- Present curriculum from whole to part, with an emphasis on big ideas.
- Develop curriculum around themes and issues significant to humans.
- Pursue student-generated questions.
- Use authentic materials and planning time for experimentation.
- Organize activities and projects as group work, with diverse group members.
- View students as critical thinkers with insights built on prior knowledge and experiences.
- Interact with students, modeling the learning process collaboratively.
- Explore students' points of view and preferred methods of expression.
- Assess through observation, conversation, and demonstration.

I have students design and perform a lab experiment. It has to be about bacteria, but they come up with a question, a hypothesis, and a procedure on their own. They submit it to me and I ask some clarifying questions to guide them in refining their experiments. Then they collect and analyze the data, and present their finding to the class. They think it is fun and I am always impressed with how creative they are with both their experimental questions and designs.

—Tenth-grade biology teacher

BOX 6.1

History of Science

The Gold Foil Experiment

Little Jack Horner sat in a corner eating his Christmas pie. He put in his thumb and pulled out a plum, and said "What a good boy am I!"

("Little Jack Horner" in Wright, 1994, *The Real Mother Goose*)

Can you imagine that at one time in history, the structure of the atom was believed to be a large plum pudding? The model featured electrons surrounded by a soup of positive change, much like plums in a pudding. If you were to "stick your thumb" in an atom, you'd be lucky if you "pulled out" an electron, as they were thought to be sparingly distributed throughout the atomic structure. This early model was proposed in 1904 by Englishman J. J. Thomson, who discovered the electron in 1897.

In 1991, Ernest Rutherford, a New Zealand scientist, questioned the accuracy of this model and devised an experiment to refute Thomson's theory. The plan was to shoot alpha particles through a very thin sheet of gold. If the positive charges were dispersed throughout the structure, as the plum pudding model dictated, then the alpha particles would pass through undisturbed. Surprisingly, observations found that although most particles did indeed pass through the thin sheet of metal, a small portion of the particles were deflected, indicating a small, concentrated, positive charge strong enough to repel an alpha particle.

From this experiment, Rutherford concluded that the atom might be mostly empty space, with most of the atom's mass and a large fraction of its positive change concentrated in a tiny center, which later became known as the nucleus.

This experiment is also known as the Geiger-Marsden Experiment, for the two graduate students, Johannes (Hans) Geiger and Ernest Marsden, who designed and conducted the study. And yes, this is the same Geiger who with Rutherford in 1908 coinvented the Geiger counter, which is used to detect radiation. Read more about atomic theory and Rutherford's Nobel Prize in Chemistry at the link below.

- **Ernest Rutherford:** http://nobelprize.org/nobel_prizes/chemistry/laureates/1908/rutherford-bio.html.
- **Atomic Theory I: The Early Days:** www.visionlearning.com/library/module_viewer.php?mid=50. Vision Learning is an innovative educational resource designed for students, teachers, parents, or anyone interested in learning. It provides an interactive glossary and a range of tools, simulations, links to current events, primary documents, quizzes, and other resources.

CLARIFY MISCONCEPTIONS

Students have many misconceptions about science. A first-grade student told a story that her teacher had her picking up lead on the playground with a magnet. There are several misconceptions in that statement. First, lead is quite poisonous and is (hopefully) not found on a playground at all. Second, lead is also not magnetic. In fact, the teacher was probably having her students look for elemental iron on the playground—which *is* magnetic and small particles of which may be found in dirt and sand. (You can even pick up iron from certain vitamin-enriched cereals if you soak the flakes in water and then use a magnet.)

Misconceptions about science are started with the best of intentions—by teachers, parents, and other well-intentioned adults. Poor models and images in textbooks may also be the culprit. One famous example of a scientific misconception is the significant number of people—including Harvard graduates—who believe that the reason it is hotter in the summer and colder in the winter is because the Earth orbits closer to or further away from the sun during these seasons. It has been suggested that textbooks that provide a flattened image of the Earth's orbit (from a 3-D sphere into a more elliptical 2-D representation) have contributed to this misconception. Read more about the Private Universe Project at www.learner.org/teacherslab/pup.

As a science teacher, you will encounter misconceptions in every area of science. These preconceived notions, nonscientific beliefs, naive theories, and conceptual misunderstandings are held strongly by students (Thompson & Logue, 2006), and you will need to ask open-ended questions and truly listen to students' ideas in order to identify the context for the misconception. Then you can structure experiences and the learning environment so that there are opportunities for students to "test out" their ideas and prove the correct concepts to themselves. This method is often referred to as *teaching for conceptual change*. When you focus the learning on what your students know, what they want to learn, and their reasons for learning, you have transformed your class into one that is constructivist in nature. We think that the more often you can incorporate constructivist approaches into your classes, the more your students will learn and enjoy science.

SELECT QUESTIONS EFFECTIVELY

Select and use questions effectively during teacher talk to stimulate student responses. The critical question posed earlier (How does science impact my personal life and society?) can frame an entire course as well as individual units in the science disciplines: How does the function and structure of our immune system impact society and our personal lives? How does our knowledge of the universe shape our personal lives and society? The question can also frame ongoing discussion of current events and new discoveries in science (i.e., How will this new discovery impact my personal life and society?).

There are eight main types of questions (Callahan, Clark, & Kellough, 1998). Each has a different purpose. Box 6.2 shows the eight types of questions with examples. Be deliberate in phrasing your questions to achieve your goals and provide students with ample time to reflect on your questions and their responses.

BOX 6.2

Eight Types of Questioning With Examples

- *Focusing.* Directing attention and energy: "Who needs a copy of the experiment?"
- *Convergent thinking.* Narrowing the choices and searching for a single answer: "What would you say was the cause?"
- *Evaluating.* Making a judgment or placing a value: "Why do you think global warming is an international crisis?"
- *Clarifying.* Delving into associated thought processes: "What would be a situation in which it would be appropriate to conduct tests on animals?"
- *Probing.* Asking for additional information and examples: "What types of trash do you recycle regularly?"
- *Cuing.* Providing clues to connect with a bigger idea or concept: "What would this piece of evidence lead you to believe?"
- *Divergent thinking.* Broadening the choices and encouraging possibilities promoted by higher-order thinking responses: "If you could do that differently, what would you do?"
- *Socratic thinking.* Conducting a dialogue where students must think critically about the problem, reflecting mindfully on their individual beliefs, and applying contextually their insights igniting student interest and energies (Brogan & Brogan, 1995).

Source: Adapted from Callahan, Clark, & Kellough (1998).

CONSIDER VARIOUS APPROACHES TO ASKING QUESTIONS

There are several approaches to keep in mind when asking questions in your classroom. One way is to create questions in advance of the discussion by following Bloom's Taxonomy. Be sure you make them easy to understand, avoiding confusing terminology and/or double negatives. Or you can look into the teacher's manual for key questions that the textbook authors may already have developed.

As you ask questions, be open to the various directions in which the discussions may go. Additional questions you pose during discussion will enable you both to probe deeper into a particular topic or issue and to expand the conversation to reflect your students' growing interests. The secret is to have extra questions prepared in advance.

Another approach is to place your students in pairs or small groups and ask them to write a few questions on different sections of the assigned reading. Give each group clear instructions as to who is leading the group, who is recording the questions, and so forth. After a specified amount of time, collect the questions, review them quickly to make sure they are appropriate, and then redistribute the questions for others to answer individually, in pairs, or in groups. You will also need to decide whether they are to write a response or discuss the answer, and whether further research will be allowed.

If you are teaching more than one section of the same course, you can ask the students in each section of the course to write questions to use with another section of the course. This technique will fascinate your students as they will not be in the same room with the students who wrote the questions. Now your students can analyze the questions more openly and honestly. The resulting conversations may be very different!

There are many ways to use questioning effectively with your students. It is essential that you are ready, and that you vary your approaches so your students feel comfortable yet challenged. Keep a record of what works for you, for your students, and for various science topics and issues. This is one area that you definitely want to succeed and where you will improve with time, practice, and experience.

ANALYZE CURRENT EVENTS TO PREPARE INFORMED CITIZENS

There are always current events in science. For example, did you know that Pluto is no longer considered a planet? The distant, ice-covered world is no longer a true planet, according to a new definition of the term voted on by scientists.

Some current events that we have talked about in science are about the whole story of Hurricane Katrina.

—Jon, age thirteen, seventh grade

Current events in science can be used as part of the regular assignments or as extra credit. You will want to come up with a simple format for students to use—such as the "who, what, where, why, when, and how" set of questions. Below are a few good Web sites for current event topics, but any newspaper will have plenty of ideas on local environmental issues and other science-related topics.

- **Science News for Kids:** www.sciencenewsforkids.org: This Web site is devoted to science news for children aged nine to fourteen, with an updated weekly newsmagazine; it also has an audio format subscription.
- **Science News Online:** www.sciencenews.org: This publication is available every other week in print and online in a new, updated format.

Students will enjoy their science classes much more if you can make the curriculum relevant to their everyday lives.

Students are very interested in current events relating to keeping Earth green. We can easily find articles to share on CFS lightbulbs, recycling, saving gasoline, and so on.

—Elementary science specialist

ADDRESS CONTROVERSIAL ISSUES

Either alone or with your students, you can select controversial topics and issues to investigate and discuss. We suggest that you always maintain the right and responsibility to decide the topics, and clearly communicate your expectations with your students. You will need to be careful that students do not have an agenda that they are attempting to convey within the confines of your science class. The topics and issues may be of interest internationally, nationally, and locally, as well as representative of individuals or groups.

When using controversial issues in your science classes, be sure to do the following:

- Allow enough time to select, delve into, and discuss them.
- Involve all students fairly and equitably.
- Provide access to plenty of information and resources.
- Explore multiple perspectives and opinions.
- Connect the learning with standards and content to illustrate big ideas and to advance science knowledge, skills, and dispositions.
- Model sensitivity if (and when) the discussion becomes heated and uncomfortable for some students or misrepresents you and the school.
- Maintain dignified control to reroute or end the discussion, if necessary.
- Allow time for closure and debriefing that may lead to alternative outcomes and social action.

You may find that your district has specific guidelines for discussing controversial issues. There may be a list of topics you are not allowed to discuss in class or with students, formally or informally, such as evolution, acquired immune deficiency syndrome (AIDS), or sexually transmitted diseases (STDs). Though students may confront you with questions or statements, you will need to explain your district's policy.

Teachers must be careful to address all points of view, and presentations must be suitable for the age and development level of their students. If you are caught off guard by a turn in conversation, discuss with students the need for preparation and return to the topic another day. For extremely sensitive issues, you may want to inform and consult with your appropriate administrator.

Hess (2005) reminds teachers to be aware of their own political views and how their words and actions can influence students. She identifies four approaches teachers commonly take: (1) denying that an issue is controversial and there is one correct position;

(2) teaching toward a particular perspective; (3) avoiding the issue because of strong feelings; and (4) promoting a balanced approach that considers various positions. Teachers must understand that their own positions influence their decisions.

Using current events and controversial issues makes the learning active and fun. Information is examined critically and in depth in ways that the students find authentic, purposeful, and relevant to their lives (Flick & Lederman, 2004). These are some of those wonderful teaching moments in science where teachers overhear their students saying, "I didn't know that . . ."

DRAW ON THE ESSENTIAL QUESTIONS OF SCIENCE

One way to engage students in science is to ask questions for which we do not yet have answers. In a special collection of articles, *Science* magazine celebrated the journal's 125th anniversary in 2005 with a look at the most compelling puzzles and questions facing scientists today. The top 25 are noted in Box 6.3, and another 100 may be reviewed at their Web site at www.sciencemag .org/sciext/125th.

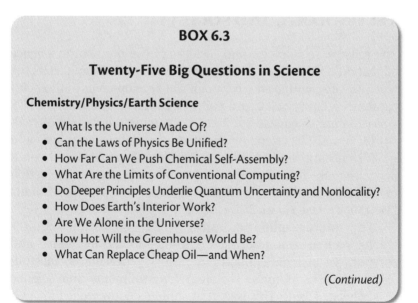

BOX 6.3

Twenty-Five Big Questions in Science

Chemistry/Physics/Earth Science

- What Is the Universe Made Of?
- Can the Laws of Physics Be Unified?
- How Far Can We Push Chemical Self-Assembly?
- What Are the Limits of Conventional Computing?
- Do Deeper Principles Underlie Quantum Uncertainty and Nonlocality?
- How Does Earth's Interior Work?
- Are We Alone in the Universe?
- How Hot Will the Greenhouse World Be?
- What Can Replace Cheap Oil—and When?

(Continued)

(Continued)

Biology/Life Science

- What Is the Biological Basis of Consciousness?
- Why Do Humans Have So Few Genes?
- To What Extent Are Genetic Variation and Personal Health Linked?
- How Much Can the Human Life Span Be Extended?
- What Controls Organ Regeneration?
- How Can a Skin Cell Become a Nerve Cell?
- How Does a Single Somatic Cell Become a Whole Plant?
- What Determines Species Diversity?
- What Genetic Changes Made Us Uniquely Human?
- How Are Memories Stored and Retrieved?
- How Did Cooperative Behavior Evolve?
- How Will Big Pictures Emerge From a Sea of Biological Data?
- How and Where Did Life on Earth Arise?
- Can We Selectively Shut Off Immune Responses?
- Is an Effective HIV Vaccine Feasible?
- Will Malthus Continue to Be Wrong?

Source: Adapted from *Science* (2005).

MAKE LINKAGES AMONG SCIENCE, TECHNOLOGY, AND SOCIETY

The science, technology, and society (STS) movement in science education is an outlook on science education that emphasizes the teaching of scientific and technological developments in their cultural, economic, social, and political contexts. The goals of STS curricula are to engage students in examining a variety of real-world issues (i.e., genetic engineering, global warming, and nuclear testing) and to develop students' capacities and confidence to make informed decisions and to take responsible action to address issues arising from the impact of science on their daily lives (Flick & Lederman, 2004; Yeager, 1996).

The interdisciplinary nature of STS education requires teachers to present information from various disciplines and perspectives, including philosophy, history, geography, social studies, politics, economics, sociology, environment, and science (Aikenhead, 1994). This is so that students' knowledge base can

be appropriately scaffolded to enable them to effectively participate in discussions, debates, and decision-making processes.

The major goal for STS efforts is the production of scientifically and technologically literate persons after thirteen years of
involvement with science in school. NSTA defines the scientifically
and technologically literate person as an individual who:

- uses concepts of science and of technology as well as an
  informed reflection of ethical values in solving everyday
  problems and making responsible decisions in everyday life,
  including those about work and leisure;
- engages in responsible personal and civic actions after
  weighing the possible consequences of alternative options;
- defends decisions and actions using rational arguments
  based on evidence;
- engages in science and technology for the excitement and
  the explanations they provide;
- displays curiosity about, and appreciation of, the natural
  and human-made world;
- applies skepticism, careful methods, logical reasoning, and
  creativity in investigating the observable universe;
- values scientific research and technological problem solving;
- locates, collects, analyzes, and evaluates sources of scientific and technological information, and uses these sources
  in solving problems, making decisions, and taking action;
- distinguishes between scientific and technological evidence
  and personal opinion, and between reliable and unreliable
  information;
- remains open to new evidence and the tentativeness of
  scientific/technological knowledge;
- recognizes that science and technology are human endeavors;
- weighs the benefits and burdens of scientific and technological development;
- recognizes the strengths and limitations of science and
  technology for advancing human welfare;
- analyzes interactions among science, technology, and society;
- connects science and technology to other human endeavors,
  such as history, mathematics, the arts, and the humanities;
- considers the political, economic, moral, and ethical
  aspects of science and technology as they relate to personal
  and global issues; and

- offers explanations of natural phenomena that may be tested for their validity. (NSTA Position Statement on Science/Technology/Society: www.nsta.org/about/positions/sts.aspx.)

I particularly enjoy marine biology because of the complexity and diversity of the animals that live in the ocean. I plan to continue as a marine biology major in college, so taking science influenced my decision.

—Ronnie, age seventeen, twelfth grade

ADVANCE YOUR CLASSROOM DISCUSSIONS

Most likely, you will encourage your students to participate in classroom discussions every day. You want to hear their reactions to reading assignments, previous classroom discussions, and their connections to various activities in your class, in other classes, and in their personal lives. The secret to success in your classroom discussions depends on your ability to facilitate or lead the discussion, to motivate students to participate through speaking and listening (incorporating both cognitive and emotional responses), and to link the discussion with your purposes for learning.

Discussion is both content and the process. That means you can teach using discussion to explore a subject, and you can teach about having discussion as a way to articulate and exchange ideas. Each of these approaches is extremely important in science. After all, scientists must be able to communicate their ideas effectively.

Discussions can be planned or spontaneous. The key is to ask important questions that focus on the science topics and issues while probing the students' knowledge, drawing upon recall and rationale. Discussion plays an important place in the STS curriculum, where the emphasis is on responsible decision making in the real world of the student, of which science and technology are components. Discussion of an issue might center on the following questions:

- Is it a problem or issue?
- How did it become a problem or issue?
- What areas of science and other disciplines might lend themselves to the solution?

- What are some alternative approaches to its solution?
- What are the potential effects of applying the alternatives on individuals and/or society?

CONDUCT A BENEFIT/RISK ANALYSIS

A benefit/risk analysis is the comparison of the risk of a situation to its related benefits (Pimentel & Coonrod, 1987). Such an analysis can be determined qualitatively and, in some cases, quantitatively. If the ratio of benefits to risks is greater than 1, then the benefits outweigh the risks. If the ratio of benefits to risks is less than 1, then the risks outweigh the benefits. Both personal and societal benefits and risks need to be considered.

Conducting a benefit/risk analysis is a good way to get students thinking about science-related issues—from smoking and drug use to the environment and global warming. It promotes higher-order thinking through a process that allows students to first analyze the issue by breaking it down into two major components (the benefits and the risks) and then synthesizing their findings into a judgment.

You might use the four questions below to engage students in small- and large-group discussion on any number of scientific issues and discoveries:

1. What five to ten scientific discoveries or technological inventions of the last one hundred years do you think have had the most impact on people and history? You will want to include inventions and discoveries that you feel are generally positive or negative.

2. For one of your discoveries/technological inventions: In what ways has the impact been positive, or beneficial? In what ways has the impact been negative, or risky? Identify both personal and societal benefits and risks.

3. For the same discovery or invention, evaluate the personal and societal benefits you have identified. Overall, is the discovery/invention worth it?

4. Are there any possible scientific discoveries or technological inventions that should not be pursued under any circumstances? Why?

INVOLVE STUDENTS IN PROJECT-BASED LEARNING

Project-based learning, or PBL (also known as problem-based learning), is a specific approach to instruction that begins with the teacher or students posing a problem to be solved. Students are then asked to investigate the real-world problem. Investigations require students to integrate subjects across the curriculum and involve them in collaborative research projects. Typically, the process requires these steps:

- Teacher/students pose a critical question.
- Students design a plan for the project.
- Teacher monitors the students and the progress of the project.
- Students and teacher assess outcomes and evaluate the experience.

The National Science Education Standards identify that a major goal of science education is to develop scientifically literate citizens who can function in their adult stages with skills necessary for lifelong learning. In a PBL approach to instruction, the teacher attempts to catalyze student learning through critical thinking and an increased ability to seek and find information related to problem situations (Gallagher, 1995).

Science projects can be formal or informal, short term or long term, single task or multitask. You can assign projects to be completed individually, with partners, in small groups, or as a whole group. They can be conducted in the classroom or outdoors. With a little extra planning, they can be interdisciplinary, incorporating mathematics, social studies, English/language arts, art, and other areas.

Science is a lot of fun and it's my favorite subject. I enjoy observing live animals, and using a microscope because with both of these activities you learn more about the subject.

—Ann, age sixteen, eleventh grade

Projects can be highly academic or a combination of academic and social interaction. The projects can extend beyond the classroom into the school and community, and include a service-learning component. You can design a sense of community around the organization and completion of the project.

The most important feature of the PBL instructional approach is the voicing of the problem itself. Greenwald (2000) recommends that the problem be "ill-defined, unclear, and raises questions about what is known, what needs to be known, and how the answer can be found. Because the problem is unclear, there are many ways to solve it, and the solutions are influenced by one's vantage point and experience" (p. 28).

As you guide and direct projects, it is important for you to step forward to develop clear directions and provide the resources and supplies for students to be successful. Then you need to step back as students go to work. Your main role is to be the resource person guiding and facilitating the process for students who need help. Box 6.4 provides a list of ideas and resources for PBL activities.

INTEGRATE TWENTY-FIRST-CENTURY LEARNING SKILLS

Educators, policy makers, and members of the business community have identified the skills that students will need to be effective, contributing members of society and active citizens of the twenty-first century, and science education plays a critical part in this (Bybee & Fuchs, 2006). These skills resonate with the scientific process skills, but signal an increased emphasis on communication and collaboration. These skills may be applied to all of the content areas of science. Skills definitely should not be fragmented or taught in isolation; they reach across the curriculum, offering interconnected proficiencies for students to apply throughout the learning process.

The Partnership for 21st Century Skills has developed a unified, collective vision for twenty-first-century learning that can be used to strengthen American education. Its vision (*Framework for 21st Century Learning*, 2004) includes the following elements:

- Teaching core subjects (English, reading or language arts, mathematics, science, foreign language, civics, government, economics, arts, history, and geography)

- Teaching twenty-first-century content (global awareness; financial, economic, business, and entrepreneurial literacy; civic literacy; and health and wellness awareness)

BOX 6.4

Project-Based Learning Ideas for Science

• *Supersize My Cancer.* High school chemistry students are asked to research and analyze the benefits and risks of acrylamide, found in fried and baked foods like French fries and potato chips. It is also a known carcinogen in animals when administered in high doses, and a neurotoxin when humans are exposed to large amounts in the workplace. (From The National Center for Case Study Teaching in Science Case Collection: http://ublib.buffalo.edu/libraries/projects/cases/case.html.)

• *Don't Trash the Earth.* The local landfill is about to close because it is too full, and middle school students play the role of waste management consultants to analyze past and current waste management practices at their school and community. Teams devise a cost-effective and user-friendly recycling program. (From Intel Education Designing Effective Projects: http://educate.intel.com/en/ProjectDesign.)

• *Outbreak at Water's Edge.* Students are introduced to the world of public health as they help discover the source of the outbreak that has hit the small community of Water's Edge and stop it before more residents get sick. (From Access Excellence Mystery Spot: www.accessexcellence.org/AE/mspot.)

• *Riverside's Dilemma.* Riverside citizens have watched the town's many factories close down over the years, due to changing market forces and other economic factors. But now a chemical company wants to start up three new operations: a metal-refining center, a paper mill, and a fine chemicals synthesis unit. Students play the role of the town councilors and decide whether to approve the sale of properties for this intended use. (From PBL at the University of Delaware: www.udel.edu/pbl/problems.)

• Requiring that students effectively use learning and thinking skills, including critical thinking and problem-solving skills, communication skills, creativity and innovation skills, collaboration skills, contextual learning skills, and information and media literacy skills

• Developing students' information and computer technology (ICT) literacy, including the ability to use technology to develop twenty-first-century content knowledge and skills, in the context of learning core subjects

- Developing students' life skills, including leadership, personal responsibility, ethics, people skills, accountability, self-direction, adaptability, social responsibility, and personal productivity

- Utilizing twenty-first-century assessments that measure all five results that matter, including core subjects, twenty-first-century content, learning and thinking skills, ICT literacy, and life skills

See the following sites for additional resources on developing twenty-first-century skills in your classroom:

Route 21: www.21stcenturyskills.org/route21/index.php. The Partnership for 21st Century Skills offers this one-stop shop for twenty-first-century skills-related information, resources, and community tools.

Twenty-First-Century Teaching and Learning Resources: www.intel.com/education/resources/index.htm?iid=teach+resources. Intel Education's bank of resources includes *An Innovation Odyssey*, a searchable database of technology-enriched projects from classrooms around the world, and *It's a Wild Ride*, an interdisciplinary project that uses roller-coaster design to engage students in math, science, and language arts.

The Gateway to Twenty-First-Century Skills: www.thegateway.org. NEA and state affiliate resources site for meeting the challenges of teaching and learning in the twenty-first century.

LOOK FOR MORE IDEAS

We have just begun to skim the surface of the many ways you can expand your teaching repertoire. Keep these in mind as we now look at literacy, lesson planning, and collaborating with colleagues. We will return in Chapter 9 to discuss how to bring science materials and guest speakers into the classroom, as well as how to take your students on field trips and where you might go. Chapter 10 looks at how to use technology and the wealth of information and resources provided by the Internet. Chapter 11 is filled with more projects and programs by subject area, which provide students with opportunities to demonstrate the science skills presented here.

REINFORCE HOW SCIENCE IMPACTS SOCIETY AND OUR PERSONAL LIVES . . .

Nothing is more exciting than the process of discovery! As you enable students to seek and find answers to their own questions, they will develop the skills they need to become independent learners. They will apply what they learn in their own lives and share it with others. They will see how science encompasses both the content and the processes that are essential in today's world.

Suggested Activities

1. Identify an upcoming science topic or issue. Select one or two skills from each area of science to coordinate with the topic or issue.

2. Review the top twenty-five questions in science with students and have them vote on the three most important, the three most difficult to solve, the three most controversial, or other categories. Have students defend their choices.

3. Ask your students what kinds of projects they would like to design for the upcoming units of learning.

4. Talk with other science teachers about their current PBL activities to see whether there is one you and your students could either join or extend as your own project.

CHAPTER SEVEN

Develop Literacy
to Build
Science Skills

We live in a world of constant scientific discovery. All citizens need to be scientifically literate to appreciate the world around them and make informed personal decisions.

—Robert Hazen (2002), research scientist,
Carnegie Institution of Washington's
Geophysical Laboratory

As you guide your students through both day-to-day activities and major assignments, you will build their literacy skills so they are equipped to better comprehend and use science concepts and vocabulary. You must cover a huge amount of content quickly, and the secret is that much of everyone's success will depend on your students' abilities to make important text connections. The good news is there are many ways to prepare your students to understand science effectively.

INTRODUCE LITERACY PROCESSES AND OUTCOMES

Literacy entails the whole experience of interacting with text through reading, writing, speaking, listening, and viewing. Literacy is both a process and an outcome, where the participant is an observer, a consumer, a producer, and a critic. Fluency, articulation, communication, and expression are proficiencies set within a context for the participant to function responsibly, to feel ownership, and to take action. These qualities certainly pertain to understanding, applying, and appreciating science.

Development of literacy in reading and writing contributes to scientific literacy. As a consumer and citizen, we have to form opinions about science-related issues, such as cloning, genetically engineered food, and lead poisoning, in order to fully participate in society. More and more, scientific and technological issues dominate the national discourse, and understanding these debates is essential.

When science is taught well, students grasp the fundamentals of systematic observation, scientific thinking, problem solving, science vocabulary, science concepts, and the physical world. These elements promote progress in literacy development by enhancing student schemata as well as important related linguistic and thinking processes.

DEVELOP VOCABULARY AND CONCEPTS

The most powerful thing that can be done is to name something.

—Albert Einstein

Vocabulary building is important because the difficulty of the vocabulary in text affects students' ability to comprehend. The secret is to spend time looking at words and what they mean. Students develop a lifelong interest in learning new words primarily through interaction with teachers who are intrigued with words.

Effective vocabulary instruction demonstrates strategies for learning word meanings; includes integration, repetition, and meaningful use of new words; and is anchored in relevant experiences and associations. Teachers can help students learn vocabulary by emphasizing the importance of vocabulary, teaching pronunciation, making dictionaries available and necessary to complete assignments, and engaging students in vocabulary development activities, such as a writing roulette vocabulary story (where a group of students composes a story using science words, rotating the recorder of the story); learning Greek and Latin roots, prefixes, and suffixes; or comparison of the science and nonscience use of words.

Science textbooks and documents are overflowing with new and precise vocabulary. It is important to select words and concepts that students will need to learn, which will enable them to read text (Schmoker, 2006). These words should be practical— that is, commonly used words and those found frequently in the study of science. Use the terms in context and with concrete examples consistently and regularly.

> *I emphasize the etiology of the words. For example, when we start talking about genetics, the roots homo, hetero, and zygo are covered that week, so students will better understand what homozygous and heterozygous mean. They are also better prepared when the words zygote or homeostasis come up later as they have had these roots already.*
>
> *—Tenth-grade biology teacher*

As you introduce new words, pronounce them clearly and ask students to repeat them. Give a synonym or a brief definition. Have students complete a form or make vocabulary cards on which they also include a picture and/or a sample sentence using the new word. Finally, provide opportunities for students to both see and use the new words in context.

Many teachers post and maintain a vocabulary list in the form of a "word wall" to reference during silent reading and class activities. The visual display will reinforce the new learning, especially if you use bold colors such as yellow, red, and black, and you incorporate the display as a natural learning strategy during class.

> *I teach new vocabulary by having students create illustrated dictionaries with the words being studied. I also have students create posters with the word, picture, and definition to hang up in the classroom.*
>
> *—Seventh-grade life science teacher*

We also suggest that you post and maintain a list of key concepts. Again, science concepts frequently are foreign and unique to your students. You probably are teaching the concepts within a particular context, and you want your students to understand the concept within that context. One effective way to display the concepts is with graphic organizers. For example, if the concepts are related to chronological events, use a timeline. If the concepts are related to parts of an organism, use a concept web. Graphic organizers are ideal for structuring the reading in meaningful ways.

> *On Tuesdays and Thursdays I would post a picture and a short crossword puzzle with clues using the unit vocabulary for students to complete at their seats. Then, with a partner, they write a short paragraph summarizing the main concepts.*
>
> *—Tenth-grade chemistry teacher*

DEVELOP CHARACTERISTICS OF EXPERT READERS

The characteristics of an expert reader are greatly compatible with the characteristics of a scientifically literate person, as defined by the NSTA:

> The scientifically literate person has a substantial knowledge base of facts, concepts, conceptual networks, and process skills which enable individuals to continue to learn and think logically. (NSTA Position Paper on *Beyond 2000*, 2003)

Expert readers approach text strategically. Science teachers help students by using a structured reading approach in their classrooms. They teach students to select strategies according to where they are in the reading process: prereading, during reading, or after reading.

Before reading, guide students to activate schema and set a purpose for reading. This involves:

- looking for organizing concepts;
- recalling related information, experiences, attitudes, and feelings;

- deciding how easy or difficult the reading selection is likely to be;
- setting a purpose for reading; and
- trying to develop a personal interest.

During reading, guide students to monitor comprehension and use additional strategies as needed. This involves:

- translating ideas into their own words;
- comparing ideas to personal experience;
- trying to identify main ideas—stopping and questioning when this is unclear;
- noting important details;
- rereading whenever necessary for clarification;
- consolidating ideas into meaningful groups;
- noticing unfamiliar vocabulary;
- forming mental pictures;
- evaluating the author's purpose, motive, or authority when appropriate;
- inventing study strategies as needed; and
- managing time to sustain concentration.

After reading, guide students to check basic comprehension, build schema, and decide on relevant applications of the new information. Elements of this process include:

- checking basic comprehension by reciting (What did I learn?);
- organizing information into chunks (How can I remember it?);
- deciding what is important (How much should I understand this?);
- trying to clarify ambiguous ideas (Did I really understand this?);
- evaluating new information in terms of previous knowledge and experience (Does this make sense?);
- developing study strategies according to class demands or personal purposes (What should I do to remember this?); and
- reviewing material periodically (How much do I remember now?).

Take time to model these strategies for students. Explain what you are doing and why as you read aloud. We now look at how to prepare students to use the textbook, how to support students who have difficulty reading, and then how to follow reading assignments with meaningful literacy activities, to reinforce the acquisition of new content and retain new vocabulary and concepts.

USE THE TEXTBOOK AS A TOOL

The readability of science textbooks has greatly improved in recent years (Chiappetta & Fillman, 2007). Today's science texts are better grounded in compelling and interesting issues; stress scientific thinking; offer opportunities for integrated reading, writing, and science skills; and make casual use of and reference to prose and poetry as a means of building familiarity with knowledge. However, they also tend to exceed the mental and social maturity levels of most students, and some topics can be controversial in some communities.

Most likely, the textbooks were selected prior to your arrival. In the future, you may have some choice about which textbooks you want to use or use most of the time. And, at some point in your career, you probably will be asked to evaluate textbooks as new series are considered for adoption. A list of criteria to consider when evaluating textbooks can be found in Resource B at the end of the book.

Many students cannot read the textbooks comfortably, and just the sight of a science textbook may stress some students. Not only do the textbooks appear overwhelming, many students have had science teachers in the past who did not know how to use the textbooks effectively with their students.

There are several major problems that compromise students' ability to read science content. These problems include:

- inadequate background or information;
- misconceptions about the physical world;
- inconsiderate or assumptive and inadequately explained text;
- difficulty in handling esoteric or technically overwhelming items; and
- inadequate preparation and orientation of teachers, particularly at the elementary level in the basic sciences.

It is essential for you to keep the reading assignments developmentally appropriate and reasonably manageable. Provide the background material, both visually and orally, that students need to be able to understand the text. Graphic organizers of main concepts will help them to follow the material. Review the text features: chapter introductions and previews; headings and sub-heading; charts, pictures, and other visual aids; and glossary. Table 7.1 provides sample structured reading activities.

> *We go through the chapter together at the start of a unit. We look at chapter titles and the section titles and try to identify how they are related. We look at the visual aids and try to identify what concepts are being emphasized. We read the statements or questions at the beginning of the chapter and the section or chapter review questions to help focus on what the author thinks is important. It's a bit tedious, but for those students who aren't very textbook savvy, it is helpful to prepare their brains by setting up some memory "files" for the content that is to come.*

> —*Ninth-grade biology teacher*

Table 7.1   Structured Reading Components and Activities

Before Reading Activities	• Draw upon or build background knowledge (i.e., use anticipation guides or KWL). • Establish a purpose for reading (i.e., graphic organizer). • Present new vocabulary and academic language. • Preview text features, including headings, visual aids, summaries, glossary.
During Reading Activities	• Focus attention on lesson objectives. • Ask questions to check comprehension and stimulate discussion. • "Think aloud," showing how you use context clues and make inferences as you read. • Relate prior knowledge to the text, asking students to predict what will happen next. • Relate new concepts to existing knowledge.
After Reading Activities	• Reflect, discuss, and write on meaning of text (i.e., KWL, quick writes, summaries). • Engage students in higher levels of thinking that go beyond the text.

Source: Adapted from Kottler, Kottler, & Street (2008).

Consider the average reading abilities of the students enrolled in each course you teach. Read an assignment yourself and note the time it takes you to read the selection slowly and carefully. Now add ten minutes. This will be closer to the length of time your students will need to read the selection superficially. You will need to add more time if you want them to read it meticulously.

START WITH READING ANTICIPATION ACTIVITIES

To connect your students with reading their text and all other documents, start with some anticipation activities outside the textbook (Readence, Bean, & Baldwin, 1998). You may use these tasks as your lesson openers. They can be completed individually, with partners, in small groups, or as a whole group. Table 7.2 has examples of ten types of prompts you might use before a reading assignment.

ASSIGN READING

If you are allowing your students time to read a selected passage for the first time in class, you cannot expect all of your students to either complete the reading or to glean from it all you want them to. Some students will be distracted and unable to concentrate fully. Reduce and eliminate as many distractions as possible. For students who cannot focus on their reading for even short periods of time, consider recording the passages ahead of time and having them listen to as much as they can, using earphones with the text in front of them.

You may want to assign your students to read a selected passage outside of class—that is, during a study hall or at home—to be discussed the next day. In this situation, you will want to give your students one to two minutes to review the reading at the start of the discussion. Again, state your reason for reading to initiate a lively conversation.

FACILITATE READING RESPONSE STRATEGIES

Reading responses are used by students during and after reading. Reading responses may relate to anticipation activities, correlating

Table 7.2   Ten Reading Prompts for Science Text

Given . . .	Students will . . .
1. A list of ten vocabulary words with two columns labeled *Know* or *Do Not Know*	Mark the ones they know and write a synonym or give an example.
2. Some key concepts with columns labeled *Agree* and *Do Not Agree*	Mark a column for each concept item; students may also give a rationale.
3. A diagram of a process that may or may not be correct with boxed numbers at significant steps	Indicate the boxed numbers as *True* or *False*.
4. A graphic organizer with column labels, *Before, During,* and *After,* and a list of items	Place the items in the appropriate column.
5. A table of data and description	Mark interpretations of data as either *I think it is correct* or *I think it is not correct.*
6. A statement stem that may be a fact or an opinion	Link the statement stem to their own perspectives or that of someone in the text.
7. A topic or issue	Write two questions about the upcoming reading assignment.
8. A concept map	List all the possible outcomes related to a particular event.
9. A series of continua	Identify how much they either agree or disagree with a series of statements.
10. Some sentence starters	Use appropriate vocabulary words and terms to complete the sentence.

the information acquired during the reading or in a different place. Responses may be kept as a journal entry, or on a poster, a graphic organizer, an overhead transparency, and so forth. Box 7.1 provides eleven examples of reading responses.

BOX 7.1

Reading Responses for Science

- Describe the meaning of a science cartoon.
- Recap as a news account, using appropriate vocabulary and concepts.
- Develop a list of questions as a police investigation.
- Construct a perspective from a particular point of view in a letter.
- Promote an issue or agenda in a speech.
- Organize vocabulary words and key concepts in a graphic organizer.
- Write a response and pass it to a partner or group member for comment.
- Organize the information in a table or chart.
- Summarize the information for a younger student.
- Draw a picture or diagram of the information.
- Link the new learning to something already covered in class.

INCLUDE ALL KINDS OF TEXT

In addition to your textbook, there are many kinds of text useful for teaching your science curriculum. Some are primary sources and some are secondary sources.

Primary sources are original items from the past and documents written by individuals who provide information about their own direct experiences during an event. They include speeches, letters, diaries, and oral histories, as well as their photographs, sketches, and other personal belongings. Primary sources can be a wonderful way to help students understand the process of discovery in science. Examples include the diary of Jim Watson (*The Double Helix*) and Isaac Newton's letters to the Philosophical Society of London.

Secondary sources are documents written by individuals who have researched information and offer an interpretation or analysis based on primary resources. Secondary sources include science journals and encyclopedias. Table 7.3 provides a list of varied texts suitable for students that we urge you to investigate.

Table 7.3   Different Types of Science Text

Abstracts	Essays	Presentation slides
Anatomical drawings	Experimental reports	Procedures
Autobiographies	Graphs	Schedules of investigations
Biographies	Hypotheses	Science fiction
Blogs	Illustrations	Speeches
Calendars	Instruction manuals	Statistics
Charts	Journals	Synopses of investigations
Databases	Laboratory notes	Tables
Diaries	Letters	Theories
Documents	Magazine articles	Timelines
Drawings	Manuals	Weather patterns
Editorials	Maps	Web sites
E-mail messages	Newspaper articles	Wikis
Equations	Periodic table	

Help students to differentiate between primary and secondary sources and the purposes for each one. Explain the importance of citing their sources and model the process of writing a citation. As there are different citation styles, be sure to let them know which one(s) they should follow. Typically, science fields require American Psychological Association (APA) format.

SUPPORT STRUGGLING READERS AND ENGLISH LANGUAGE LEARNERS

Some students need additional support. For struggling readers and English language learners, shelter your instruction. The SIOP

(Sheltered Instruction Observation Protocol) Model (Echevarria, Vogt, & Short, 2005) consists of eight components. The Preparation component, for example, suggests planning lessons carefully by selecting language objectives along with content objectives, choosing supplementary materials, and incorporating meaningful activities to create context for learning.

The SIOP Model emphasizes adapting the textbook by rewriting selections of the text that cover the key concepts (with topic sentence and supportive details) to give to students. Additionally, the SIOP Model encourages keeping a few copies of the text set aside in which you add notes in the margins. Rather than write in the book, you can add notes on overhead transparencies to fit over the pages or you can create or a handout that fits around the text. Some teachers reserve texts in which they have highlighted the main idea, significant vocabulary, key concepts, and summary statements for students to read first. Another idea is to add notes to students on Post-it paper. Building background, using comprehensible language, and modeling expectations are other important features in working with English learners and all other students.

INTEGRATE VARIOUS TYPES OF WRITING

Literacy involves not only all kinds of text, it also involves all types of writing. Many literacy experts (Strong, 2006; Zinsser, 1988) purport that students better understand what they read when they write, as they are visibly and authentically engaged in their learning. They personalize their knowledge. Daily or weekly quick writes or journal entries provide students with records of what they have learned. They may want to reference this work as they study for tests or create a project/presentation.

When your students are writing, they tend to listen more attentively to what is being said by you and others, process information, and select more precisely what they are recording. They use critical thinking skills. During the writing process, students realize that teachers and peers can or will see what they are producing, especially when they present in front of their peers or write for assessment purposes. When students are writing in science, you want them to:

- use science vocabulary and concepts correctly—this means contextualizing the meanings accurately and precisely;
- transfer the vocabulary and concepts correctly to new and different contexts, either literally or figuratively; and

- construct their own uses of vocabulary and concepts to new and different contexts and applications to advance their thinking.

Writing can be expressed in ways that include the following:

- *Expository.* Conveys information or explains what is difficult to understand, such as documents, summaries, news reports, magazine articles.
- *Narrative.* Tells a personal story or fictional experience based on real or imaginary events, such as results of project-based learning or descriptions of life in the future.
- *Persuasive.* Attempts to convince the reader to accept a particular point of view or to take a specific action—for example, an editorial or focused analysis.
- *Technical.* Relates scientific information or principles, such as laboratory reports, evaluations, instructions, directions, hypotheses, formal arguments, problem solving.

Table 7.4 offers a list of science writing exercises.

GRANT YOUR STUDENTS WRITING P.O.W.E.R.

To teach the writing process, use P.O.W.E.R. (Street, 2002). Students follow five steps when expressing their ideas on paper. Students begin with **P**rewriting (brainstorming thoughts), such as free writing, asking questions, talking and listening, and reading. Then comes the task of **O**rganizing (meeting a purpose). Next, students engage in **W**riting (capturing ideas), followed by **E**scaping (taking a break). Finally students turn to **R**ewriting (polishing the work). Teachers serve as coaches to support students in their efforts as they become empowered in writing.

TRY THE DRAFT WRITING PROCESS

One creative way to engage and empower students in writing is to use DRAFT (Gallavan, 1997). DRAFT is a strategy where students **D**esign a written piece that allows them to write from a unique and personalized perspective. Students select the **R**ole of the writer, the **A**udience that will be reading or hearing the writing, the **F**ormat of the writing, and the **T**opic. For example, students can assume the **R**ole of a newspaper editor, address the **A**udience of newspaper readers and citizens in general, write in the **F**ormat of a persuasive editorial, and discuss the **T**opic of air pollution.

Examples of DRAFT

Earth Science: Students can take the Role of Copernicus. The Audience is a group of scientists from his time period. The Format is a speech. The Topic is his theory that the sun is the center of the universe, and not the Earth as was previously believed.

Chemistry: Students can take the Role of an element. The Audience is a group of molecule makers who must buy atoms. The Format is a persuasive argument. The Topic is what physical and chemical characteristics make the element an important purchase.

Take time to brainstorm a variety of DRAFT ideas with your students so they can select the writing combinations that suit them.

Table 7.4   Different Types of Science Writing Exercises

Autobiography	Investigation report
Advertising campaign	Journal entry
Analysis of data	Laboratory report
Biography	Letter
Blog	Magazine article
Brochure	Mission statement
Contract	Mystery
Diary	Newspaper article
Editorial	Obituary of scientist
Essay	Play
Evaluation	Report
Eyewitness account	Review of book or article
Fiction	Scientific criticism
Hypothesis	Speech criticism
Interview	Wiki

DEVELOP OBSERVATION SKILLS

Whether working with inanimate or animate objects, students need to develop observation skills, one of the most critical of the scientific processes. Teach appropriate vocabulary related to the object and procedures for the experiment. Ask students to objectively describe what they see, then describe their subjective reactions to it. With photographs, discuss what or who might be missing and whether it is a posed or candid shot, the composition of the picture, and what might have happened before and after the picture was taken. Table 7.5 provides a sample Science Observation Guide.

REFERENCE CURRENT AND HISTORICAL EVENTS

Using current events exemplifies authentic application of qualities of powerful science teaching and learning, as well as the skills of literacy. Plus there are many visual aids available. Pictures, graphs, charts, and maps provide effective visual references to support student learning. Newspapers, magazines, and television programs often present bulleted summary points to guide understanding. Students make immediate connections.

Find local issues that are interesting and meaningful to your students. Perhaps there is a new construction or transportation project being considered for development. How will that impact their lives? Look for current events in the school and local newspapers to share in class and to post on the bulletin board. You can also use the current events as the context when introducing and reinforcing concepts. The sample four-week unit on microbiology presented in Chapter 8 (see Table 8.3, Sample Science Unit) includes several current events to promote interest in science.

Some schools use the "Newspaper in Education," program (for which there is now an online resource at http://nieonline.com) with lesson plans, quizzes, and other resources. Other schools use student newspapers or student magazines targeted at grade and reading levels. One choice in science, *Scholastic Science World Magazine* (www.teacher.scholastic.com), for Grades 6–10, includes feature articles and hands-on activities in every area of the science curriculum. Teacher Guides are included with every issue.

Along with current events, the opportunity to consider the historical, social, and cultural contexts of scientific discovery can also engage students. Although it may take a few minutes to decipher the peculiarities of seventeenth-century terms in Newton's letter to the Philosophical Society of London, his careful articulation of his thinking is charming. (See Box 7.2.)

Table 7.5 Science Observation Guide

Science Observation Guide*

Item, origin	Frame of Reference/Perspective	Physical Description (Written)	Image	Personal Reaction	Questions
Name or description of item	What context it relates to . . .	What it looks like, including color, texture, pattern, size, shape, and other measurements as appropriate, such as temperature, volume, weight, speed	Drawing of item (or photograph)	How it makes you feel . . .	What you wonder about . . .
Dependent and Independent Variables					
Resulting Changes					

*Teachers and students should expand this form as needed.

BOX 7.2

History of Science

The Hole in the Blind: Newton's Prism

To perform my late promise to you, I shall without further ceremony acquaint you, that in the beginning of the Year 1666, I procured me a Triangular glass-Prisme, to try therewith the celebrated Phænomena of Colours. And in order thereto having darkened my chamber, and made a small hole in my window-shuts, to let in a convenient quantity of the Suns light, I placed my Prisme at his entrance, that it might be thereby refracted to the opposite wall. It was at first a very pleasing divertisement, to view the vivid and intense colours produced thereby; but after a while applying myself to consider them more circumspectly, I became surprised to see *them in an oblong form; which, according to the received laws of Refraction, I expected should have been circular.* (*Philosophical Transactions of the Royal Society*, No. 80 (19 Feb. 1671/2), pp. 3075–3087)

It all began with a damaged window shade, as English mathematician and scientist Sir Isaac Newton notes in the beginning of his famous letter for the *Philosophical Transactions of the Royal Society*. Even before Newton's 1665 experiments with light, people were using prisms to experiment with color, and thought that somehow the prism colored the light. Newton's simple observation that the colors were in oblong form instead of circular prompted him to experiment further.

After considering and accepting/rejecting several small hypotheses, Newton performed his *Experimentum Crucis* (key experiment) to prove that the prism was not coloring the light. He put a screen in the way of his spectrum. This screen had a slit cut in it, and let only the green light go through. Then he put a second prism in the way of the green light. If it was the prism that was coloring the light, the green should come out a different color. However, the pure green light remained green. This led him to theorize that light was composed of colors, rejecting the idea that the prism itself was coloring the light. In another experiment with two prisms, he placed a second prism upside down in the way of the light spectrum created by the first prism. The band of colors combined again into white sunlight.

In these experiments, Newton had proved that white light was made up of colors mixed together, and the prism merely separated them. He was the first person to explain the presence of a rainbow, but his discovery did not end there. As a result of these experiments with light and refraction, Newton designed the refractive telescope, which greatly improved our ability to see objects at a distance. His work also led to improvements in the microscope. In addition, his process of posing and

(Continued)

(Continued)

testing hypotheses, conducting the *Experimentum Crucis,* and then using experimental findings to accurately predict and explain behavior of other phenomena led to the development of the scientific method. Read the rest of his famous letter at the links below.

- **The Newton Project:** www.newtonproject.sussex.ac.uk. This link provides a comprehensive set of resources, including his letters to the *Philosophical Transactions of the Royal Society.*
- **Newton's Prism Experiments:** http://micro.magnet.fsu.edu/ primer/java/scienceopticsu/newton/index.html. This site includes an interactive version of Newton's experiment with two prisms.

In the next chapter, we look at how to develop a lesson plan with instructional strategies to captivate and keep students' attention. We will share specific ideas for selecting themes and concepts, opening and closing your lessons, guiding in-class activities, and selecting out-of-class assignments successfully.

EQUIP YOUR STUDENTS TO COMMUNICATE SCIENCE . . .

Literacy skills prepare your students to interact on their own as participants, consumers, producers, and critics of science knowledge. In short, the development of literacy results in the scientifically literate student. These skills enable students to communicate science in oral and written forms. Teachers rely heavily upon learners' levels of literacy, and their abilities to read, write, and view objects and images objectively and from multiple perspectives. Integrating literacy and science helps prepare your students as lifelong learners.

Suggested Activities

1. Reflect upon your interactions with science textbooks and laboratory manuals. Which features will you want students to use?

2. List three forms of text that inform and support your science knowledge. Discuss how you will share these with students.

3. List three types of writing that express your science knowledge. Which types will you integrate into your classroom?

4. Make a list of five current events in your content area and identify where they might fit into your curriculum.

CHAPTER EIGHT

Plan With Students in Mind to Prepare Your Teaching

If you want to live a happy life, tie it to a goal, not to people or things.

—Albert Einstein (1879–1955)

The best approach to use when planning your science curriculum, instruction, and assessments is to find connections that are relevant to your students. Unfortunately, many students do not feel positive about science when they come to school. They think it is too difficult, or too abstract, or too disconnected from their everyday lives. Your challenge is to develop your curricular content, design your instructional practices, and align your authentic assessments so the learning is captivating and meaningful in ways that are pertinent to them on a personal level. The secret is to strategically identify concepts, themes, and issues when planning your lessons.

SELECT YOUR UNITS OF LEARNING

Let's begin with the big picture. Most of you will be responsible for creating and implementing your own units of learning that you develop for your particular style of teaching and your specific group of students. After you are assigned your courses and the grade levels, we suggest that you concentrate on the curriculum: lay out the state standards, keep the school district expectations handy, and open the textbooks. Now think about your students' interests as well as your own energies.

Many of you will follow the chapters as they are presented in the textbook. By doing this, the chapters in the textbook most likely will determine your units of learning. You may think you are compelled to follow this plan as some of the information and vocabulary in the second chapter will build upon the first chapter, and so on throughout the book. Perhaps you will be more confident if you adhere to this plan during your first few years of teaching.

However, you have choices. You can teach the textbook chapters in your own order, supplement them with other materials, or reorganize the material to fit your own curriculum design. Alternatively, your school site or district may have a standard outline that you should follow. You may have joined a department where teachers follow a pacing guide, and benchmark tests are administered on a set schedule. In some schools, resources have to be shared, and teachers rotate the materials and units they teach. In this situation, you will need to collaborate with the other teachers. You may find you will not have as much freedom as you would like to have in making curricular planning decisions. By talking with the other science teachers at your school, you can learn more about how best to organize your units of learning.

HIGHLIGHT CONCEPTS

All of your units should include concepts (McCarthy, 1997). Usually the state standards and school district expectations include an extensive list of important concepts. Concepts are single words or short phrases that represent high-level, abstract ideas or beliefs key to their academic discipline; concepts symbolize large bodies of knowledge and reference a hierarchy of knowledge that increases and decreases by generality, complexity, and abstractness (Taba, 1962).

EMPHASIZE SIGNIFICANT THEMES OF SCIENCE

Teach the concepts by emphasizing the significant themes related to your subject area (Manning, Manning, & Long, 1994). Themes connect the concepts or big ideas that address essential understandings with science standards and academic expectations mentioned in Chapter 2. Themes can be dissected through assorted approaches and viewed from multiple perspectives. Rather than presenting informative passively, invite students to explore significant themes to involve them in their own learning processes. To fully understand a theme, students will rely upon previous learning not only in this subject area, but they also must utilize concepts and practices learned in other subject areas.

> *I try to have a theme or overarching question for each unit—so each concept is taught in relation to that theme. For ecology, it might be "How are humans impacting the environment?"*
>
> *—Tenth-grade biology teacher*

The American Association for the Advancement of Science advocates the use of common themes to assist in the development of scientific literacy (AAAS, 1990). There are four major themes that unite the study of all areas of science—systems, models, constancy and change, and scale. However, even these themes are interrelated—as you will note in the following descriptions.

- *Systems.* A system is a group of interdependent items that form a unified whole. A system is more than the sum of its parts. It is an arrangement of components that act together to perform functions not possible with any of the individual parts. Examples include the respiratory, digestive, and circulatory systems of the body; the solar system; simple to complex molecules; the water cycle; the processes of photosynthesis and respiration; transformation of energy into different forms; and chemical reactions.
- *Models.* Models are tools for learning about the things they are meant to resemble. They may be physical objects, often built to scale, that represent another object. Examples of models include models of the very large (i.e.,

the solar system) and the very small (i.e., cells and mole-cules). They may also be conceptual, such as a description of a system, theory, or phenomenon that may be used for further study. Finally, they may be mathematical, such as those for evolution, population growth, Newton's laws, and behavior of ideal gases.

- *Constancy and Change.* "Much of science and mathematics has to do with understanding how change occurs in nature and in social and technological systems, and much of tech-nology has to do with creating and controlling change" (AAAS, 1990). A major consideration is the rate at which things change, and how we can represent change in math-ematical and conceptual models. When things *don't* change is another point of interest in scientific discovery. The state of equilibrium, conservation, and the symmetry of objects are all examples of constancy.
- *Scale.* Most of nature's variables, including time, tempera-ture, distance, speed, and size, show extreme differences in magnitude. Because of the very, very large (i.e., distance to the sun, geologic time) and the very, very small (i.e., nanotechnology, the Whos in Whoville), representing these numbers in terms of powers of ten makes it easier to under-stand them.

Table 8.1 provides examples of AAAS benchmarks organized by scientific theme and grade level.

TEACH SOCIETAL ISSUES

Next, take a look at the dominant topics and relevant issues con-nected to your concepts and themes. The National Science Teachers Association promotes the use of issues in the Science, Technology, and Society curriculum, documenting research that this approach results in students with more sophisticated concept mastery and ability to use process skills (NSTA, 1990). The organization offers a position paper, *Science/Technology/ Society: A New Effort for Providing Appropriate Science for All* (www.nsta.org/about/positions/sts.aspx).

Table 8.1   Science Themes and Selected AAAS Benchmarks by Grade Level

By the end of the grade below, students should know that . . .				
	Grade 2	*Grade 5*	*Grade 8*	*Grade 12*
Systems	Something may not work if some of its parts are missing.	In something that consists of many parts, the parts usually influence one another.	Any system is usually connected to other systems, both internally and externally. Thus a system may be thought of as containing subsystems and as being a subsystem of a larger system.	Even in some very simple systems, it may not always be possible to predict accurately the result of changing some part or connection.
Models	A model of something is different from the real thing but can be used to learn something about the real thing.	Geometric figures, number sequences, graphs, diagrams, sketches, number lines, maps, and stories can be used to represent objects, events, and processes in the real world.	Models are often used to think about processes that happen too slowly, too quickly, or on too small a scale to observe directly, or that are too vast to be changed deliberately, or that are potentially dangerous.	The basic idea of mathematical modeling is to find a mathematical relationship that behaves in the same ways as the objects or processes under investigation.

(Continued)

Table 8.1 (Continued)

	Grade 2	Grade 5	Grade 8	Grade 12
Constancy and Change	Things change in some ways and stay the same in other ways. Some changes are so slow or so fast that they are hard to see.	Often the best way to tell which kinds of change are happening is to make a table or graph of measurements.	Physical and biological systems tend to change until they become stable and then remain that way unless their surroundings change.	Most systems above the molecular level are so sensitive to tiny differences in conditions that their precise behavior is unpredictable.
Scale	Things in nature and things people make have very different sizes, weights, ages, and speeds.	Almost anything has limits on how big or small it can be.	As the complexity of any system increases, gaining an understanding of it depends increasingly on summaries and descriptions of typical examples of that system.	Representing large numbers in terms of powers of ten makes it easier to think about them and to compare things that are greatly different.

Source: Adapted from AAAS, 1990.

Most science teachers identify ten to twenty main topics and issues to guide their units of learning during a school semester. Concepts and themes give your students a context for understanding the topics and issues. Students may examine many different ideas and issues that impact their lives now as well as in the future. They become more active and engaged in the learning when the learning is connected to their lives. Below are examples of issues that may be appropriate for each of the scientific disciplines.

- *Biology*—biodiversity, genomics, biotechnology, population control, evolution, disease
- *Chemistry*—pollution, chemical sensitivity, drug and nutrition chemistry, feeding the world's population
- *Physics*—nuclear power, radiation and radioactive waste, energy
- *Earth science*—the environment, space technology, climate change

There are many Web sites that provide ideas on science, technology, and society issues:

- **NSTA Learning Center:** http://learningcenter.nsta.org. A search for personal and social issues results in a list of free and inexpensive curriculum guides and resources for teaching an STS curriculum.
- **Seven Bioscience Challenges**: www.actionbioscience .org. This educational resource of the American Institute of Biological Sciences promotes bioscience literacy with incredible links to articles and teaching resources. Select what would be developmentally appropriate for your students and consistent with your subject area.
- **Physics and Ethics Education Project:** www.peep.ac.uk/ content/index.php. This United Kingdom interactive Web site and virtual learning environment for secondary school science teachers and their students is a teaching resource developed to highlight the moral, ethical, social, economic, environmental and technological implications and applications of physics.

After you identify the concepts, themes, topics, and issues, then you specify your objectives and reading passages, and isolate the vocabulary and thinking skills. These items will help you organize your learning experiences, incorporate various forms of expression, balance assignments throughout the unit, and select alternative assessments. All the while, you want to break the learning into manageable pieces for students to master. Figure 8.1 contains a list of the factors to consider in planning a unit.

ENVISION YOUR PLANNING SCHEMA

Many teachers like to develop patterns for their units. By developing schema or a specific and consistent approach for planning your units (Yildirim, 2003), you and your students will feel comfortable, participate more easily, and enjoy the teaching and learning readily. Setting a pattern will help the students have a sense of order when, for example, they can anticipate how much they are expected to read for each unit, how many assignments they have to complete on their own and with others, how many

Figure 8.1   Checklist to Follow When Planning a Science Unit

- ❏ Science course and grade level
- ❏ State standards
- ❏ School district expectations
- ❏ School mission statement
- ❏ Students' special interests
- ❏ Concepts
- ❏ Themes
- ❏ Topics and issues
- ❏ Texts and other resources
- ❏ Educational goals and objectives
- ❏ Vocabulary and thinking skills
- ❏ Learning experiences and forms of expression
- ❏ Assignments
- ❏ Assessments and evaluation

presentations they are expected to make (again on their own and with others), and how they will be assessed.

Typically, it takes about six days to cover a topic or textbook chapter if you are going to allocate at least one full day for assessment and two for investigations and experiments. Consider the unit template outlined in Table 8.2. Regardless of the time, you must consider how each day will be allocated to achieve your goals and the students' objectives. Some topics take longer, such as the example of a four-week science unit in Table 8.3. This type of schema helps students plan their lives and take control. You, your students, and their parents will appreciate this approach.

You will want to plan your entire unit of learning as far in advance as possible and with as much detail as is feasible. This process helps you to attend to all parts of the unit, look at it from multiple perspectives, locate resources, and make special arrangements with plenty of time to ensure that one unit of learning flows seamlessly with the previous unit and into the next unit, and matches your students' energy levels.

Table 8.2   Blueprint for Six-Day Science Unit

Day 1	*Day 2*	*Day 3*
Introduce unit Assess entry-level knowledge Preview vocabulary and concepts Use textbook as resource	Conduct investigation or experiment Connect with current events and personal experiences	Engage in problem solving Reinforce vocabulary Continue investigation or experiment Monitor student progress
Day 4	*Day 5*	*Day 6*
Show video segment or otherwise demonstrate application of topics and issues in the real world Jigsaw cooperative groups	Review vocabulary, concepts, and types of problems to be solved Revisit textbook Summarize learning	Assess learning

Table 8.3 Sample Science Unit (Four Weeks)

Unit: Microbiology

Course/Grade: Biology, Grades 9–12

State Standard: Biology/Life Sciences (California)

1. *Cell Biology:* c. Students know how prokaryotic cells, eukaryotic cells (including those from plants and animals), and viruses differ in complexity and general structure.

10. *Physiology:* d. Students know there are important differences between bacteria and viruses with respect to their requirements for growth and replication, the body's primary defenses against bacterial and viral infections, and effective treatments of these infections.

National Education Standard: Life Science

Content Standard C: As a result of their activities in Grades 9–12, all students should develop understanding of the cell; molecular basis of heredity, biological evolution, and interdependence of organisms; matter, energy, and organization in living systems; and behavior of organisms.

	Day 1	*Day 2*	*Day 3*	*Day 4*	*Day 5*
Week 1	**Lecture:** Bacterial classification, size of structures, and morphology **Textbook Walk:** Chapter 10	**Demonstration:** Technique of Simple Stain **Laboratory Activity:** Simple Stain of Bacteria	**Lecture:** Two divisions of Bacteria, Gram Stain **Demonstration:** Gram Stain	**Video:** Bacterial Growth and Reproduction **Textbook:** Questions and Vocabulary	**Lecture:** Moneran Growth and Respiration **Individual Work:** Venn Diagram

146

	Day 1	Day 2	Day 3	Day 4	Day 5
Week 2	**Quiz:** Audience Response Quiz **Lecture:** Medical Microbiology and Defenses	**Computer Group Activity:** Research on Anthrax and Other Gruesome Diseases	**Group Activity** Sharing on Anthrax and Other Gruesome Diseases	**Video:** Viruses **Lecture:** General Properties of Viruses	**Video:** HIV/AIDS **Group Activity:** Modeling of Synthetic Epidemic
Week 3	**Reading Activity:** *In Search of Salmonella's Smoking Gun*	**Video:** *Andromeda Strain* **Group Work:** Worksheet	**Video:** *Andromeda Strain* **Group Work:** Worksheet	**Laboratory:** Bacteriology Project	**Laboratory:** Bacteriology Project
Week 4	**Laboratory:** Bacteriology Project	**Laboratory:** Bacteriology Project	**Laboratory:** Bacteriology Project	**Review:** Jeopardy Game	**Unit Exam:** Written

FOLLOW A CONSISTENT
LESSON PLAN FORMAT

Preparing a lesson plan will give you a specific road map to follow once the class period begins. On the plan you will list your standards and objectives. You will anticipate the order of events, from a "warm-up task," to introducing the lesson, to activities. Then you will identify instructional adaptations and modifications for specific students and your assessments. Finally, you will indicate what your closure activity will be. You can anticipate your homework assignments and include any announcements. Listing the resources you need for the lesson will enable you to quickly gather any special supplies you will need for a given period. Using a consistent lesson plan format will help ensure that you have thought out all parts of your lessons. A detailed lesson plan format can be found in Resource C and an abbreviated lesson plan format is provided in Resource D at the end of the book. The sections that follow present suggestions for the various sections of a daily lesson.

UNDERSTAND ATTENTION SPAN

Most likely, you can hold your students' attention with one activity for approximately thirty minutes, and probably less for younger and less mature students. Today's students are conditioned to a limited amount of concentration, a heightened sense of immediacy, and a reduced level of self-sufficiency, partly due to their habits with television and movies, computer games and the Internet, e-mail, and cell phones. You are a part of this generation too, only now you are the teacher, and you must channel these habits into effective science teaching and learning.

In a traditional class period, your class can be subdivided into three main segments to facilitate effective teaching and learning opportunities: (1) opening the learning; (2) leading students through the body of the lesson, such as facilitating in-class activities, investigations, experiments, or projects; and (3) closing the learning. In this chapter, we describe strategies to exemplify each time segment. You may discover that some of the examples listed in one can be modified and used in a different way for another. We strongly encourage you to find more strategies and add them to your repertoire as your science teaching career develops.

CAPTIVATE STUDENTS
AS YOU OPEN LESSONS

> *I teach new concepts by relating the idea to something students are already familiar with. For example, when teaching students about density of substances, I bring in Italian salad dressing. I then pose a question, such as "Why is the oil floating at the top while the rest of the ingredients are beneath it?"*

> —*Seventh-grade life science teacher*

The first time segment involves opening the learning process so that you can grab your students' attention immediately and completely. When students arrive, make sure you have set up the classroom explicitly for that group of students by arranging desks, organizing teaching strategies, and preparing learning activities. You might want to follow an established daily routine, or you might want to introduce something different every day or every few days. There are many different models of teaching (Joyce & Weil, 2003). Whatever approach you prefer, you will want to set the stage for the entire class period. Consider the following ten easy-to-implement activities.

Ten Opening Activities

1. *Hand a prompt.* Greet students at the door, and hand them a paper or other item related to the upcoming learning experience. Instructions can be written on paper or posted on a board or screen.

   a. Hand all of your students the same item, such as copies of a question to answer or problem to solve in the first few minutes of class. Students can work independently, with partners, or in small groups.

   b. Hand your students different items such as puzzle pieces to form a huge puzzle assembled by the entire class or papers of different colors to be used in small groups.

2. *Post a prompt.* Post information on the board or a screen with an overhead. Ask a question, give directions, and provide the worksheet, overhead transparency, or chart

paper for students to complete individually, with partners, or in small groups. The prompts may:

a. reflect the reading, listening, or viewing;
b. connect topics and issues with the real world;
c. survey current beliefs and behaviors; or
d. ask for predictions and/or suggestions.

3. *Display a specimen or model.* Place the item in a highly visible location and ask students to discuss what they observed. You may have students make hypotheses based on some characteristics or their questions. You can conduct this opener individually, with partners, or in small groups, as an oral or written response. Pass the item around if possible.

a. Have students name the item, describe the item, or formulate hypotheses or questions about the item.
b. Have students pose questions that enhance their critical thinking.

4. *Perform a demonstration or discrepant event.* Conduct the demonstration and ask students to discuss what they observed. Have students hypothesize about what happened. You can conduct this opener individually, with partners, or in small groups, as an oral or written response.

a. Have students record the steps of the mini-experiment, including materials, data and observations, and results.
b. Have students pose questions that enhance their critical thinking.

5. *Show a video clip, audio recording, or take a virtual Internet tour.* Show a segment from a video, DVD or Web site.

a. Have students describe what they have seen, and discuss observations in either small groups or the entire class.
b. Have students express their feelings connected with the viewed selection or predict how the viewed selection related to a particular topic or issue.

6. *Read aloud.* Start the class by reading a selection aloud. The selection may be any kind of narrative, serious or humorous.

a. Have students report what the reading makes them think and how the reading makes them feel.

      b. Have students write a similar piece individually or in small groups.

7. *Introduce a guest speaker.* After students are settled, introduce a guest speaker. The speaker's visit may be planned, and students may have constructed questions in advance. Or the speaker's visit may be a surprise.

      a. If the speaker's visit is planned, have students listen for responses to previously identified questions during the talk or ask the questions at the appropriate time.

      b. If the speaker's visit is a surprise, give students a few minutes to record some questions before the speaker talks.

8. *Conduct silent reading.* Provide a reason for reading, preferably written on the board or on a handout, and instruct students to read a short passage silently for the first five to ten minutes of class. The passage maybe from the textbook or supplementary material. The History of Science topics in each chapter of this book are very good resources for this type of activity. Box 8.1 features DNA.

      a. Have students respond to the purpose for reading.

      b. List key vocabulary words and concepts from the passage and have students describe the concepts using vocabulary.

9. *Pose a problem.* Provide students with a problem to be solved. The problem may be on a science issue or it may be mathematical. It could include analysis of data in a table or chart.

      a. Individually or in small groups, have students solve the problem. Students should record their process of arriving at a solution as well as the solution.

      b. Have students write questions they could ask or identify investigations they could take to find out more information.

10. *Play a game.* Games used to start class should be mastered activities that you can lead without direction. They can be used in previewing upcoming learning, scaffolding or revising prior learning, reviewing or applying new learning, or preparing for assessments. When using games as an opener, be sure to:

      a. distribute all necessary materials in advance;

      b. follow previously established rules;

   c. limit to the first ten minutes of class; and

   d. connect the purpose of game with upcoming learning.

Select a strategy that will spark interest and draw students into the topic of the day. Your introductory activity should stimulate their thinking while relating to the objectives you will cover in the lesson.

BOX 8.1

History of Science

The Race for the Structure of DNA

The race to discover the structure of DNA began shortly after World War I, with four young scientists. This was when Rosalind Franklin, an English scientist, joined the Laboratoire Centrale des Services Chimiques de l'Etat in Paris and became an authority on the techniques of x-ray crystallography. In 1950, she returned to England to King's College, London, where her responsibility was to upgrade the x-ray crystallographic laboratory for work with DNA. Her colleague was Maurice Wilkins, born in New Zealand, who proposed that they study DNA by x-ray crystallographic techniques.

While Franklin and Wilkins took an experimental approach, analyzing x-ray diffraction images of DNA, Cambridge researchers Englishman Francis Crick and American James Watson offered a different perspective. Their approach was to make physical models to narrow down the possibilities and eventually create an accurate picture of the molecule. Watson and Crick rapidly put together several models of DNA and attempted to incorporate all the evidence they could gather.

In 1951, Watson attended a lecture by Franklin. From her x-ray images, she had deduced that the phosphate part of the molecule was on the outside. Based on this information, Watson and Crick realized that their model was a failure. Their supervisor even told them to stop DNA research! But they couldn't let it go.

Continuing her work, Franklin determined that her x-ray diffractions showed that the form of DNA had all the characteristics of a helix. She suspected that all DNA was helical but did not want to announce this finding until she had sufficient evidence. Wilkins showed Franklin's results to Watson (apparently without her knowledge or consent).

Watson and Crick reconceptualized the molecular structure to be made of two chains of nucleotides, each in a helix as Franklin had found, but with one going up and the other going down. Their proposed structure so perfectly fit the experimental data that it was almost immediately accepted.

DNA's discovery has been called the most important biological work of the last hundred years, and the field it opened may be the scientific frontier for the next hundred. It was the foundation for modern molecular biology, biochemistry, biology, genetics, and medicine. By 1962, when Watson, Crick, and Wilkins won the Nobel Prize for physiology/medicine, Franklin had died.

James Watson (1968) characterizes science as an exciting race for knowledge in *Double Helix: A Personal Account of the Discovery of the Structure of DNA*. Francis Crick (1988) describes it as a "mad pursuit" (*What Mad Pursuit: A Personal View of Scientific Discovery*), in which he and Watson, with Wilkins and Franklin to a lesser degree, were in pursuit of discovery against Linus Pauling and scientists in the United States. Anne Sayer (1975), author of *Rosalind Franklin and DNA*, represents the race as unequal, with Rosalind Franklin deserving much more of the glory than was given to her. You may read more about this scientific contest and contested discovery on the following Web sites:

- **DNA From the Beginning:** www.dnafb.org. An animated primer on the basics of DNA, genes, and heredity sponsored by Cold Spring Harbor Laboratory.
- **DNA PBS:** www.pbs.org/wnet/dna. The PBS site of the comprehensive history of DNA science.

BEGIN THE LEARNING EXPERIENCE

If you spend the first ten minutes for the lesson opener, you have approximately thirty-five minutes remaining for the body of the lesson, with five minutes left for closure and five for any administrative tasks (announcements, cleanup) in a traditional period.

You want to move into the learning experience quickly and smoothly. If your students figure out that you can be distracted or drawn off the subject, most likely it will occur at this time. Be aware that your students will know exactly when and how to start unrelated conversations to delay the start of your planned lesson.

After assessing your students' prior knowledge or schema, begin the starting point of your teaching and their learning. If gaps have been identified, you can build new knowledge by introducing additional experiences and visual references. At this point, you need to make a decision to take one of two paths: *indirect teaching* or *direct teaching*.

> *I build on prior knowledge. For example, in learning about the respiratory system I ask students to recall prior knowledge of the cell, muscular system, and blood. Then I begin to relate it to the lungs. I ask students about life experiences related to the topic, such as asthmatics and smokers in their families.*
>
> *—Seventh-grade life science teacher*

START WITH SOME DIRECT TEACHING

If you follow the direct teaching path, information is given to your students either by you, via lecture and example, through shared reading, or through another medium, such as video or a guest speaker. Direct teaching allows you to cover a huge amount of content quickly and with control of the pacing, engagement, and expectations. It is essential that teachers begin by stating the objective for learning and providing graphic organizers for students to take notes and make connections. Direct teaching certainly plays an important role in science classes.

Most teachers primarily rely on talking with students formally and informally to provide information. These personal conversations also provide feedback, contributing to your assessments of students' understanding and achievement. Effective teacher talk (Callahan, Clark, & Kellough, 1998) both encourages and requires students to listen in a way that constitutes active engagement in the learning process.

Guidelines for Direct Teaching

- Outline your talk to have a beginning, middle, and end, with a logical order of information and events that provides background or extends rather than repeats what is in the text.

- Provide an outline or study guide, preferably in the form of a graphic organizer, for students to follow your talk, take notes, and make connections (Ausubel, 1963).
- Use visual aids, such as illustrations and artifacts, slides, transparencies, charts, drawings, videos, physical demonstrations, and so forth.
- Incorporate vocabulary, concepts, and examples naturally within the body of your talk.
- Apply familiar examples to connect the learning with your students' prior knowledge and experiences.
- Consider diversity in the content and examples.
- Use notes to guide your talk; be sure you speak to and *not* read to your students unless you are reading explicit directions that must be followed precisely.
- Encourage participation with and among your students.
- Monitor your voice quality (tone and volume) and eye contact.
- Move around the classroom and speak from various locations; this technique helps make all students feel included in the conversation and forces students to stay alert.
- Reinforce key ideas and significant outcomes with closure.

Expository teaching provides an explanation using facts, ideas, and other vital information to transmit basic knowledge and essential skills specified by the curriculum. *Demonstration teaching* involves showing, telling, and/or conducting performances relating knowledge, skills, and dispositions through efforts and endeavors that may be planned or spontaneous, frequently combined with the modes of exposition and inquiry. Table 8.4 compares the structure of expository and demonstration teaching with respect to the teacher's role, the student's role, and the nature of assessment.

Both types of teaching are often used in a given lesson. Here is an example in physics. Using *expository teaching,* you might lecture on Newton's three laws of motion. Using a mobile cart and other equipment, you would likely include demonstrations of each of the three laws, but that is not what we are referring to when we define *demonstration teaching.* Students would take notes and then be assessed with a quiz, essay, or alternative assessment.

Using *demonstration teaching,* you would model for students how to solve problems involving speed, force, momentum, and

Table 8.4   Comparison of Structure of Expository and Demonstration Teaching

	Expository Teaching	*Demonstration Teaching*
Teacher's Role	To direct the learning, primarily through teacher talk and media presentations	To plan, organize, and execute the demonstration clearly
Student's Role	To listen, to record notes	To observe, listen, and follow the presentation carefully
Assessment	Based on recalling and reproducing correct answers of a predetermined curriculum	Based on the ability to participate, replicate, or respond to questions and discussion during or following the demonstration

acceleration. Students would observe what you do and, first with guided and then independent practice, follow your model for solving problems. Both knowledge and skills are involved in this unit. Teachers choose their methods to achieve their objectives. Again, they would take notes and be assessed with a quiz, essay, or demonstration of their own.

FEATURE INDIRECT TEACHING

The indirect teaching path engages your students in their own learning. The teacher becomes a facilitator of learning, guiding with questions and providing resources. There are several steps to follow with indirect teaching.

Guidelines for Indirect Teaching

- *Introduce the activity.* You can give an overview and all the details at once, or you can give an overview and inspect each detail individually at a later time.
- *Provide reading response mechanisms.* Most activities conducted in class will relate to the textbook; you and your

students will benefit from guided reading response strategies and reviewing the text features. Some options are listed in Chapter 7.

- *Monitor student progress*, keeping an eye on the time. Allow plenty of time. Students may be slow in getting started. Be prepared for the activity to grow and change as students get involved and take ownership of their own learning and outcomes. As you interact with students, give fair, frequent, and positive oral feedback on their work.
- *Collect products with students' names on them at the end of the activity* to use during upcoming class sessions, to give written feedback, and to record their participation in your grade book.

There are many different types of indirect activities for you to try with your students (Hoge, Field, Foster, & Nickell, 2004). The amount of time and kinds of materials that are needed vary with each teacher, group of students, and course content. Student grouping is another factor to consider. Indirect teaching allows for *differentiated learning* as students address objectives with a variety of activities and resources. The presentations that result give you and the students a wonderful opportunity to share their learning with others, such as students in other grade levels, parents, and the community.

Ten Indirect Learning Activities

1. *Inquiry.* Stimulate students to develop questions when investigating new events or building on prior knowledge and experiences resulting in description (telling what it is), significance (telling how it is relevant), and justification (telling why it is relevant) (Costa, 1991).

Inquiry-based or problem-based learning uses immediate problems as the foundation of study. The teacher selects a topic, or has students participate in the selection of a problem to be solved, and provides the tools and supplies needed. Students work as a class or in small groups to define the problem, research the background, propose various solutions, and then choose the best solution for presentation. Having an authentic problem and audience makes these experiences especially meaningful. Students learn how to work together and how to solve problems, as well as how to master the issue or topic under study. You may want to review information covered in Chapter 3 on inquiry methods.

2. *Data Analysis.* Introduce topics and issues substantiated with research-based information and statistics along with narrative descriptions of situations and incidents (quantitative and qualitative data). Have students examine causes and effects, trace interconnections, consider multiple perspectives, and evaluate implications related to concrete and abstract, real and fictitious conditions and events.

3. *Investigations and Experiments.* Facilitate learning experiences by placing students in new situations where they can observe, react, question, describe, compare, contrast, explain, and interpret events in their own terms and through their own means (Brunner, 1959; Taba, 1962). Tell students they are detectives responsible for determining what they know, what they need to know, what they do not need to know, what others may or may not know, and so forth. Investigations and experiments may be conducted deductively or inductively.

4. *Critical Thinking.* Develop learning experiences that challenge students and cause them to wonder, doubt, and question the given situation or status quo (Beyer, 1995). Ask students to consider a topic or issue from a different perspective, a viewpoint that they probably would never take on their own, then research and defend it to a group through a presentation, debate, or staged event such as a trial.

5. *Concept Attainment.* Formulate significant ideas for students to comprehend, explain, apply, and appreciate both simple and complex issues generalized or transferred from meaning and experience (Parker, 2005). Concepts are big ideas that tend to be somewhat difficult for students to realize and apply to new or different contexts. Introduce and reinforce concepts slowly and deliberately with many explicit examples for complete attainment.

6. *Cooperative Learning.* Organize students to function in small groups where they draw from one another's wisdom and strengths to understand given information, to construct new knowledge, and to teach themselves and others (Johnson & Johnson, 1989). We strongly recommend that you teach your students cooperative learning techniques early during the school year using a relatively easy concept so your students fully

understand the roles, responsibilities, and rationale of cooperative learning. Then, after some practice and debriefing the group process, you can use cooperative learning activities as a technique that your students can apply readily to more complex concepts and skills.

7. *Role Play and Simulation.* Have students role-play historical or current events. They must conduct research and present their findings. Simulations help students develop social justice and critical thinking skills.

Simulations seem to work best when teachers have participated in the simulation themselves and a careful debriefing takes place following the interaction (Singleton, 2006). This way, the teacher is fully aware of what learning takes place; the length of time, the kinds of materials, and the type of setting that are needed; and the level of stress experienced if the simulation is presented in front of an audience. Clearly explained objectives and directions are critical for success using simulations. A follow-up discussion is equally important to give students the opportunity to summarize and clarify what they gained from the experience, the degree to which their thinking changed, how well they have worked with others, and how the simulation relates to real life.

8. *Debate.* Select an age-appropriate, relevant topic for your students about which ample reference material is available. Present the debating procedures to the students. They need to understand the roles played by participants, the impact of the rules, and how the debate will be judged. Then students need time to research, write, and practice their delivery. What better way for students to distinguish fact from opinion and explore different points of view? What better way to integrate listening, speaking, and literacy skills in the classroom? You can even consider engaging students in a different location in a debate using technology (Hess, 2005).

9. *Project-Based Learning.* Design long-term, interdisciplinary, student-centered, collaborative learning experiences for students to take stock of current situations and accepted norms and then propose viable solutions integrated with real-world issues and practices (Evans, Newmann, & Saxe, 1996). Project-based learning requires several steps that you want to develop completely before starting them with your students. Usually the steps involve reading, writing, inquiry, interviewing, field trips, drawing, technology, and presenting. Think of project-based

learning as a real-life event that adults commonly have to perform around their homes or at their work. Students attach themselves quickly to project-based learning as they can apply their personal touches to the outcomes.

10. *WebQuests.* Take students on a virtual "quest" for information to answer a question, solve a mystery, or create a product or other predetermined task. Bernie Dodge, with the help of Tom March, developed the model of inquiry-based research on the Web in 1995 at San Diego State University. WebQuests provide students with specific directions and Web links so they do not have to spend needless time searching for information. Allow one to three class periods or longer for students to complete their "quest."

Select a WebQuest your students will find interesting and provide some background information. Then give the directions for completing the task, including resources and organizational tools to be used. Provide an assessment rubric to guide students. At the end, have students present and summarize their learning.

Teachers have experienced great success in assigning students to groups or teams for WebQuest activities. With time and experience, students can create their own Web Inquiry Projects (WIPs), which are open-ended tasks with limited teacher scaffolding. In WIPs, students select their own data to analyze and present to their peers. Two good references for reading and educational materials can be found at http://webquest.sdsu.edu, where Bernie Dodge also maintains a free Web site with 2,500 examples for WebQuests, and at http://edweb.sdsu.edu/wip for WIPs (Molebash & Dodge, 2003).

REINFORCE LEARNING DURING CLOSURE

Just as you wanted to motivate learners when you opened the lesson, now you want to reinforce the learning during closure. Too often, closure is simply the ringing of the bell followed by the closing of books. We recommend that you leave the last five to eight minutes of class to bring the learning to a close. By capturing the most important points and relating them back to your objectives, you enable your students to process what they have learned. By having students record their findings, the learning will be strengthened. Box 8.2 shows a variety of ideas for closure.

BOX 8.2

**Ten Closing Activities Applicable
to Effective Science Learning**

1. Write one statement, question, comment, or connection on a note card.

2. Make a daily entry in a journal.

3. Record information on a graphic organizer.

4. Summarize results on a group paper or poster.

5. Vote on a prediction.

6. Take a stand on an issue.

7. Ask a question of a partner.

8. Make a connection and share with a group.

9. Write a summary, with each member of the group adding a sentence.

10. Construct a quick quiz question for everyone else in the group to answer.

ASSIGN HOMEWORK

A question you may often hear from your students is "Why do we have to do homework?" In fact, this is a good question! What is the purpose of homework? Often, it is used as a means for students to review content learned in class. However, homework should also serve a wider range of purposes—for both students and teachers. Homework can help students:

- review, apply, and integrate prior knowledge with current content;
- develop mastery of skills;
- develop self-direction;
- explore topics more fully than class time permits; and
- prepare for the next class session.

Homework can also help teachers assess student understanding and provide for differentiated instruction. You may vary the types of assignments you want your students to experience and build upon individual learning styles. Sometimes, you may be able to give students a choice of assignments. You may also use homework as a conduit for students to share personal interests and involve family members in the learning experience. Homework is the perfect opportunity to include families and to make meaningful connections outside of the classroom. For example, you may ask students to interview a parent, grandparent, or neighbor to find out how the world has changed since they were children and what we know now that was unknown then.

Homework assignments need to have clear purposes related to your science topics and issues. Students must be able to complete the work on their own and communicate expectations with their parents. While typical assignments involve reading and studying notes, some types of homework assignments are new tasks given to students to complete explicitly outside of the classroom, and perhaps specifically at their homes. The homework assignment may be a written product or a presentation preparation that students must complete outside of class using the library, Internet, or other resources. Each of these types of assignments may be difficult, if not impossible, for all students to complete if the students are not given appropriate access, and supplies, time, or opportunities are not available to them outside of school. Not all students have even minimal supplies at home. In these situations, you should provide supplies or offer alternative assignments. Check with your students to make sure each one is capable of achieving success.

Don't forget to consult the homework policies for your school district, school building, and teaching team. There may be clear guidelines as to the frequency, amount, and types of homework that you can and cannot ask your students to complete.

USE BLOCK SCHEDULING WISELY

Block scheduling, in which students have ninety minutes or more for a class period, provides a great setting for science. Students have longer amounts of uninterrupted time for research, experimentation, discussion, and presentation than in a traditional period. Teachers can easily combine elements of direct teaching and indirect teaching during one class session. Students can engage in one major concentrated learning experience or a variety of activities during one period. You can revisit content in a multitude of ways.

Managing block scheduling periods effectively requires you to be well prepared with plans, materials, and patience. You need to know exactly what you expect to happen throughout the entire block. Both you and your students will find your energies fluctuating, so it is important to give explicit instructions along with appropriate time limits to complete activities. Most students are not able to sustain their attention for ninety minutes on a single assignment. Either you will want to start and stop the entire class at regular intervals to monitor progress and comprehension and vary activities, or you will need to meet with groups during the block to check on your students' ability to complete their tasks. Including activities that involve movement and time to work with others will be appreciated by all during a block period.

MAKE THE MOST OF YOUR TIME . . .

Ideas are endless, but time is limited. You must be aware of the time as you teach your classes, knowing exactly when to start and stop each activity, moving through the opening, guiding the lesson activities, and closing each day. The secret is to make the most of your time in the classroom and your students' time outside of the classroom. Try new strategies. Evaluate to see which ones are best for your students. In the next chapter, we will explore how to incorporate a variety of resources inside and outside the classroom.

Suggested Activities

1. Plan a lesson from introduction to closure using both formats in the Resources section of this book. Discuss the advantages and disadvantages of each.

2. Make a large chart with the segments of a typical class and use sticky notes to start designing your teaching strategies for your units of learning.

3. Observe teachers to see how they implement and transition through the parts of a lesson plan to make learning relevant for their students. Discuss with a colleague.

4. Ask your students to give you feedback on their favorite topics and learning experiences.

CHAPTER NINE

Include Resources to Make Science Real

To smash the simple atom, all mankind was intent. Now any day, the atom may, return the compliment.

—Ogden Nash, American poet (1902–1971)

Topics and issues will leap off the written page when you and your students bring a variety of resources to class to share with one another. When your students can see and touch objects that are discussed in the textbook, the focus of learning shifts. Instead of being on the outside looking in passively, now you and your students are inside, taking an active role in the learning process. Your students make connections and build community as they share their questions, thoughts, findings, and feelings.

SET THE STAGE

There are many different types of resources and many different ways of using them in your classes. It is essential that you are well prepared and plan far in advance. You will have to arrange for supplies or reserve equipment early in the school year. Therefore, it is important to be extremely organized and forward thinking as you order materials to be sent to your school, invite guests, coordinate field trips, and so on. For some activities, you may need to obtain administrator and/or school board approval. Here is a guide to follow as you get started.

Resource Planning Guide

- Identify all of your units of learning for the entire school year with the approximate amounts of time you want to allocate for each one.
- Check all of the applicable calendars, such as activities, substitute availability, testing dates, and so forth, to avoid schedule conflicts.
- Share your plans with your department head, science department members, and team members, and add their suggestions. They will let you know if additional approval is required.
- Brainstorm three to five types of resources that would enhance each of your units of learning; perhaps you can brainstorm with a colleague.
- Inquire about the resources available in your media center and school district; there may be many resources right at your fingertips.
- Talk with your library/media specialists, who may have already coordinated resources pertinent to your anticipated units of learning in the past.
- Acquire some heavy cardboard boxes or large plastic crates, along with colorful files for each anticipated unit of learning, to collect and organize your own collections of resources.
- Develop a filing system of folders or a three-ring notebook divided into your anticipated units of learning for each course you will be teaching; record your unit ideas and the contacts in each subdivision of the notebook. If you record your plans and contacts on your computer and other electronic organizers, be sure to make a hard copy to keep in your file or notebook. You may want to carry the information with you when you go to the telephone, when you visit off-site locations, and when you go home.

The secret to using resources is to know your subject, your audience, and your purpose. As you select resources—especially when inviting guest speakers and taking field trips—investing your time and energy efficiently and effectively will be appreciated by your students.

INTRODUCE MODELS AND SPECIMENS

My favorite way to study science is by doing things, rather than just reading a textbook or doing a worksheet. For example, when I learned bones, my teacher had a model skeleton and we learned the bones by looking at the skeleton.

—Ann, age thirteen, eighth grade

Science concepts and practices will make much more sense when you bring in the actual objects, specimens, or models representative of the objects that you are describing. These objects and models are vital to effective science. For instance, if you are studying rocks, you should display a variety of rock types and examples. These may be purchased from a science supplier or collected during your travels and investigations. Pictures may also be used.

Once you show your students your samples, they will want to bring their personal collections to share with the class. Continuing with our example, some students may have collected geodes, gemstones, or other rock and mineral samples. You might want to send a note home to parents or via e-mail to let them know what you are studying and how students can get involved. With younger students, we suggest that you ask students to bring the items to you first thing after they arrive at school for you to keep. Have a box of zip-lock plastic bags and some markers handy so you can write the name of the student and the item brought to school. Ask your students whether you can share the item in your other classes, as you want to be sure you can share their personal objects with other students before doing so.

BRING IN PLANTS AND ANIMALS

Many science teachers like to keep plants and/or animals in their classrooms. NSTA supports the decision of science teachers and their school or school district to integrate live animals and in the K–12 classroom because "observing and working with animals firsthand can spark students' interest in science as well as a general respect for life while reinforcing key concepts as outlined in the *National Science Education Standards*" (NSTA, 2008).

Plants are much easier than animals to care for, but some equipment is required, including special lighting, special soils and food, and water. Some plants are particularly fun for students—consider a Venus Fly Trap, for example. Plants that bloom in different colors in different soils may also be an interesting choice.

Animals can stimulate and enhance learning, and should be handled safely in the laboratory/classroom. Whenever animals are to be used in science activities with students, it is imperative that both the animals and the students are protected. Because increased activity and sudden movements can make animals feel threatened, *all* student contact with animals should be highly organized and supervised. Wild or poisonous animals should never be allowed in the classroom. You should also require your students to use gloves and wash their hands after handling.

For some students, the science classroom is their only experience with a small animal such as a hamster, rat, snake, gecko, fish, hermit crab, or bird. There are many things that need to be considered when selecting a classroom pet:

1. Does your school and district allow you to keep a pet? How will the project be funded?

2. What pet(s) should you choose? What eating, sleeping, social, and activity patterns should be considered?

3. What amount of space is available in your classroom? Where is the best location for the pet?

4. What are the safety considerations of keeping the pet? How will the pet be safe from curious fingers? (And how will students who have curious fingers be safe from pets?)

5. What kind of cage will provide a good habitat for the pet while also allowing students to view its daily activities?

6. How will the pet be cared for on weekends and over holidays?

7. How will the cage be cleaned?

8. How will the pet be fed and watered?

9. What will you do if the pet becomes ill?

10. What science may be taught by keeping this pet?

TEACH WITH TOYS

Remember our History of Science topic in Chapter 7? Well, Newton's discoveries all began with a simple toy. In 1665, Sir

Isaac Newton came home with a new toy he had purchased at the local fair—a prism! He couldn't wait to get into his room and see how the prism broke the light into the colors of the spectrum. However, as he was playing with the toy, he noticed an interesting anomaly. Newton's simple observation that the colors were in oblong form instead of circular prompted him to investigate—and the rest, as they say, is history!

Science education is at its best when students have opportunities to make connections between their own world and scientific concepts. What could be more natural than using toys as learning tools? For teachers and students alike, toys can provide motivational and experiential links between science concepts and everyday experience. Teaching science with toys is a way to start where your students are. Consider toys in these content areas:

- *Chemistry*—soap bubbles, Silly Putty®, helium-filled balloons, candies, slime, Floam®, bubble gum, Tinkertoys®, and crystal formation kits
- *Physics*—magnets, wind-up cars, tops, holographs, Boomwhackers®, Circus Sam Balancing Man®, robots, rubber band propelled paper airplanes, parachuting man, kites, periscopes, yo-yos, hula hoops, whistles, and Etch-A-Sketch®
- *Geology*—K'NEX®, geyser tube, tornado tube, boomerangs, Cartesian diver, telescopes, Slinky®, rock tumbler kit, Lego®, magnets, fool's gold, sand and water sifters and funnels
- *Biology*—microscopes, whirligig and propeller stick, ant farm, butterfly garden and net, bug magnifiers and bug jars, Ladybug Land™

FEATURE SCIENCE LITERATURE, POETRY, AND HUMOR

Have you heard the one about the atom who had lost his electrons? When asked if he was sure they were really lost, he replied, "I'm positive." Yes, this is a silly joke—but it serves to underscore an important point: To "get" a joke, you have to have the appropriate background knowledge. Using poetry, puns, humor, and literature will increase student understanding of, and favorable attitudes toward, science. There is plenty to find on the Web and in print, and students may also compose their own poetry, children's stories, news articles, want ads, and other journalistic compositions, as well as other fiction and nonfiction works on science-related topics.

Science Verse, by John Scieska (2004), is a great example for all science classrooms. The story begins when a boy hears a teacher remark that "if you listen closely enough, you can hear the poetry of science in everything." What follows is a series of poems that parody the styles of Joyce Kilmer, Edgar Allan Poe, Lewis Carroll, Robert Frost, and many others, as well as familiar songs and nursery rhymes. "Once in first grade I was napping/When I heard a scary yapping" begins a lament about studying dinosaurs year after year. Our favorite is "Astronaut Stopping by a Planet on a Snowy Evening," where the narrator bemoans the fact that he can't figure out what planet he's on because "In science class I was asleep . . ."

Singing songs with tunes from Chemistry Carols for the holidays is also a fun activity. Who can resist joining in with "I'm dreaming of a white precipitate, just like the ones I used to KNO_3," or "Oh chemistry, oh chemistry, how lovely is thy stoichiometry!" A quick Google search will find many different choices. And don't forget to write your own! See Table 9.1 for "The States of Matter: A Poem in Three Phases" by your author, Victoria Costa.

DRAW FROM SCIENCE FICTION TO TEACH SCIENCE FACTS

"You canna' change the laws of physics," Scotty used to tell Captain Kirk, even though his *Star Trek* spaceship often seemed to. But you might be able to teach the laws of physics through some good—or bad—science fiction. Films like *Fantastic Voyage, The Day the Earth Caught Fire, 2010 Space Odyssey,* and *Them!* provide students with challenges to identify the nonsense—or nonscience—in these stories. Dubeck, Moshier, and Boss (2003) have found that by teaching students through science fiction instead of traditional techniques, students gain a better understanding of the scientific principles. See examples of topics and corresponding science fiction films in Table 9.2.

Using science fiction to teach science facts is one way to tap into its popularity with young people, and use it as an educational tool to build interest in and awareness of real science. *The Science of Star Trek* is a television documentary that compares and contrasts the scientific principles in *Star Trek* with current science. Many clips from the *Star Trek* movies and TV series are used to illustrate the concepts of faster-than-light travel, time travel,

Table 9.1   The States of Matter

"The States of Matter: A Poem in Three Phases", by Victoria Costa		
LIQUIDS	**GASES**	**SOLIDS**
I went to the pool On a hot summer day, Jumped in the water And made it spray.	I got out of the pool And I felt a warm breeze Then the wind yanked my towel	I sat down on the chair And the chair stayed there No dripping or spilling Anywhere!
I splashed the lifeguard And my best friend, too. The clear, cool water I dove right through.	From my hands to my knees. Although I couldn't see it It must be the air. I can feel it around me So I know it is there.	I didn't fall off And I didn't fall through. That makes my chair A solid, true.
How can this be? *Oh, how wonderful! Oh, how strange!* *How the particles of water must be arranged!* *Not too near or far away,* *Or in one place the water would stay.*	*How can this be?* *Oh, how wonderful! Oh, how strange!* *How the particles of air must be arranged!* *So far apart we cannot see* *The particles of air are moving free.*	*How can this be?* *Oh, how wonderful! Oh, how strange!* *How the particles of solids must be arranged!* *So snug and tight, with spaces small.* *Their definite shape doesn't change much at all.*
Water is a liquid, And liquids have three Properties that make them Very liq-ui-dy.	Air is a gas With particles so far apart That gases seem like nothing But we can see them if we're smart!	Some solids are metals, Such as iron and tin. They are shiny and sturdy, Like the coins that we spend.
The space between their particles Makes room for plenty more, So we can make Kool-Aid, And sugar tea we pour.	A gas makes up the bubbles Of a can of soda pop. The gas makes the pop go everywhere If you shake the can a lot!	Other solids are soft Like powder and lead It is even a solid That makes up your bed!

"The States of Matter: A Poem in Three Phases" by Victoria Costa		
LIQUIDS	**GASES**	**SOLIDS**
The particles of liquids Are free to slip and slide, That's why milk can spill on tables And rain puddles form outside. Liquids are shaped like their containers Like a bowl, a jar, or cup Mom pours our juice inside one Before we drink it up.	Helium is a special gas That is lighter than the air. I love balloons with helium You buy at the County Fair!	*Oh, how interesting! Oh, how strange! How the particles of matter must be arranged! In the pool, in the wind, on a chair with my friend Matter is everywhere! All we need to do is look around, and we'll find matter there!*

anti-particle physics, medical imaging, extraterrestrial life, artificial intelligence, and matter transmission. Below are some additional resources for teaching science through science fiction.

- *Fantastic Voyages: Learning Science Through Science Fiction Films* (Dubeck, Moshier, & Boss, 2003).
- *Teaching Science With Science Fiction Films: A Guide for Teachers and Media Specialists* (Cavanaugh & Cavanaugh, 2004).
- Center for the Study of Science Fiction: www2.ku.edu/~sfcenter. This University of Kansas site provides information and links to other resources about teaching science fiction.

EXPLORE THE RICH HISTORY OF SCIENCE

As you have seen throughout this text, science enjoys a rich history of discovery. Familiarizing students with the lives and accomplishments of the men and women who have made contributions to science will help students understand that what they learn in science class is the product of the hard work of those who have come before them, and will encourage them to be future contributors to our understanding of how nature works. In addition, it fulfills the *National Science Education Standards* for students to understand science

Table 9.2   Science Fiction Films and Science Topics

Topic	Science Fiction	Summary
Biology/Life Science		
Cellular biology, origin of life	The Andromeda Strain (1971)	A group of scientists investigate a deadly new alien virus.
Viruses, disease	Outbreak (1995)	A deadly airborne virus finds its way into the United States and starts killing off people at an epidemic rate.
Multicellularity	The Blob (1958 and 1988)	A strange life form consumes everything in its path as it grows.
Plant structure	The Thing (1982)	Scientists in the Antarctic are confronted by a shape-shifting alien, which assumes the appearance of the people it kills.
Plant movement	The Day of the Triffids (1962)	Triffids are experimental plants that escape and are capable of moving themselves around and attacking people.
Circulatory system	Fantastic Voyage (1966)	Scientists attempt to save a life by shrinking a submarine to microscopic size and injecting it into his bloodstream with a small crew.
DNA	Gattaca (1997)	A genetically inferior man assumes the identity of a superior one and travels in space.
DNA, extinction	Jurassic Park (1993)	To create a theme park, scientists clone dinosaurs, which escape during a security breach.
Evolution	Planet of the Apes (1968 and 2001)	An astronaut lands on a planet inhabited by humanlike apes who rule the planet with an iron fist.
Physical Science		
Electricity	Mary Shelley's Frankenstein (1994)	A man-made monster comes to life with the help of electricity.

Nuclear energy	*Them* (1954)	Early atomic tests in New Mexico cause common ants to mutate into giant monsters.
Nuclear energy	*Silkwood* (1980)	The story of Karen Silkwood, the Oklahoma nuclear-plant worker who blew the whistle on dangerous practices at the Kerr-McGee Corporation.
Time travel	*The Time Machine* (1960 and 2002)	A nineteenth-century inventor travels 800,000 years into the future, where he finds humankind divided into two warring races.
Earth Science		
Meteors and comets	*Meteor* (1979)	After a collision with a comet, a piece of the asteroid heads towards Earth.
Earthquakes	*Earthquake* (1974)	An earthquake devastates Los Angeles.
Volcanoes	*Dante's Peak* (1997)	Dante's Peak is threatened by a volcano.
Space	*2001: A Space Odyssey* (1968)	Mankind finds a mysterious artifact on the moon, and scientists work with an intelligent computer to understand its meaning.
Pollution, environment, natural resources	*The Lorax* (1972)	A ruined industrialist tells his tale of his environmentally self-destructive greed despite the warnings of an old forest creature.
Earth and space science	*October Sky* (1999)	The story of Homer Hickam, a coal miner's son who studied rocketry against his father's wishes.
Global warming	*The Day After Tomorrow* (2004)	A climatologist tries to save the world from global warming.
Global warming, overpopulation	*Soylent Green* (1973)	A look at life on an overpopulated futuristic Earth ruined by global warming.

Source: Adapted from Firooznia (2006); Dubeck, Moshier, & Boss (2003); and Cavanaugh & Cavanaugh (2004).

as a human endeavor, the nature of science, and the history of science. In the History of Science boxes in each chapter of this book (including the one in Box 9.1), we have included stories of scientists of many different cultures and national origins working independently and collaboratively, and advancing the accepted theories of their time period or dangerously challenging the status quo.

BOX 9.1

History of Science

Phlogiston Theory

My husband soon will show that much depends on vital air—that he calls Oxygen. You boast that Phlogiston's the key to fire and rust, but why not credit vital air? Could it not feed the flames or lead to rust? Combined with carbon, say, or iron, it must!

—Madame Lavoisier, playing Oxygen in *Oxygen*

Phlogiston theory, stated initially in 1667 by the German Johann Joachim Becher, maintained that in addition to the classical four elements of the Greeks (Earth, Water, Air, and Fire), there was an additional firelike element called "phlogiston" that was contained within combustible bodies, and released during combustion. The theory was an attempt to explain oxidation processes, such as combustion and the rusting of metals. The theory holds that all flammable materials contain phlogiston, a substance without color, odor, taste, or mass that is liberated through burning.

Phlogiston remained the dominant theory until the French-man Antoine-Laurent Lavoisier showed that combustion requires a gas that has weight (oxygen), which could be measured by means of weighing closed vessels. For this and other experimentation, Lavoisier is often considered the "Father of Modern Chemistry."

On a side note, Lavoisier was branded a traitor during the Reign of Terror by French Revolutionists (not due to his work as a chemist, but attributed to his profession as a tax collector) and was guillotined at the age of fifty.

At the following links, you may read more about phlogiston theory and Lavoisier's contributions to chemistry, which were recounted in the two-act play *Oxygen*, by chemists Carl Djerassi and Roald Hoffmann.

- **Antoine Lavoisier—the First "Modern" Chemist:** www.timeline science.org/resource/students/phlog/lavois.htm. This timeline outlines one thousand years of scientific thought in the period AD 1000 to 2000. Educational activities are provided to help science students and their teachers explore changes in how we understand the world.

- **Combustion and the Attack on Phlogiston:** http://acsweb content.acs.org/landmarks/chemrevolution/combustion.html. The National Historic Chemical Landmarks Web site provides information and teacher resources on places, discoveries, and achievements identified by the American Chemical Society as historic chemical landmarks.
- *Oxygen,* **a two-act play by Carl Djerassi and Roald Hoffmann:** www.djerassi.com/oxygen11/oxygen.htm.

INCORPORATE MULTIMEDIA SELECTIONS

Multimedia presentations offer you and your students the opportunity to see as well as hear, or hear about, and understand people, places, objects, and events that your textbook and discussions cannot communicate completely. You have many different video choices, such as documentaries, investigations, historical timelines, and so forth. Whatever you choose, select only the portions that are relevant to your lesson.

After you determine that a particular video or DVD matches your standards and expectations, you need to decide the appropriate time in your unit of learning to show it. You can show it at the beginning of the unit to initiate interest and inquiry, and to provide background knowledge. You can show it midway through the unit to introduce new information and to build upon prior learning. You can show it at the end of the unit as review and extension. If you are involved in team teaching, you can show it in your class and integrate instruction with your colleagues. For example, you might show a National Geographic video about water. In social studies, you connect it to rivers and environmental issues. In science, students relate it to natural resources, animal habitats, and human usage and abuses. In language arts, students use the video as the basis of a debate. In math, students conduct a survey and evaluate data on water usage.

After deciding the purpose(s) and timing for showing a particular video, identify how you will guide your viewers before watching the video, and how you will ask your learners to respond during and after watching the video. Take time to communicate your expectations for students' behaviors. If you are expecting your students to take notes, you have to provide lighting or know exactly when to stop the video for your students to write. Likewise, if you plan to stop for discussion, you need to know when to pause the video for such interaction. The goal is to create a seamless series of learning experiences throughout your unit, with the video as just one more event.

There are several items to consider in determining the suitability of any media selection.

Media Previewing Questions

- *Length.* Can you show/play the piece or selected segment during one class session?
- *Content.* Does the medium address main ideas essential to your theme, topic, or issue?
- *Vocabulary.* Does the medium use appropriate vocabulary, and can your students understand the language?
- *Scenery and Displays.* Does the video show developmentally appropriate scenes?
- *Quality.* Is the piece of high quality, or does it experience any difficulties?

TAKE FIELD TRIPS

> *Our school science and math club walked across the street to see a local vet perform a simple operation on a cat. We also visited the local fast-food restaurant to see how workers maintained a clean and germ-free environment.*
>
> —*Tenth-grade chemistry teacher*

Field trips offer one of the most effective ways to help your students learn about science. The field trip could be a walking trip or one that requires transportation, such as using vans, buses, or private cars. Many cities have local science museums. You could partner with another teacher on your team so that two classes could go at one time and extend your time away from school for the two class sessions. Often it is school field trips that provide the unique opportunities for your students to leave their immediate neighborhoods. Otherwise, your students might not ever see the local college, central park, beach or other landform, museum, or other site of community, and perhaps state and national, interest. Many teachers refer to these experiences as "field school" so as to indicate learning will be taking place and proper school behavior is expected.

> *I took students to a wastewater treatment plant that was nearby. The students were really blown away that water from a sewer can*

be cleaned so thoroughly and recycled. It solidified the water cycle for them.

—Ninth-grade biology teacher

Unfortunately, taking field trips requires more time and money than most schools can allocate. However, certain agencies and organizations will reimburse bus transportation. You may be allowed to take only one or two field trips per school year, so choose wisely. The trips may be selected as a team, grade level, or science department on a rotating schedule, with a different subject area or a different aspect of science featured each year. Field trips usually are identified early in the school year so detailed arrangements can be made well in advance, and coordinated with curriculum and instruction.

Our second-grade curriculum includes how organisms depend on one another, so we take the students to observe tide pools. Our third-grade curriculum includes adaptations. Then we take our students to see the wetlands.

—Elementary school teacher

FOLLOW GUIDELINES FOR TAKING FIELD TRIPS

You may discover that docents are available to visit your school before the field trip. They may bring handouts, posters, worksheets, or workbooks to help prepare your students for their visit. They will also explain the procedures ahead of time so everyone will know what to expect.

There are several factors to keep in mind when planning field trips:

1. *Identify some locations fairly close to the school.* The less time you spend getting there, the more time you can spend being there.

2. *Know the purpose for selecting particular sites.* Everyone wants to know that you are spending time and money well.

3. *Select sites that most students have not visited or would not visit on their own or with their families.*

4. *Contact the potential sites to make appointments to visit them.* You will want to investigate:

    a. alignment of standards and expectations with the field trip experience;

    b. availability of a tour guide;

    c. content and vocabulary quality of the displays and tour guides;

    d. whether the tour includes experiential, hands-on learning and any materials such as brochures or worksheets;

    e. choices, costs, and lengths of tours;

    f. easy access for buses and parking;

    g. easy access to restrooms;

    h. elements of universal design needed for students with disabilities;

    i. convenient place(s) to eat sack lunches and dispose of trash;

    j. predominance of souvenir shops and whether you can avoid them; and

    k. procedures involved in arranging a field trip.

5. Know both the procedures and paperwork at your school for arranging a field trip, including transportation, chaperones, admission fees, funding, and permission slips.

6. For collecting or observing in the field, determine what materials students will need to take with them and what you will provide, such as notebooks, observation forms, probes, cameras, binoculars, magnifying glasses, containers, drawing paper, graph paper.

Inform students of both the content related to taking this particular field trip and the behaviors to be used during the field trip. You need to make the consequences for not complying with expectations quite clear to students and their parents.

> *I take my students to the California Science Center. The students love the chance to touch things and gain a hands-on opportunity to learn about sound, light, and human body systems.*
>
> —*Seventh-grade science teacher*

CONSIDER VIRTUAL FIELD TRIPS

When time and funds are scarce, consider virtual field trips on the Internet. Many museums, universities, and agencies host their own sites. Alternately, you can have your students plan virtual field trips as a project involving technology.

Virtual field trips are wonderful for students who live far away from resources. There are even Web sites dedicated to virtual field trips! One example is the Tramline Virtual Field (www.field guides.com/vft/index.htm), which includes virtual field trips to salt marshes, wildfires, and the Columbia River watershed. Other examples include the Spokane Aquifer Virtual Field Trip (www.spokaneaquifer.org/vft/trailhead.htm) and NASA's Jet Propulsion Laboratory Virtual Field Trip (http://virtualfieldtrip .jpl.nasa.gov/smmk/top). There are also e-quariums, such as the Monterey Bay Aquarium (www.mbayaq.org/efc/cam_menu.asp), which offer live Web cams of aquatic life as well as podcasts, a video library, and interactive activities. See Box 11.1 for a link to a virtual exhibit on Gregor Mendel at the Chicago Field Museum.

CONDUCT VIRTUAL DISSECTIONS AND EXPERIMENTS

Several sites have been set up to allow research scientists and educators to post videos of their experiments, lab projects, or results. They provide a chance to see real science in action. One of our favorites is the Access Excellence Virtual Dissections, Labs, and Field Trips (www.accessexcellence.org/RC/virtual.html). The Net Frog Dissection program provided at this site includes a tutorial, pictures, and an interactive section that allows you to virtually dissect the frog. Also at this site is access to Geology Labs Online.

There are also virtual dissection software programs for purchase, one of the most popular of which is Froguts (www .froguts.com). Click on the demos in the upper right-hand corner of this site to see a frog, owl pellet, or squid dissection. Additional resources include the following:

- **DNA Tube:** http://dnatube.com. This video site is a visual scientific resource for its visitors, and makes scientific concepts easily understandable.
- **SciVee:** www.scivee.tv. Created for scientists by scientists, SciVee moves science beyond the printed word and lecture by taking advantage of the Internet as a communication medium where scientists exchange ideas.
- **Lab Action:** http://labaction.com. This is a wonderful set of resources on biotechnology, cloning, human genetics, genetic disorders, stem cell research, and marine biology.
- *Journal of Visualized Experiments:* http://jove.com. This online research journal employs visualization to increase reproducibility and transparency in biological sciences.

- **Virtual Chemistry:** http://neon.chem.ox.ac.uk/vrchemistry. Created by the Department of Chemistry at Oxford University, this site offers experiments, webcasts, and tutorials.

BECOME A ROLE MODEL OF RESOURCEFULNESS . . .

Whether you are aware of your influence or not, how you interact with science resources will communicate volumes to your students that you could not teach in any other way. You will be a model to your students on how to handle specimens and samples, how to ask questions either as general or philosophical inquiries of specific guests, and how to make connections among prior learning and new explorations. Incorporating a variety of resources into your science classes will help your students see the presence and power of science everywhere, and learn to become resourceful themselves. We strongly encourage you to consider your responsibilities as a role model seriously. These opportunities will establish a keen sense and orientation about the world for your students now and as lifelong learners.

Resources for science abound. The secret is to keep your units of learning in mind when you shop, travel, or visit museums, national parks, and different areas of the world. With time and experience, you will refine your abilities and expertise to ask your students to suggest and bring in resources too. While this chapter examined physical resources and guest speakers, Chapter 10 turns attention to developing technology skills and using techno-logical resources in the classroom.

Suggested Activities

1. Visit a teacher supply store or thumb through science supply catalogs to find resources you might want to order, or to initiate ideas for future resources that you can acquire.

2. Write a science poem and share it with your students.

3. Obtain a list of your school's videos and CDs, and begin to preview ones you think would be appropriate for a unit of study.

4. Attend a state or national science conference and acquire all kinds of resources and resource ideas.

CHAPTER TEN

Integrate Technology to Enrich Learning

We should all be concerned about the future because we will have to spend the rest of our lives there.

—Charles Francis Kettering (1876–1958),
Seed for Thought, 1949

W ith the increase in the use of school desktop and laptop computers, as well as handheld devices, teachers and students have additional venues for information and communication in the classroom. Technology is a wonderful way to facilitate student-centered learning. In addition, it may be used to promote twenty-first-century skills and enhance learning through research, exchanging ideas, collaboration, and productivity strategies and tools (Salpeter, 2003). Technology can also encourage student self-direction and higher-order thinking (*Learning for the 21st Century,* 2003).

On the other hand, technology can also be daunting: Which resources are most important? Do we have evidence that their use improves student learning? Which are even available at your school site? How will you use technology to support communication, collaboration, research, and productivity in your classroom? This chapter will explore some of the answers to these questions.

TAKE A TECHNOLOGY INVENTORY

First things first! Determine what types of technology access, equipment, and resources are available to you. Then look for resources, including grants and donations, to acquire what you need to be successful in the classroom. Use Table 10.1 to inventory your current technology resources. Do you have an overhead projector? An ELMO electronic imager? A multimedia computer? Most schools today have at least one computer in the classroom, although it may not be a new one. You may have a microscope that projects onto a screen. You may or may not have a projection system. If you have a television monitor, you can project from your computer with a cable device, such as a TVator. This will enable your whole class or a large group to view the screen at one time, rather than having small groups crowd around the computer monitor. Perhaps you have a few computers in your room that students can use by themselves or in pairs.

Sometimes equipment is shared among teachers. Your school may have a traveling bank of laptops or AlphaSmart™ keyboards, for example. Or you may need to reserve time in a media center or a computer lab. In these situations, you will have to plan ahead to coordinate scheduling with your lessons.

Additional factors in your planning will be not only the level of proficiency of your students but also the district, school, and department expectations for student technology proficiency development. Does your school require students to take computer classes that address the National Educational Technology Standards for Students (2007)? These standards include demonstrating basic operations, understanding ethical and other issues, and using tools to record information, produce work, communicate with others, conduct research, solve problems, and make decisions.

A basic computer course is now often part of the eighth-grade curriculum to prepare students for technology use in high school. Teachers are now expected to engage students in the use of technology as research, collaborative, communication, and productivity tools. How often will you be able to offer technology-rich lessons? Do you meet the National Educational Technology

Table 10.1   Technology Inventory

Access	*Hardware*	*Tools and Licenses*
Acceptable use policy	TV monitors, VCRs, projection screens, laser disc players, CD/DVD players	Windows/Vista operating system
Wired Internet connectivity	Color, dot matrix, or laser printers; photo printers	MAC operating system
Wireless Internet access	Digital still cameras	Grade book program
Teacher desktop	Digital video cameras, camcorders	General utility tools (Snag It, survey instruments)
Teacher laptop	Interactive whiteboards, also known as SMART Boards	Teacher utility tools (crossword puzzle or word search generator, rubric maker, quiz generator)
Networked computers in classrooms	Assistive/adaptive devices; classroom amplification system	Student thinking tools (Inspiration, InspireData™)
Multiple networked computers per classroom	LCD projection	Subject-specific software and interactives (Gizmos, BrainPOP)
Computer labs/media center may be utilized for whole-class instruction	AlphaSmart™ or IntelliKey keyboards and word processors	Video editing (Camtasia, Garage Band, iMovie, MovieMaker)
Portable carts of laptops may be checked out for class use	Handhelds (Palms, PDAs)	Online course delivery systems (Blackboard, Moodle)
Computer labs/media center opened before, during, and after school for student use	Graphing calculators, including overhead graphing calculator	Microsoft® Office (Word, PowerPoint, Publisher, FrontPage, Excel, Outlook, Access)

(Continued)

Table 10.1 (Continued)

Access	Hardware	Tools and Licenses
Smart keyboards or laptops may be checked out for home use	Scanners/digitizers	Reference and research tools (WorldBook Online, United Streaming)
Teacher e-mail accounts	Videoconferencing units	Assessment manager and data bank (Data Director, Edusoft)
Student e-mail accounts	Document camera	Plagiarism prevention (Turnitin)
Online courses offered to students	Audience response system	CDs, DVDs, laserdiscs, film checkout
Online professional development offered to teachers	Web cams	Web publishing
Cable or satellite access	Individual SMART Boards (Airliner Tablets)	Subscriptions to online newspapers, magazines, and other periodicals
Student access to teachers' Wikis and blogs	Global Positioning System (GPS) unit	
Student use of cell phones and cameras for learning purposes	Science probeware (PASCO, Vernier)	
Student Web lockers	Digital microscopes or telescopes	

Standards for Teachers? Some of them are the same as the student standards! See a comparison of these standards for students and teachers in Table 10.2.

Your school district and/or your school may have policies and procedures for you to follow. Most districts have filtering software that prevents your students from accessing inappropriate sites. Most likely, they also have established an Acceptable Use Policy (AUP) for all students and employees about what is appropriate and inappropriate behavior with respect to using computers and

Table 10.2   National Educational Technology Standards (NETS) for Students and Teachers

National Educational Technology Standards (NETS) for Students and Teachers	
NETS for Students (2007)	*NETS for Teachers (2008)*
Technology Operations and Concepts: Students demonstrate a sound understanding of technology concepts, systems, and operations.	**Student Learning and Creativity:** Teachers use their knowledge of subject matter, teaching and learning, and technology to facilitate experiences that advance student learning, creativity, and innovation in both face-to-face and virtual environments.
Digital Citizenship: Students understand human, cultural, and societal issues related to technology and practice legal and ethical behavior.	**Digital-Age Learning Experiences and Assessments:** Teachers design, develop, and evaluate authentic learning experiences and assessment incorporating contemporary tools and resources to maximize content learning in context and to develop the knowledge, skills, and attitudes identified in the NETS for Students.
Research and Information Fluency: Students apply digital tools to gather, evaluate, and use information.	**Digital-Age Work and Learning:** Teachers exhibit knowledge, skills, and work processes representative of an innovative professional in a global and digital society.
Critical Thinking, Problem Solving, and Decision Making: Students use critical thinking skills to plan and conduct research, manage projects, solve problems, and make informed decisions using appropriate digital tools and resources.	**Digital Citizenship and Responsibility:** Teachers understand local and global societal issues and responsibilities in an evolving digital culture, and exhibit legal and ethical behavior in their professional practices.
Communication and Collaboration: Students use digital media and environments to communicate and work collaboratively, including at a distance, to support individual learning and contribute to the learning of others.	**Professional Growth and Leadership:** Teachers continuously improve their professional practice, model lifelong learning, and exhibit leadership in their school and professional community by promoting and demonstrating the effective use of digital tools and resources.

(Continued)

Table 10.2 (Continued)

NETS for Students (2007)	NETS for Teachers (2008)
Creativity and Innovation: Students demonstrate creative thinking, construct knowledge, and develop innovative products and processes using technology.	

Source: Adapted from *NETS for Students* (2007) and *NETS for Teachers* (2008), International Society of Technology Education.

Web sites, including e-mail communication. Many districts are looking at Web lockers for students to store and retrieve their work. Some provide access to a Web-based course delivery system. Others may prohibit teachers from using commercial Web sites for classroom use. You will want to find out what is possible and appropriate at your district level and in your school.

PLAN FOR COMPUTER USE

How you use technology and the Internet will depend on expectations, time, space, abilities of the students, your expertise, and the amount and quality of hardware, software, and infrastructure available. Consider the following ways to integrate technology (Kottler & Gallavan, 2007).

- *Demonstration for Whole-Group Instruction.* A projection screen or TV monitor (consider two if possible!) is placed where all students can see the display. The teacher guides the students through the content. Students participate firsthand in the experiential learning by posing inquiries, guiding the operations, recording data, and analyzing outcomes. Interactive whiteboards, such as SMART Boards® and Promethean® boards, increase student engagement during presentations.
- *Cooperative Group Stations.* Computers are located to one side or in a corner of the classroom where a small group of students can gather around. Groups may be working on the same or different parts of the same unit of learning, and

can share results with one another. Time is given during the day for different groups to work at the stations; the teacher can assist each group.

- *Learning Centers.* Different forms of instructional technology are located to the sides or in the corners of the classroom, where individuals or small groups can work. Assignments at the learning centers can be related to the units of learning directly or indirectly. All students can go to any learning center at once at your direction, or the students may go to their assigned centers when they have completed other tasks.

- *Independent Research/Communication Stations.* Computers are located to the sides or in the corners of the classroom where one to three students can work as they desire. Sign-up sheets will ensure equitable access and use. Factors to consider include length of time at stations, supplies needed, and measurements of productivity.

- *Computer Lab.* Computers are located in such a way that each student has individual access to a computer at the same time. The science teacher or the computer teacher leads students through lessons giving time for personalized practice and application. Students may work on individual or group projects as well.

- *One-to-One Laptop Classroom.* Each student or group has access to a laptop, either as part of a classroom set or for concentrated individual use.

ORGANIZE YOUR RESOURCES

Far more information and many more resources are available to you now that you have access to the Internet. Some of this may be stored on your computer or on portable storage devices, while other resources will be accessed via the Web when needed. We recommend that you set up a comprehensive set of folders on your desktop computer so that you can easily drop in newly created documents. Otherwise, it is easy to misplace your hard work!

You will also want to organize your Web addresses in a "Favorites" file for easy access. Or you might also want to use an online bookmarking site so that you can access your sites from any computer. Free examples include Portaportal (www.portaportal .com), del.icio.us (http://del.icio.us), and Furl (www.furl.net/).

The latter two are social bookmarking utilities, which allow you to share and tag sites so that others can see your notations. You will need to decide how much socializing you want to be able to do with your Web resources. See a sample list at http://guest.portaportal .com/sample. Now compare that with the Hotlist found at http://del.icio.us—you can view the tagging comments and also see the tag names that were assigned. The Portaportal list is simple yet useful, and is easily accessible by anyone who has your guest access log-in. However, it is nowhere near as interactive as what is available at del.icio.us or Furl.

IMPROVE ADMINISTRATIVIA

A good grade book program can make your life easier. Although you can still record your student grades on paper or use a spreadsheet, grade programs allow for Web access, generation of individual and class reports, and integration with assessments and attendance systems; they also include parent access features. You'll be able to record and store student assessment information and provide individualized assessment data on students. Grade books may also be Web based so that you can access them from school or home. Examples include SnapGrades (www.snap grades.net) and InteGrade Pro (www.pearsonschoolsystems.com/ products/sasi/gradebook.htm).

You'll be expected to use your school e-mail to communicate with colleagues, administrators, students, and parents. Many schools use electronic communication to share announcements with teachers, staff, students, parents, and the community. Some districts require the student referral process to be completed with online forms and communications. Many districts now use online reporting for report cards and Individual Education Plans (IEPs). Some districts require that all professional development be tracked online so that teachers may print out a list of their yearly activities.

The telephone is being used in new ways to increase communication with families. Districts have the ability to send out programmed messages to parents, while parents can also call for prerecorded messages related to assignments, field trips, school events, and other announcements.

IMPROVE TEACHING
WITH TECHNOLOGY TOOLS

Teaching through technology will transform how you present and share information (*Learning for the 21st Century*, 2003; Salpeter, 2003; Schacter, 1999). Many of you will have access to large viewing screens on which you can project Web sites for viewing together as a whole class. You and your students can share information using PowerPoint and other slide presentation systems, ELMO and other projection systems, and overhead transparencies. You might have interactive whiteboards or plasma display with the new Smart DVIT™ (Digital Vision Touch) technology where you and students interact with content by touching the screen or with a "pencil" tool. You will be able to enrich your classroom presentations with the use of images and content you incorporate into your lectures.

Most importantly, you will want to get technology into the hands of your students. Science students should be using technology on a daily basis—to research information, collaborate with classmates, communicate with experts, produce reports and multimedia projects, and conduct experiments and investigations. You will improve your teaching as your improve student learning.

Students enjoy "surfing the Web," and certainly Web-based research can be beneficial, but it can also be very time consuming without meaningful results toward your learning outcomes. Therefore, most teachers preselect what they consider to be "good Web sites" from which students can choose to conduct research. These are known as "Webliographies," and may even be annotated. Post your Webliographies online (either on the student desktops or via a class Web site, Wiki, or blog) to make it easy for the student to simply click on the links instead of having to type in lengthy URLs. Narrowing the search will economize on time, yet offer choices for students. You and your students want to be able to scan a Web site quickly and critically to see whether the information you are seeking is available, whether the Web site offers creative possibilities to expand one's thinking, and whether the Web site is safe and trustworthy. See Box 10.1 for five sets of questions to ask when looking at Web sites. Remember that information on Web sites is self-published.

BOX 10.1

Evaluating a Web Site

1. What can you learn from the URL description before navigating to the Web site? What is the domain? Who is the publisher? Is it a personal page?

2. What is listed on the home page? How current is the information? Who is the organization or author? What are the organization's or author's credentials?

3. What is the quality of the information on the Web site? Can you see and understand the pictures and words easily? What kinds of links are available? Can you navigate in and out of the Web site readily? Is the information research based and authentic? Does the information have footnotes and citations?

4. What do others say about the Web site? Are there links to other resources? Are there links to reputable reviews?

5. What is your reaction to the Web site? What is the purpose of the Web site? Does the Web site fulfill or exceed your expectations?

We suggest you visit Kathy Schrock's "Guide for Educators" at http://school.discovery.com/schrockguide/eval.html to guide you in evaluating Web sites that you may want to access for yourself and with your students. This site has evaluation surveys at the elementary, middle, and secondary school levels. There are also evaluation forms for blogs and podcasts that are easy to use and student-friendly.

HAVE STUDENTS COMMUNICATE ELECTRONICALLY

Computer software provides many new ways that students can organize and communicate information, such as the results of their investigations or experiments. There are many resources to help with using Microsoft® Word, Access, Excel, and PowerPoint in the classroom—from how-to guides to PowerPoint and Publisher templates, and lesson plans for every content area.

I like to show my students how to make charts, graphs, tables, and other graphic organizers. They think it is a great way to share information and not write another report.

—*Veteran science teacher*

There are also many Web 2.0 tools to assist students in communicating within and beyond the classroom—with the teacher, other students, the community, and science experts. "Web 2.0" refers to the supposed second generation of Internet-based services. Whereas first-generation services were mainly unidirectional, Web 2.0 services—including social networking sites, Wikis, blogs, communication tools, and collaborative documents—let people work together and share information interactively. Research is showing some positive effects on literacy development, including fluency, vocabulary development, and comprehension (Banister, Ross, & Vannatta, 2008). How might your students use Wikis, blogs, and Google Docs or other Web-based file-sharing documents to gather, share, analyze, and understand data and information? Consider the ideas in Table 10.3.

CALCULATE AND PROBE HANDS-ON SCIENCE

Science students need access to scientific calculators, and you will want to be very clear about the features you will and won't allow—for class work, homework, and examinations. Will you need scientific notation, logarithms, trigonometry, or exponents? You will need to make sure that students don't attempt to cheat by using a calculator to store information they should know, or by slipping a piece of paper between the calculator and its cover.

It is also critical that you have a way to ensure equity. A classroom set of calculators is helpful, but you still may need extras for students to check out. In addition to student calculators, you need one of your own. Even better, you need an overhead calculator to use with an overhead projector so that you can model effective calculator usage for your students. Scientific calculators can improve students' ability to solve algebra problems, and stoichiometry and unit analysis calculations, as well as analyze graphs, collect and manipulate data, and perform basic statistical manipulations.

Table 10.3   Web 2.0 Tools

Web 2.0 Tool	Description	Instructional Uses	Examples
Online collaborative documents	Allows users to create and upload documents to the Web where they can then be edited and shared	Collaborative writing, creation of spreadsheets, presentations	Google Docs www.google.com/docs
Wiki	A collaborative Web site that is edited by designated users	Collaborative writing and other collaborative activities	PB Wiki www.pbwiki.com WikiSpaces www.wikispaces.com
Blog	A Web log that is used to electronically share information and opinions	Journals, reflections, Webliographies,	Edublog www.edublog.com
Online surveys	Online survey that is used to gather and analyze data	Data collection	Survey Monkey www.surveymonkey.com Zoomerang www.zoomerang.com

Graphing calculators and calculator-based laboratory equipment are great tools for teaching integrated math and science. They promote inquiry learning and are relatively inexpensive.

Handheld computers are the latest technology making its way into the classroom—imagine having the periodic table in the palm of your students' hands! Apple's iTouch is being marketed for its educational uses, including quick access to the Internet without the necessity for an expensive computer. Handhelds also offer numerous Earth science applications, unit conversion software, and quizzing software, and many can now be used with probeware for hands-on lab activities. Additional educational resources and professional development opportunities for handheld devices may be found at the following sites:

- **Texas Instruments:** www.ti-nspire.com
- **Casio Education**: www.casioeducation.com
- **Palm Programs for Teaching and Learning:** www.palm
  .com/us/business/solutions/education_programs.html
- **iPod Education:** www.apple.com/education/itunesu_
  mobilelearning/ipod.html
- **Vernier Software and Technology:** www.vernier.com

POSITION YOUR STUDENTS FOR LEARNING

A Global Positioning System (GPS) unit is an electronic device that can determine your approximate location (within around 6–20 feet) on the planet. Coordinates are normally given in latitude and longitude. You can use the unit to navigate from your current location to another location. Some units have their own maps, built-in electronic compasses, and voice navigation, depending on the complexity of the device. The United States Geological Survey Web site describes the GPS as an excellent, multidisciplinary, inquiry-driven, field-based, standards-based tool applicable to many subjects, including mathematics, geography, Earth science, environmental studies, and more. Additional information is provided at:

- **United States Geological Survey (USGS):** http://education
  .usgs.gov/common/lessons/gps_in_education.html. GPS
  in Education.
- **GPS: The New Navigation:** www.pbs.org/wgbh/nova/
  longitude/gps.html. PBS demonstration of how global positioning systems work.
- **Geocaching:** www.geocaching.com. This treasure hunting sport uses GPS devices to locate caches of "treasure" that have been stashed all over the world.

INVESTIGATE CRITICAL
THINKING INTERACTIVES

Critical thinking is an important skill to develop in your students, and the Internet is just the resource to assist you! There are a variety of wonderful interactive tools available online—and many are completely free. Some are generic; others are content specific. Consider these wonderful possibilities:

- **Google Earth:** www.earth.google.com. Google Earth is an excellent resource for science education. Students may study science topics like Earth's Holocene volcanoes, including images, links, and descriptions, with information about thousands of volcanoes around the globe. Students can also use Google Earth to explore topics like the impact of civilization on the natural environment, and the impact of natural disasters like Hurricane Katrina in New Orleans. There is even a free tool for Windows users that enables you to create charts and graphs inside Google Earth using data sites, such as the U.S. Census Bureau. And with Google Earth's new Sky feature, you can view incredible images of distant galaxies and nebulae from the Hubble Space Telescope. At www.google.com/educators, you will find a teacher community and additional resources and tools, including printable posters on Google "how-tos."

- **Intel Education Thinking Tools:** www.intel.com/education/tools. Intel Education has created a number of free interactive tools that promote higher-order thinking and the development of twenty-first-century skills. These include the *Visual Ranking Tool*, where students identify and refine criteria for assigning ranking to a list, and then debate differences, reach consensus, and organize ideas; the *Seeing Reason Tool*, where students investigate relationships in complex systems, creating maps that communicate understanding; and the *Showing Evidence Tool*, where students construct well-reasoned arguments that are supported by evidence. Teachers create their own workspaces that store student work, allow for collaboration and communication between students and teachers, and facilitate formative and summative assessment. Each tool includes project ideas in science (see below), but teachers are encouraged to develop their own as well. Examples of ways to use the tools are:
  - *Visual Ranking Tool.* Students devise their own animal classification system, and analyze how human actions affect the quality of nearby rivers.
  - *Seeing Reason Tool.* Student groups simulate civil engineering firms to design and construct a bridge, take on the role of meteorologist to understand and prepare for a weather phenomenon, and study the conflicting needs of humans and animals when habitats overlap.

○ *Showing Evidence Tool.* Students conduct benefit/risk analysis of space exploration and biotechnology applications; chemistry students apply gas laws to determine the most likely source of a potential toxin.

I love the Seeing Reason Tool *and have used it for many chemistry topics, including the study of chemical reasons. I have students create a causal map on what can increase or decrease the rate of a reaction, such as temperature and pressure changes or addition of a catalyst.*

—Eighth-grade physical science teacher

- **Inspiration:** www.inspiration.com. With integrated diagram and outline views, students create graphic organizers. This software program utilizes visual learning, in which ideas, concepts, data, and other information are associated with images and represented graphically. This tool is useful for both teachers and students to organize and analyze ideas, an important prereading and prewriting skill. Teacher resources, such as concept maps of Newton's laws, physical and chemical changes, the path of red blood cells, and radioactive decay, are available by grade level. A free trial is available.

- **The JASON Project:** www.jason.org. A nonprofit subsidiary of the National Geographic Society, JASON connects young students with great explorers and great events to inspire and motivate them to learn science. Its core curriculum units are designed for fifth-through eighth-grade classrooms, but are flexible enough to be adapted for higher or lower grades. One unit focuses on the investigation of the biological, chemical, and physical interactions and resiliency of the Earth's ecosystems. A second unit focuses on dynamic weather systems and their impact on societies. Student tools include online articles, digital labs, journals, message boards, and worldwide community challenges. Teacher tools include online curriculum, interactive events with scientists, a digital library, lesson builder, assessment builder, and usage, assessment, and progress reports.

- **Explore Learning:** www.explorelearning.com. Explore Learning offers modular, interactive simulations in math and science for teachers and students in sixth through twelfth grades. Called Gizmos, these interactive simulations allow students to practice skills and apply knowledge. Students balance equations and see the conceptual models of the compounds, complete Punnet squares for chicken and mice, and experiment with Newton's laws using the motion of a cart. All Gizmos include a free five-minute trial, and there is also a subscription rate that includes a classroom workspace.

- **Science Interactives:** www.learner.org/interactives. Sponsored by the Annenberg Channel, this site includes interactives for seventh through twelfth grades on amusement park physics, DNA, garbage, the periodic table, volcanoes, and the rock cycle.

- **Computing Life:** http://publications.nigms.nih.gov/computinglife. Created by the National Institute of General Medical Sciences, this site examines how physicists, biologists, and artists are using computers to advance our understanding of biology and human health.

UTILIZE TEACHER UTILITIES

There are many free online resources that can assist teachers in their daily activities. Would you like to make a crossword puzzle, build a rubric or quiz, or create an online survey? Do you need step-by-step instructions on how to use PowerPoint? Check out the links below.

- **Puzzlemaker:** http://puzzlemaker.discoveryeducation .com. Create and print customized word searches, crossword puzzles, and more using your own word lists.
- **Survey Monkey:** www.surveymonkey.com. This software allows you to quickly create online surveys and summarize results.
- **QuizStar:** http://quizstar.4teachers.org. With QuizStar, you can manage class quizzes, attach multimedia files to questions, make quizzes in multiple languages, and access your creations from any Internet-connected computer. A free trial is available.
- **RubiStar:** http://rubistar.4teachers.org/index.php. RubiStar is a free tool to help teachers create quality rubrics.
- **Assessing Projects:** http://educate.intel.com/en/Assessing Projects. This Intel Education site helps teachers create

assessments that address twenty-first-century skills; it also provides strategies to make assessment an integral part of their teaching.

- **Help Guide:** www.intel.com/education/helpguide. Here you will find step-by-step instructions for hundreds of technical skills for commonly used software applications.
- **Filamentality:** www.kn.pacbell.com/wired/fil. This is an easy, fill-in-the-blanks tool that guides you through selecting a topic, searching the Web, gathering good Web links, and turning them into online learning activities.
- **SoftChalk:** www.softchalk.com. This software enables teachers to create interactive Web pages and engage students with lessons that include pop-up text annotations, self-assessment quizzes, and interactive learning games.

TAP THE AUDIENCE WITH A RESPONSE SYSTEM

Many schools are acquiring interactive software where students can respond to prompts or questions with handheld response mechanisms frequently described as clickers, and have results automatically presented in charts and displays in slide presentations. For example, students can vote, take a position, rank items, or answer questions on an issue. This technology helps keep students involved during direct instruction. It can also be used to check entry-level knowledge of a topic and for quick assessments.

Audience response systems are gaining in popularity because they allow for student interactivity and support, and engage all learners—including English learners and students with special needs. Examples of manufacturers include Turning Technologies®, OptionFinder®, Quizdom, CP Wireless, Promethean, and iRespond. The teacher creates multimedia slides that include questions for student responses. Teachers pose the questions at pedagogically strategic moments during a lecture or demonstration, and students use handheld devices to respond with their answers. The responses are recorded via infrared, radio frequency, or wireless, and the data are presented on a follow-up slide for class discussion. Data are also recorded by the device (and thus by students) in spreadsheets so that teachers may use the system to assess students. All versions include a variety of multiple-choice question options;

some also allow for the keying in of text for short answers and the creation of spontaneous prompts. Responses may be anonymous or collected, reported, and recorded for the student or group.

There are a variety of benefits to using an audience response system: students receive immediate feedback; the learning environment is enhanced through increased student participation; and use of audience response systems also provides the ability to gather data for reporting and analysis of student performance.

CONSIDER A FEW MORE WEB RESOURCES

Throughout this text, we have identified rich Web resources wherever appropriate, but there are some we just did not have a good place to put. Listed below are additional Internet sites with which we have had positive experiences.

Science and Technology Museums

- **Exploratorium: The Museum of Art, Science, and Perception:** www.exploratorium.edu. This site includes access to a digital library and online exhibits on a microscope imaging station, the origins of biodiversity, earthquakes, sports science, and global climate change.
- **Boston Museum of Science:** www.mos.org/events_ activities/virtual_exhibits. This site has online exhibits on the universe, secrets of the ice, scanning electronic microscope, and fireflies. The museum also offers podcasts and videocasts on topics including how cancer develops, unusual frogs, exercise and the heart, and a drug-resistant fungus.
- **Oregon Museum of Science and Industry:** www.omsi .edu/explore/online.cfm. OMSI offers a variety of online activities and exhibits, including a RatCam; an Air Travelers Lab on the basic principles of buoyancy, properties of gases, temperature, and the technology involved in hot-air ballooning; and exhibits on aging and sound science.

Pedagogical Resources

- **The Why Files: Science Behind the News:** http://why files.org
- **Nova Interactives:** www.pbs.org/wgbh/nova/hotscience

- **Learning Science:** www.learningscience.org
- **Earthquake Hazards Program:** http://quake.wr.usgs .gov/recenteqs/latest.htm
- **NASA:** http://quest.nasa.gov
- **Create a Graph:** http://nces.ed.gov/nceskids/createa graph/default.aspx. This simple but effective tool allows students to create a graph from start to finish, using their own data. It is most appropriate for the middle school level.
- **Federal Resources for Educational Excellence (FREE):** www.free.ed.gov. More than 1,500 federally supported teaching and learning resources are included from dozens of federal agencies. New sites are added regularly. You may receive new resources delivered to you several times a week by signing up for the FREE RSS.

Women and Minorities in Science

- **The Faces of Science: African Americans in the Sciences:** http://webfiles.uci.edu/mcbrown/display/faces .htm. Maintained by faculty at the University of California at Irvine, this site provides biographies of current and past African American men and women who have contributed, or are contributing, to the advancement of science and engineering.
- **Women in Science:** www.fieldmuseum.org/exhibits/ exhibit_sites/wis. This exhibit of the Chicago Field Museum presents interviews of thirteen women about why they chose science as a career.
- **Biographical Snapshots of Famous Women and Minority Chemists:** www.jce.divched.org/JCEWWW/ Features/eChemists/index.html. This column provides demographic information and description of contributions to chemistry.
- **Society for Advancement of Chicanos and Native American Students (SACNAS):** www.sacnas.org. The mission of this organization is to encourage Chicano/ Latino and Native American students to pursue graduate education and obtain advanced degrees necessary for science research, leadership, and teaching careers at all levels.
- **Association for Women in Science (AWIS):** www.awis .org. This organization promotes equity for women in science, mathematics, engineering, and technology.

Emphasizing the contributions of women and minorities to science will motivate all students to consider careers in science-related fields, including the medical fields. The History of Science topic in this chapter (see Box 10.2) focuses on the contributions of Dr. Daniel Hale Williams, an African American who performed the first open heart surgery.

BOX 10.2

History of Science

The First Open Heart Surgery

African American Dr. Daniel Hale Williams (1858–1931) was the first doctor to operate successfully on the human heart. While working as a barber, he met Dr. Henry Palmer, a leading surgeon and the Surgeon General of Wisconsin. Dr. Palmer took Daniel on as a medical apprentice and facilitated his admission to the Chicago Medical School. Dr. Williams graduated with his medical degree in 1883 and began to practice surgery and medicine at the South Side Dispensary. At the same time, he held a position at Northwest University, as an instructor of anatomy.

During this period in history, African American patients were routinely subject to second-class medical care. Opportunities for most black physicians were extremely limited, and it was difficult for African Americans to gain admission to medical and nursing schools because of institutionalized racism. This prompted Dr. Williams to establish the first African American–owned hospital in the United States. Provident Hospital started as a twelve-bed facility and nursing school for African Americans. Dr. Williams employed African American and white doctors at Provident Hospital, emphasizing the need to provide the best available care to everyone.

On July 9, 1893, a young man named James Cornish was injured in a bar fight, stabbed in the chest with a knife. By the time he was transported to Provident Hospital, he had lost a great deal of blood and was in shock. In the operating room, Dr. Williams decided to open up Cornish's chest and see what could be done before he bled to death internally. The surgical team found a pierced blood vessel and a tear to the pericardium tissue around the heart. Fifty-one days later, James Cornish walked out of Provident Hospital and would go on to live another fifty years. Newspaper headlines reported: "Sewed Up His Heart! Remarkable

Surgical Operation on a Colored Man!" It was the first successful open heart surgery ever performed. It is also noteworthy that Williams was the first surgeon to open the chest cavity successfully without the patient dying of infection. His procedures would therefore be used as standards for future internal surgeries.

Dr. Williams went on to become Surgeon-in-Chief at Freedmen's Hospital in Washington, DC. He helped organize the National Medical Association, which at the time was the only medical organization open to African Americans. He was the first black physician named as a Fellow in the American College of Surgeons. Williams is immortalized for his achievements in the Stevie Wonder song "Black Man," from the album *Songs in the Key of Life*.

Read more about Daniel Hale Williams at the following links:

- **Daniel Hale Williams:** www.africanamericans.com/DanielHale Williams.htm. The host site, AfricanAmericans.com, has over 750 Web pages on the African American community. This link provides a nice biography and list of illustrations.
- **Daniel Hale Williams:** www.pbs.org/wnet/aaworld/reference/ articles/daniel_hale_williams.html. Resources on African American history and culture, supported by PBS and *Encyclopedia Britannica*.

DEMONSTRATE THE CUTTING EDGE OF SCIENCE . . .

We find that most students are fascinated with the abundance of resources available on the Web. The field of science includes every aspect of our lives, and the Internet allows us to access rich and diverse resources to inform and support our teaching in every way. We think you will discover all these secrets and "bookmark" your own favorites soon. In the next chapter, we will present a wide range of activities to include during class, information on how to incorporate guest speakers and community resources, along with service learning and extracurricular activities.

Suggested Activities

1. Develop specific rubrics for your students to reference to evaluate particular Web sites.

2. Talk with your technology specialist to develop strategies to apply technology to maximize student learning in one of your units.

3. Create a Webliography for a specific unit or for Web sites that you will frequently use for your science courses. Be sure to consider teaching sites too.

4. Find an online exhibition on a topic in your content area, and plan a lesson around a Web-based activity.

CHAPTER ELEVEN

Seek Powerful Activities to Engage Learners

The important thing in science is not so much to obtain new facts as to discover new ways of thinking about them.

—Sir William Henry Bragg, winner
of Nobel Prize for Physics, 1915

Teaching science is both exhilarating and exhausting! You are tackling challenging content knowledge that includes depth, breadth, and diversity with an audience of diverse students. Plus, it changes every day. We encourage you to look for ways that make your classes active and engaging. A central component of all of these endeavors is making science real, and extending it beyond your classroom and the textbook. In addition to all of the strategies, resources, and Web sites shared with you in previous chapters, this chapter contains suggestions for activities that you can incorporate either into your teaching, at your school, or within your school district and state. Choose those you feel will benefit your students the most.

PARTICIPATE IN COMPETITIONS AND PROGRAMS

There are myriad programs, contests, and competitions available. Most are free, some cost a little, and a few are expensive. Explore the ones that seem interesting to you and that you think will have appeal to your students. Beyond intrinsic rewards, there may be recognition of student achievement as well as awards for participation. Check rules for eligibility and deadlines for enrollment. Talk to teachers whose students participate in these activities about their experiences. Watch how their students demonstrate their expertise through new knowledge, refined skills, and positive dispositions as a result of their involvement.

In its Position Statement on Science Competitions, the National Science Teachers Association (1999a) recognizes that science competitions, such as science fairs, science leagues, symposia, Olympiads, scholarship activities, and talent searches, can contribute significantly to the education of students of science. They advocate that participation (by both students and teachers) be voluntary and open to all students; emphasize that the focus should be on the learning experience rather than on the competition; and encourage scientific competitions to foster partnerships among students, the school, and the science community. Read more on this position statement at www.nsta.org.

To get started, conduct some research on the Web, and attend a local professional development workshop or a presentation at a local, state, regional, or national conference. If possible, attend a contest or competition in person. You can go it alone or partner with another teacher. The class time needed for these activities may range from a few sessions to ongoing time throughout the school year. The following sites provide helpful information:

- **Science Buddies:** www.sciencebuddies.org/science-fair-projects/top_science-fair_overview.shtml. Along with project ideas and information about science competitions, this site includes links to blogs written by students who have competed in some of the individual competitions discussed below.
- **Science Competitions:** www.osti.gov/sciencelab/Science Competitions.html. The U.S. Department of Energy Office of Science provides a list of science competitions, including some not listed below.

- **Pre-Engineering Competitions:** www.engineeringedu
.com/competitions.html. The Engineering Education Service
Center provides a list of engineering-related competitions.

SHOWCASE SCIENCE FAIR PROJECTS

E. W. Scripps created Science Services as a nonprofit organization
in 1921. The purpose was to bridge the gap between scientific
achievement and the public's knowledge of such achievement.
The organization began sponsoring the notion of a science fair
competition, and the rest is history!

Science fairs are now ubiquitous in elementary, middle, and
high schools. Today's science fair project involves students in use
of the scientific method to investigate or experiment with a science research question. Each step of the process is documented for
the written report and visual display board. Students present their
research question, problem statement, hypotheses, procedures,
materials, observations, findings, results, data, and conclusions.
They also conduct a review of the research on the topic. Students
perform at their ability levels. Teachers provide access to, or help
students obtain, reference materials and supplies. They guide
students to set realistic deadlines and monitor their progress, real-
izing that they may be the sole adult support for the students in
their classes.

Teachers may assign science fair projects for a class assignment without competition in mind. Or they may require students
to compete at the school level, with winners going on to compete
at the district, regional, state, and national levels. At each level,
competition becomes more rigorous and the possibility for scholarships and awards increases as well. Consider these Web
resources to help teachers and students:

- **Exploratorium Science Fair Information:** www
.exploratorium.edu/ls/pathfinders/scifairs
- **Free Science Fair Projects:** www.free-science-fair-
projects.com
- **Science Fairs:** www.cdli.ca/sciencefairs
- **Science Fair Projects:** www.all-science-fair-projects.com
- **Super Science Fair Projects:** www.super-science-fair-
projects.com

ENCOURAGE INDIVIDUAL COMPETITIONS

Many students prefer to engage in research on their own. Other individual competitions include:

Intel International Science and Engineering Fair: www.societyfor science.org/isef/index.asp. Winners of regional and state science fairs may be entered in the Intel International Science and Engineering Fair, an international precollege science competition. Projects are showcased on an international stage and judged by doctoral-level scientists. Students compete for millions of dollars in prizes and scholarships. Competitions are available for both high school and middle school students.

Intel Science Talent Search: www.societyforscience.org/sts. High school students may participate in the Science Talent Search. Since 1941, first in partnership with Westinghouse and since 1998 with Intel, the competition has provided a national stage for America's best and brightest young scientists to complete an original research project and have it recognized by a national jury of highly regarded professional scientists. Finalists are selected from a nationwide pool to attend a weeklong Science Talent Institute in Washington, DC. Over 3,000 finalists have received $4 million in scholarships. Of the finalists, three have become National Medal of Science winners, nine MacArthur Foundation Fellows, two Fields Medalists, and five Nobel Laureates.

Siemens Competition in Math, Science & Technology: www .siemens-foundation.org/en/competition.htm. Another program for high school students is the Siemens Competition in Math, Science & Technology. This program fosters individual growth for high school students who are willing to challenge themselves through science research. Through this competition, students have an opportunity to achieve national recognition for science research projects that they complete in high school. Administered by The College Board and funded by the Siemens Foundation, the competition provides college scholarships and awards each year for talented high school students in the United States.

Junior Science and Humanities Symposia (JSHS) Program: www.jshs.org. Sponsored by the U.S. Army, Navy, and Air Force, the Junior Science and Humanities Symposia Program invites high school students to conduct an original research investigation in the sciences, engineering, or mathematics, and to participate in a regional symposium sponsored by universities or other academic institutions. Through oral and written research presentations, students report on their contributions to the research problem and their approach to undertaking the investigation. The overall test is that students demonstrate valid investigation and experimentation aimed at discovery of knowledge.

TEAM UP FOR COLLABORATIVE COMPETITIONS

For students who enjoy working with others, some collaborative competitions include:

Science Olympiad. Founded in 1893 as an alternative to science fairs, Science Olympiad is a nonprofit organization dedicated to the improvement of science education through student participation in the tournament and noncompetitive events, teacher training, and incorporation of Science Olympiad into the classroom curriculum. Science Olympiad events are like a track meet, in which teams of students participate in over twenty events in a diverse array of science investigations. Teams and individuals win medals, trophies, scholarships, and prizes. Information about the Science Olympiad is available at www.soinc.org.

eCYBERMISSION: www.ecybermission.com/index.cfm. Sponsored by the U.S. Army, *eCYBERMISSION* is for teams of students in Grades 6–9. It is a Web-based science, mathematics, and technology competition. Students compete for regional and national awards while working to solve problems in their communities. Teams propose solutions to real problems in their community and compete for regional and national awards.

ExploraVision Awards: www.exploravision.org. Sponsored by Toshiba and NSTA, ExploraVision is a competition for students of all interest, skill, and ability levels in Grades K–12. Entrants must be U.S. or Canadian citizens or legal residents, living within the United States, U.S. Territories, or Canada. The purpose of the competition is to encourage students to combine their imaginations with the tools of science to create and explore a vision of a future technology. Winning students receive savings bonds.

National Engineers Week Future City Competition: www.futurecity.org. The mission of the National Engineers Week Future City Competition is to provide a fun and exciting educational engineering program for seventh-and eighth-grade students that combines a stimulating engineering challenge with a "hands-on" application to present their vision of a city of the future. Groups of students use teamwork, problem-solving approaches, and skills in mathematics and science, computers, and research and presentations to design cities using SimCity software. Regional contests lead to the national competition.

Odyssey of the Mind: www.odysseyofthemind.com/learn_ more.php. Another popular program is Odyssey of the Mind, an international educational program that provides creative problem-solving opportunities for students from kindergarten through college. Students apply their creativity to solve problems that range from building mechanical devices to presenting their own interpretation of literary classics. Thousands of teams from throughout the United States and other countries participate in the program each year.

CONNECT TO CAREERS

I always wanted to be a teacher. In the third grade, I brought home leftover dittos of math worksheets, which I used to "teach" my neighborhood friends in my backyard playhouse. It wasn't until my sophomore year in high school, however, that I found my second love—chemistry! Although I toyed with becoming a medical doctor and a research scientist, I eventually returned to my love of teaching. I knew that I wanted to be a teacher like my high school science teacher heroes—Ms. Bonner and Mr. Ellis.

—Eleventh-grade chemistry teacher

Everything you teach is based on one or more academic disciplines with people who have dedicated their lives and developed professional careers to preserve, communicate, and advance that particular field of study. Each field of study is filled with all kinds of careers either directly or indirectly related to it. Grab these teachable moments to make the connections between the established science concepts and practices and future educational and career possibilities. Frequently, it is a teacher who showed an object, invited a guest speaker, or took the students on a field trip that served as the catalyst for the future. Your use of resources may provide just the stimulus your students need to invest in their learning or to explore science-related careers later in life.

Science educators recognize that the seeds for becoming a scientist, engineer, or doctor are planted early, and that middle and high school science plays an important role in recruitment. School science may be considered as a rite of passage into the scientific community (Costa, 1993a). As such, it is important to include activities that help students see themselves as future scientists.

Career education is easily integrated in class activities during each unit. Consider making a chart per unit, or one continuous chart that you and your students maintain throughout the semester or school year. Students can contribute ideas throughout the unit of learning as they make connections to the community and the world. You might want to invite guest speakers who are professionals within the subject area, such as university professors or medical staff. Organizations such as the American Chemical Society (www.acs.org) and Association for Women in Science (www.awis.org) can also provide useful resources, as do the following sites:

- **Careers in Science (National Agricultural Library):** www.nal.usda.gov/kids/careers.htm
- **Cool Careers in Science (Scientific American Frontiers):** www.pbs.org/safarchive/5_cool/53_career.html
- **Careers in Science and Engineering: A Student's Guide (National Academies Press):** www.nap.edu/reading room/books/careers/contents.html
- **Science Careers (*Science Magazine*):** http://sciencecareers .sciencemag.org
- **Science Careers Job Search:** http://aaas.sciencecareers .org/js.php

It is interesting to note that, historically, many individuals who engaged in science were not employed as scientists *per se*. Instead, they worked in science as a sideline or hobby. Gregor Mendel, for example, was a friar and high school teacher! What is common to all scientists is that they, as Sir William Henry Bragg noted, were focused on new ways of thinking about facts. This passion of discovery and theorizing is what we hope to instill in students as they learn science. Read more about Mendel's life and discoveries in Box 11.1.

BOX 11.1

History of Science

Mendel's Peas

Most people know that Austrian Gregor Mendel shaped our understanding of inheritance. However, although Gregor Mendel made one of the great discoveries of science, the importance of his research on plant hybridization in the late 1860s was not recognized until years after he died.

Mendel chose a common garden pea for his first experiments. These plants exhibited a number of simple traits, which occur either in one variation or another, with no in-between seed color (i.e., yellow or green), position of flowers (axial or terminal), and form of ripe seed (smooth or wrinkled). Mendel used over 28,000 pea plants and made 287 crosses among 70 different plants. While experimenting, Mendel noticed that when breeding two peas, a particular variation of a trait in one pea (e.g., the greenness of a pea) would not appear in the next generation. However, in the following generation, when breeding the children together, this variation would appear again. He concluded that the traits were being "masked" in the second generation, to be exhibited again in the third.

Gregor Mendel never described a gene or even used the word, yet he uncovered the principles of heredity. He is given credit for discovering that parents pass distinct traits to their offspring in combinations governed by predictable laws, now known as "Mendelian genetics." Scientists eventually decided *some actual thing* must carry these traits and coined the word "gene."

Why did Mendel's discovery go unrecognized? The multiple reasons include a mismatch and gaps in both content and experimental method (Garfield, 1980). Mendel offered his theory prior to the understanding of chromosomes and mitosis (these theories were developed in 1900), resulting in gaps between what inheritance is and how it occurs. In addition, Mendel used statistical modeling at a time when few biologists believed that mathematics had any legitimate application in biological science. (*Biometrika*, the journal devoted to mathematical biology, was first published in 1901.)

Following are some resources on Gregor Mendel and his work:

- *The Monk in the Garden: The Lost and Found Genius of Gregor Mendel, the Father of Genetics* (2000, Houghton Mifflin). Author Robin Marantz Henig recounts the story of the early days of genetics and the mysterious thirty-five-year pause between its discovery and rediscovery.

- **Gregor Mendel: Planting the Seeds of Genetics:** www.field museum.org/mendel. This virtual museum uses artifacts of Mendel's life to place his work in context. In addition, interactive displays help explain genetics.
- **MendelWeb:** www.mendelweb.org. MendelWeb is an educational resource for teachers and students interested in the origins of classical genetics, introductory data analysis, elementary plant science, and the history and literature of science.

To encourage students to pursue careers related to science, take your students to visit a variety of places, such as an institute, museum, hospital, or laboratory, for a day. Materials and information on Job Shadow Day are available from www.jobshadow.org. This is a collaborative effort to have students see careers beyond what their parents do for a living. Students spend a day seeing a career that they might not otherwise consider. Coalition founders are America's Promise, Junior Achievement, the U.S. Department of Education, and the U.S. Department of Labor, along with sponsoring agencies ING, Nelnet, and Valpak.com.

Your school or district also may have career day opportunities in which your students will either meet with representatives from different occupations and government services, or travel to meet with professionals at their respective work sites. These are perfect times to collaborate with area universities and colleges too, so your students can understand why they need to earn specific degrees and apply for licenses to pursue specific career goals. Most colleges and universities have recruiting departments with personnel who will provide information and contacts for high school teachers and counselors.

I integrate careers by having science professionals in our community come to speak to my classes during our annual career day. I have had doctors, dentists, and other people involved in science.

—*Seventh-grade life science teacher*

INVITE GUEST SPEAKERS

Bringing guest speakers to the classroom is another way to help students make connections. Invite experts who specialize in particular areas or individuals who can offer particular insights about a specific science topic or issue. For example, you can invite a water treatment plant director to visit your classroom to talk about the various levels of water treatment and waste. A different example would be to invite a cosmetologist to talk about the chemistry of hair coloring and curling. This is a perfect way to connect with your students, their families, and the community. It allows your students to hear from a variety of teachers, and you learn at the same time.

Having guest speakers visit your class involves some risk. You cannot always preview the guest speaker as you would a video. Some of the guest speakers will have experience speaking to an audience and some will not. Some will be prepared; some will bring visual aids and/or handouts; others will not. Some guest speakers will know how to talk with your age group of students; other inexperienced speakers will need prompting ahead of talking to them. The checklist below has suggestions to help you get started.

Guest Speaker Checklist

❒ Make an appointment to talk in person or on the telephone with the guest speaker. It is important that you hear the guest speaker talk so you can evaluate the quality of their voice, tone, and language skills.

❒ If the speaker has experience, ask whether there is a videotape of a presentation for you to preview, or whether you can be in the audience at a forthcoming scheduled presentation.

❒ Be ready to ask some questions, either directly or indirectly, to learn more regarding their knowledge, skills, and dispositions about the content, processes, and vocabulary; outlook, biases, and agenda; and communication skills applicable to your age group and students' special needs.

❒ Discuss the length of time the guest speaker plans to talk, or tell the guest speaker how much time will be allotted. Remember to leave time for closure.

❒ Ask what visual aids and handouts, if appropriate, the speaker plans to bring and distribute.

❒ Find out whether the speaker expects you to prepare the classroom setting in any way, order special equipment, make copies of the handout, and so forth.

❏ When you invite a guest speaker, be sure that each of you is clear on the date, time of arrival, length of the talk, classroom setting expectations, equipment required, and time the talk should end.

❏ Confirm the arrangements in writing by sending a letter or an e-mail message with copies sent to either your department chair or school administrator and a copy for you. (If you invite a guest speaker well in advance, be sure you make contact a few days prior to the speaking engagement to reconfirm the plans.)

❏ If the guest speaker has a business card or brochure, request that the guest speaker send you a copy in advance. Or ask the guest speaker to send you a résumé. You can use this information to introduce the guest speaker.

❏ After the presentation, send the guest speaker a letter of appreciation typed on school stationery. You can include handwritten notes from your students if this is appropriate.

One parent was passionate about astronomy. He set up his own personal telescopes that allowed my students to look at the sun and see its spots. The students loved it! I prepared my students for this visit with the astronomy section in our book.

—*Eighth-grade life and physical science teacher*

PREPARE STUDENTS TO BE A RECEPTIVE AUDIENCE

Just as you would prepare your students when showing a video in your classroom, prepare your students when inviting guest speakers for a smooth sequence of learning experiences. We suggest that you tell your students about the guest speaker's background, what the guest speaker plans to address, and what you expect your students to do and learn.

My ninth-grade students culminated their unit on electricity with a guest speaker father who was also an electrician. He demonstrated how to replace a plug and switch and emphasized safety issues.

—*Ninth-grade physical science teacher*

You may want to dedicate a class session or part of a period to practice asking appropriate questions related to the topic or issue, and determine the order of questions and who will ask them. Doing this will tell you what your students know, what they want to know, and how they plan to ask it. In this way, you can add more background knowledge if you feel your students are not well informed and/or you are inviting a guest speaker who might address a controversial subject. For example, if you are asking a representative from the city council to talk about the pollution of a local river, you may or may not know in advance that some of your students have parents who work at the factory causing much of the pollution! Perhaps you want to invite a guest speaker who will help your students to understand multiple perspectives related to an issue. Be sure you have alerted your guest speaker for a healthy conversation.

During the presentation, listen closely to what the guest speaker says. You may want to take notes to incorporate the key points into your overall unit of learning. Monitor the talk for accuracy, perceptions, and a point of view that you may need to explain later. As the speaker is talking, you may need to assist with the equipment, provide supplies, enhance with your own visuals, or redirect inappropriate student behaviors. We suggest you establish with your speaker that you will give a five-minute warning sign to help them wrap up on time. If your speaker does not heed the warning, then you must intervene at the one-minute warning and tell them in front of the group that there is one minute. If that is not effective, you will have to say something kindly, such as: "That is where we will have to end today. Thank you Mr. or Ms. Guest Speaker."

In some cases, the guest speaker will leave before the class ends, so you can close the learning with your students. In other cases, the guest speaker will join the audience and wait to leave when the students are dismissed. You will have to provide closure with the guest speaker in the classroom. You can ask students to write two or three main points on a card and share them in small groups to recap the talk. In both cases, you want to sound supportive of the guest speaker, regardless of the talk. You can revisit the talk the next day to examine multiple points of view. Your guest speakers will be perceived experts in their fields, activists in the community, parents, or other individuals who your students know. If the guest you would like to invite isn't able to come to your room or to speak at an assembly, consider a Web chat or video conference.

> *A parent came for the day and demonstrated dry ice and liquid nitrogen. I prepared the students to understand key terms (melting point, boiling point, sublimation, elements, molecules) and to show appreciation to a guest!*
>
> —*Eighth-grade physical science teacher*

DEVELOP SCIENCE ACTIVITIES IN YOUR SCHOOL

There are many ways to incorporate science schoolwide. Students can contribute to the school newspaper, highlight special days, and take leadership roles in school events.

- *School Newspaper.* Many schools have newspapers. You could offer to take responsibility for a column or two focusing on science news and views, along with science-related events, discoveries, and investigations on the school, community, state, national, or international scene. Form student groups to write the reports and edit one another's work.

- *School E-mail List.* Some schools have school-based e-mail distribution lists. Like the school newspaper, you could oversee a student committee to post news and science-related events.

- *Poster Contests.* Offer to organize a poster contest for special events such as Safe and Drug-Free Schools Week or National Energy Awareness Month in October, Healthy Heart Day in February, Earth Day in April, or other local events. Ask students to serve as the organizers, judges, and awards committee. They will enjoy participating in these types of functions.

- *Debates.* Your school may have a debate team and host debating contests. Usually, specific topics are assigned. You can coordinate your curriculum to coincide with the topic and invite members of the debate team to share their skills with or present a debate to your science classes.

- *School Projects.* Your school may or may not yet recycle, and newspapers, plastics, and glass can be a source of income for purchasing science resources as well as a service-learning activity for your students. You can also use this activity as a scientific investigation for data collection on recycled materials or attitudes toward environmental issues. Alternatively, you might want to plant a garden or otherwise beautify the campus.

- *Elementary Student Tutoring.* If you are located near an elementary or middle school, students may benefit from cross-age tutoring during the day or after school.

CELEBRATE LEARNING THROUGH SCIENCE

All schools celebrate learning in various ways. Here are a few ideas to consider:

- *Curriculum Fairs.* Your school may create a fair in the spring for students to display their achievements. Students can construct displays that show various discussions, experiments, and discoveries. Capitalize upon these opportunities to showcase science—and don't limit yourself to the traditional display board approach to a science fair project. Invite students to use multimedia to create presentations, Web pages, Wikis, blogs, videos, and more! See additional ideas in Chapter 10.

- *Awards Assemblies.* Give out awards for your students' accomplishments. Honor those students who excel in science academically or by virtue of their participation and/or competition in programs, projects, and contests. Science needs to be celebrated just like sports, music, and other academics. Create your own awards: you can name the awards after exemplary alumni who have graduated from your school. Contact local science-related businesses to see whether they will offer a small scholarship for your awards.

- *Book Displays and Book Talks.* You might be fortunate enough to invite an author or illustrator to visit your school, or to have book clubs. Showcase the books in your science class to connect the stories with your curriculum.

- *Caught Doing Science.* Begin a new recognition of students and community members who are "caught doing science." There are all kinds of possibilities of who might be featured, and this recognition will help students make connections between science, careers, and their everyday lives.

OFFER SERVICE-LEARNING OPPORTUNITIES

Both participants and recipients benefit from service-learning projects. Students demonstrate their abilities as they take on responsibility for making a difference in their communities and meeting the real needs of its members. They like the sense that they are an appreciated and respected part of their community. They meet new and interesting people, and have stories to tell as a result. Effective service learning requires careful planning, time for implementation, and time for reflection.

Service learning provides a mechanism to bridge gaps between science and communities. Many activities are possible, but all should include hands-on experience and careful guidance so that the student gains new scientific knowledge in the form of methods or information, as well as an understanding of fundamental concepts such as the scientific process, ethics in science, and the role of today's scientists. Below are a few links to get you started, and Table 11.1 provides additional suggestions for science-related service-learning activities.

Table 11.1   Science-Related Service-Learning Activities

• Tutor children in science/math at elementary/middle school or an afterschool program.	• Teach about household chemicals and poisons (www.poison.org/prevent/house.asp).
• Read science fiction and nonfiction to children at the local library or bookstore (www.rif.org/parents/readingaloud).	• Recycle at your school, community center, or religious institution (http://earth911.org).
• Help blaze a trail at a nature center.	• Care for animals at a veterinarian's office, animal rescue center, pet shop, zoo, pet grooming center, or humane society.
• Promote earthquake, hurricane, or tornado safety at your local afterschool programs, or community agency.	• Be a docent at a local science museum.
• Plant trees, plants, or a garden for your community or school (www.kidsgardening.com).	• Talk about sea cucumbers as a touch tank volunteer at an aquarium marine life center.
• Get involved in safe and drug-free school activities.	• Volunteer at a sports clinic or hospital.
• Plant daffodil bulbs and then sell as a fundraising activity for the American Cancer Society (www.cancer.org).	• Campaign for propositions to improve the environment during the next voting cycle.
• Start a lead poisoning information campaign (http://kids.niehs.nih.gov/lead.htm).	• Participate in Earth Day (www.earthday.net).
	• Conduct items (food, soap) for the local food bank/homeless shelter.

- **National Service Learning Clearinghouse:** www
  .servicelearning.org. This comprehensive service-learning
  resource includes many ideas about service learning in science. Click on "A–Z Topics" for a quick search.
- **Kids Count: Young Citizen-Scientists Learn Environmental Activism:** www.edutopia.org/service-learning-
  citizen-science. This article provides many examples of how
  "citizen-scientists" are addressing real-world questions
  through activism.

SPONSOR A CLUB

A great way to spend time with students outside the classroom is
to sponsor a club. Away from the classroom, you take on a different role serving as a resource person helping students achieve
their goals. As a club advisor, you will be involved with students
over many years, rather than just a semester or year, and you will
be able to watch them grow and develop into mature individuals
as they take on positions of leadership and pursue their interests.

*I wanted a way to get students more involved in science and
mathematics. We formed a club—the Math and Science Society, or
MASS. Our motto played on the definition of matter (anything
that has mass and takes up space): "We matter! We have MASS and
we take up space!" We required at least a 2.5 GPA and good
citizenship to participate; we raised money to buy a centrifuge; and
our field trips included a trip to a car factory to see how parts are
manufactured and assembled and to an animal hospital to observe a
cat undergo surgery to be spayed.*

—Ninth-grade physical science teacher

Many organizations, such as the Junior Engineering Technical
Society (JETS), have brochures and toolkits for teachers to get
started. They contain suggestions for planning events, conducting
activities, and promoting the group. Information on holding
events with background information can be found on their Web
sites, along with sample forms and other documents. Resource
materials can be found online and in print.

Look in your school's student handbook or ask your department chair about science clubs and organizations. The clubs may be looking for an advisor or additional advisors. Or you might want to start a new club. Most schools have established days and times for clubs to meet at school. Some clubs meet before school, some meet at lunch, some meet after school.

> *I do a LegoRobotics and Science Club. It is so wonderful to see the students thrive as they swap programming ideas and building techniques for their robots. They also love the competitions we stage in the club.*
>
> *—Elementary science specialist*

CHECK OUT COMMUNITY RESOURCES

As you travel around your district and follow the local news, you will become aware of significant features or places of notable interest and potential personalities in your local area. See Table 11.2 for a list of potential community resources.

> *One of my favorite resources was the local plastics manufacturing plant. Each year, one of the directors would visit my classes and bring samples of the "before and after" of the manufacturing process. When funding was available, I would take students on a field trip to the plant so that they could see the plastic pellets transform into thin plastic wrap.*
>
> *—Tenth-grade chemistry teacher*

You might be surprised to find there are "science boosters" of parent groups, teacher associations, or businesses in your area that will support extracurricular activities. They may have or help raise funds for your classroom projects, provide materials and supplies, and/or have a speakers' bureau. Some agencies and organizations fund professional development and even sponsor field trips. Find out what your school's policies and procedures are, what financial assistance is already in place, and how to obtain more if needed.

Table 11.2   Community Resources: Consider the Science of a(n) . . .

arboretum	commercial laboratory	hair salon	river bottom
airport	crime/forensics unit	hospital	rock/land formation
amusement park	cultural center	industrial plant	sanitation center
apiary	dairy	library	sawmill/lumber yard
aquarium	dam	mass transit	shoreline/tide pool
archeological site	dentist/doctor office	mine	sports clinic
artist or art gallery	dock and harbor	museum	telecommunications
assembly plant	factory	newspaper plant	train station
bank	farm	nursery	university
batting cage	fire department	observatory	utility company
book publisher	fish hatchery	oil refinery	veterinary office
bookstore	food preparation	park	water reservoir
broadcast station	forest	pet shop	water treatment plant
canal lock	gas company	planetarium	weather bureau
cemetery	geological site	power plant	wildlife reserve
chemical supply	health department	recycling center	zoo

Another source of aid is through grants. Check local foundations and corporations for criteria eligibility, requirements, deadlines for proposals, and deadlines for funding. The state and federal governments are also sources of grant money. Remember, you may need school board approval to seek outside resources.

START A SCHOOL RESOURCE BANK

Some of your best resources will be your colleagues' and your students' families. As you learn more about the people with whom you are working, as well as the people in the community, start a resource bank (Epstein, 1997). You can achieve this electronically or by hand using note cards and a small file box. You will want to record valuable information to reference in the future when you plan your curriculum and get ready to start your instruction.

Design a note card that fits your purposes. Perhaps colleagues have already begun this for you, and you can use their banks as a start. See Table 11.3 for a list of information to gather from

Table 11.3   Resource Bank File Card Template

RESOURCE BANK FILE CARD TEMPLATE
Preferred format:
[ ] Field Trip Visit by Students [ ] Guest Speaker in Classroom [ ] Either
1. Area(s) of knowledge, experience, or information you could share with students:
2. Type of presentation you would like to make:
3. Length of presentation:
4. Resources you will share:
5. Equipment you will provide for your presentation:
6. Equipment we need to provide for your presentation:
7. Time needed for notification to prepare presentation:
8. Name:
9. Address:
10. E-mail address:
11. Telephone numbers:
12. Student's name, if applicable:
13. Student's science teacher's name, if applicable:
14. Comment

parents and member of the community to start a science school resource bank.

HAVE FUN WITH SCIENCE . . .

You have many choices for making science real and exciting. As you grow personally, pedagogically, and professionally, your efforts will make a huge difference for your students and for you. Everyone will be more invigorated and involved when you incorporate special activities into your science lessons. In the next chapter, we will explore how collaborating with colleagues expands your students' experiences and enriches their learning.

Suggested Activities

1. Talk with your science colleagues about service learning in your community. Explore how they got started and how their students benefit.

2. Find one special activity link in your community to incorporate into your science units. Plan how and when you will introduce it to your students.

3. Visit another school to see the kinds of science clubs that are available. Talk with the advisors.

4. Begin your resource bank on guest speakers in your area. Consider agencies, government and nongovernment organizations, and higher education, as well as business and industry in your local community.

CHAPTER TWELVE

Collaborate With Colleagues *to Expand Opportunities*

Science is a collaborative effort; each scientific advance builds upon, and is dependent upon, the work of the many scientists who have broken the original ground and build the foundation.

—Institute for Neurological Research
Web site on Alzheimer's Disease research
(Independent Scientific Contributions, 2007)

Science is a collaborative effort, and so is science education. There are many opportunities to collaborate with colleagues. You may team with teachers in different content areas in your grade level, within the same department, with those at another school campus, and with instructional aides. These multiple layers of organization empower teachers in knowing their students and understanding their school day holistically, aligning their science plans and preparing their activities with other teachers assigned the same courses, and interacting with science professionals and exchanging ideas to stay current in the field. We will describe what you can anticipate and the secrets to negotiating these layers to ensure your success.

CONTEMPLATE THE COLLABORATIVE NATURE OF SCIENTIFIC DISCOVERY

Franklin, Watson, and Crick; Marie and Pierre Curie; Rutherford and his graduate students (and Kottler and Costa, for that matter!)—what do all of these folks have in common? They collaborated! Scientists are known for being both competitive and collaborative, and it is important for students to realize that few scientists work alone. The synergy of working together, sharing ideas, and problem solving is far more than the sum of each person working alone. Many of the examples presented throughout this text demonstrate the collaboration among scientists toward a common goal— Franklin, Crick, and Watson in their search for the structure of DNA; Rutherford and his graduate students in their theorizing of the structure of the atom; and Marie and Pierre Curie in their research on radium and other radioactive substances. Read more about this husband and wife collaboration in Box 12.1.

BOX 12.1

History of Science

Marie and Pierre Curie Discover Radium

We must not forget that when radium was discovered no one knew that it would prove useful in hospitals. The work was one of pure science. And this is a proof that scientific work must not be considered from the point of view of the direct usefulness of it. It must be done for itself, for the beauty of science, and then there is always the chance that a scientific discovery may become like the radium a benefit for humanity.

—Marie Curie (1867–1934), Lecture at Vassar
College, May 14, 1921

It is clear from Marie Curie's speech that she believed in science for science's sake. However, her work revolutionized not only the fields of physics and chemistry, but ultimately the field of medicine as well. Two important discoveries led Marie Curie (Polish born as Maria Slodowska) to her life's work. In 1895, German physicist Wilhelm Roentgen discovered rays that could travel through solid wood and flesh. In 1896, French physicist Henri Becquerel developed a photographic plate that had been sitting under a small piece of paper-wrapped uranium for several weeks, and discovered that the uranium had exposed the photographic plate even though it had been covered in opaque material.

In 1897, Marie Curie, then a graduate student at the University of Paris, decided to investigate this new phenomenon for her doctoral dissertation. She decided to make a systematic investigation of the mysterious "uranium rays," and was fortunate to have access to a homemade electrometer that could measure weak electrical currents. In just a few days, Marie discovered that thorium gives off the same rays as uranium. After further study, she concluded that the ability to radiate did not depend on the arrangement of the atoms in a molecule, but was linked to the interior of the atom itself. This discovery was absolutely revolutionary, and some believe it is her most important contribution to the development of physics.

Marie Curie's French husband, Pierre Curie, a physicist at the university, found her research far more interesting than his own work on crystals. In the end, they discovered two new radioactive elements, which they named polonium and radium. In 1903, they were jointly given half the Nobel Prize in recognition of their joint research on the radiation phenomena with Professor Henri Becquerel. Marie Curie later received the Nobel Prize in Chemistry (in 1911) for her advancement of chemistry by the discovery, isolation, and study of radium and its compounds. Many chemists consider the discovery and isolation of radium to be the greatest event in chemistry since the discovery of oxygen, because it was the first time in history that an element was transmuted into another element. Read more about the life of Marie Curie, including the complete text of her speech at Vassar College, at the links below:

- **Marie and Pierre Curie and the Discovery of Polonium and Radium:** http://nobelprize.org/nobel_prizes/physics/articles/curie/index.html
- **Madam Curie and the Discovery of Radium:** www.timelinescience.org/resource/students/curie/curie.htm
- **Marie Curie's Speech: On the Discovery of Radium** (From Marie Curie, *The Discovery of Radium, Address by Madame M. Curie at Vassar College, May 14*, 1921, Ellen S. Richards Monographs No. 2 (Poughkeepsie: Vassar College, 1921), www.fordham.edu/halsall/mod/curie-radium.html

EXAMINE COLLABORATIVE CONCEPTS AND PRACTICES

Effective collaboration gives teachers a mechanism for working with a diverse collection of individuals who share interests and energies. Cooperation and creativity work together to satisfy the academic expectations and to generate new ideas. You can integrate your curriculum, instruction, and assessments in many different ways to meet the needs and interests of the teachers, students, and school (Fine, 1995). Together, you can plan, teach, and evaluate your teaching and your students.

We suggest you keep these key concepts and practices in mind:

1. Combine team members wisely, considering subject areas and individual teaching styles.

2. Establish teachers' teaming expectations regarding outcomes and processes.

3. Determine members' responsibilities for all tasks, including planning meetings, facilitating discussions, taking notes, distributing minutes, attending to details, reporting to administrators and other teachers, serving on committees, monitoring progress, communicating with parents, and so forth.

4. Identify expectations for the students, including management, rewards, and consequences that are positive, fair, and consistent.

5. Stay focused during meetings; arrive prepared to maintain positive and productive professionalism.

6. Recognize and appreciate the knowledge and skills in others as strengths; build upon the diversity to expand your own viewpoints and the educational experiences you are providing for your students.

7. Share resources, materials, ideas, responsibilities, recognition, and rewards.

8. Evaluate various teaming configurations (see below).

9. Coordinate activities, projects, and events.

10. Hold meetings with your students frequently to communicate team expectations and to celebrate achievements.

ADOPT THE SECRETS OF SUCCESSFUL COLLABORATORS

Collaboration must be based on important personal attributes held by each individual and shared mutually. The secrets to success are to adopt qualities of professionalism, such as enthusiasm, flexibility, patience, trustworthiness, commitment, resourcefulness, and risk-taking. It is important to have a sense of humor, respect others, and take responsibility for one's actions.

Effective teachers organize and operate with shared purposes related to teaching, learning, and schooling. All teachers—especially new teachers—need frequent chances to ask questions, articulate concerns, and contribute openly and honestly with receptive faculty, staff, and administrators. All teachers need opportunities to reflect. Collaboration requires an optimistic sense of adventure—one that, if conducted professionally, will serve you and your students well.

> *I have the opportunity to meet with my subject-alike teachers each week. We share a common pacing guide (which we developed together) and common assessments for our units (which we also developed). We also discuss the results of the assessments by standards. Those whose students performed well share what they did with their class. Sometimes we share a lesson or assignment that did not go as expected and together try to problem solve and improve the lesson.*
>
> *—Ninth-grade science teacher*

Surround yourself with those who have positive attitudes and genuinely want to help you succeed. You may need to stay away from the teachers' lounge if that's the location where people who complain, whine, and have negative attitudes gather. Spend your time with teachers who are excited and enthusiastic about their work.

CONSIDER VARIOUS TEAMING CONFIGURATIONS

There are various configurations for organizing teaching teams. Each configuration engages teachers and students in different scenarios to fulfill different outcomes. Some teaming configurations are permanent and some are temporary. There are advantages and disadvantages to these configurations, so weigh your options carefully (Alleman & Brophy, 1993). Here are some teaming configurations for you to consider and try:

1. *Team Planning.* Team teachers exchange ideas and coordinate events collectively but teach individually; teachers are responsible for their own classrooms but align their school agendas and share student concerns at a weekly team teachers' meeting. Usually, four or five teachers serve on the same team and teach the same grade level; team members may or may not teach the same subjects as one another. We suggest you (a) keep notes in a notebook to reference throughout the year and during future years, (b) select a team leader as the team coordinator and liaison, and (c) distribute responsibilities equitably.

2. *Teaming With Departmentalization.* This configuration is virtually the same as the previous one, but teachers share the same students. Usually four or five teachers serve on the same team and teach the same grade level, while students move among all the classes. The team consists of one teacher per subject area of language arts, math, social studies, science, and maybe reading, library, foreign language, or technology. Again, we urge you to keep notes, to select a leader, and to distribute tasks.

3. *Teaming With a Shared Resource Center.* This is the same as either of the above options, with the team sharing a resource center such as a specialized library, media center, or technology lab. In some schools, these types of resource centers are located in the center of the teaching area or pod, and are supplied with tables, chairs, and assistants. Teachers can use the resource center with students during instructional time, or teachers can arrange to send students individually or in groups to access the services available in the center.

4. *Single-Teacher Planning.* One teacher plans and prepares for all other teachers on the team who follow the stipulated instructional plan; this configuration tends to happen only on occasion to fulfill a specific purpose or when one teacher is an expert in a particular subject. The teacher gets everything ready, and all the other teachers teach according to the plan using the provided materials.

For example, the science teacher writes a lesson plan about the environment, collects the materials, and equips the three other team teachers to teach the same lesson on Earth Day.

5. *Identical Teaching Across the Team.* This is the same as number 4 above; however, all teachers on the team help with preparation and teach the same learning experience in each classroom, with all members of the team contributing parts of the planning, instruction, and evaluation. For example, all four teachers show the same video about weather emergencies and safety procedures, ask their students to write and practice informative skits in small groups, and prepare to make presentations for the entire team. This learning experience would require literacy, math, social studies, and science as well as fine arts, research, and technology.

6. *Integrated Instruction Across the Team.* Like number 4 above, this configuration requires all team members to teach an aspect of the same curriculum. In this situation, students rotate among the team teachers to learn various aspects of an overarching theme, topic, or issue. For example, science teachers plan and organize four different lessons related to geologic time, with each teacher focusing on a different era.

7. *Traditional Team Teaching.* Two teachers work together; each prepares and teaches one entire group of students two different aspects of one theme, topic, or issue. The teachers may teach the same subject area or different subject areas. For example, with two science teachers, one teaches balancing equations and the other one teaches the four major types of equations. With a science and language arts teacher, the science teacher presents information on global warming and the language arts teacher guides students through a related exercise in persuasive writing where students defend their position on the need for concern about this issue. The nonteaching teacher assists the teaching teacher by writing instructions or samples on the board, providing and/or monitoring student progress, and so forth. Both teachers remain in the classroom and actively engage with the instruction.

8. *Collaborative Team Teaching.* This configuration is a modification of the traditional configuration by involving two teachers in the teaching and learning at the same time. For example, the

two teachers introduce the fishbowl discussion strategy to explore issues related to urbanization and its effects on animal habitats. Both teachers contribute in giving students directions and both participate in the activity. This teaming configuration requires the two teachers to be equally knowledgeable with concepts and practices, as well as comfortable with an interactive teaching style.

9. *Supportive Team Teaching.* This looks like number 8 above, with one teacher guiding the initial or direct instruction for the two groups of students, then the other teacher providing follow-up practice. For example, the first science teacher introduces the concept of sound and waves; the second teacher guides in-class activities using tuning forks to experiment with pitch and amplitude.

10. *Parallel Team Instruction.* Two teachers and two groups of students work together in one space; each teacher leads one group of students through the same instruction. Students form one large group and share outcomes at the end of the learning experience.

11. *Differentiated Teaming.* Like number 10 above, groups are divided according to specific purposes: abilities, interests, learning styles, needs, and so forth. Each teacher leads instruction to one group; the instruction in each group might be similar but the content or practices will be unique to the needs of the group. The teaching team can decide whether outcomes will be shared as a whole group or within groups as a culmination.

12. *Monitoring Teaming.* Similar to numbers 8 through 11 above, one teacher guides two groups of students combined in one setting throughout the entire learning experience, and the other teacher monitors students' progress and manages behaviors by moving among the students and providing individual intervention. For example, the science teacher models how to prepare a cheek cell microscope slide. The second teacher circulates among students to prompt and assist as necessary.

We want to emphasize that you can create and combine all kinds of teaming situations throughout the school year to serve many different academic purposes and social outcomes. The variety will captivate your students' interests and help keep your teaching fresh and alive.

WEIGH THE PROS AND CONS
OF TEAM TEACHING CAREFULLY

There are many advantages as well as disadvantages to team teaching that we want to share with you now before you leap into making an uninformed decision. We know that some of you will have no choice about whether or not you team teach. This decision may have already been made before you arrived or you interviewed at a school where team teaching is the norm.

Some of the advantages of team teaching include:

- teachers specializing in their subject area, providing expertise where the content is more complex;
- teachers consolidating the materials and resources into one space and being ready to teach all related curriculum in that subject area;
- teachers getting to know their students extremely well in that one subject area;
- teachers teaching what they enjoy and expressing their passion with their students;
- students being grouped together by abilities or interests, allowing teachers to focus on particular content and skills in ways that are developmentally appropriate to differentiate instruction more efficiently;
- students being more attentive to and engaging in learning since they travel through their day with the same group of students (or most of the same students), following the same schedule;
- special service teachers working with identified students who are grouped together within the team;
- teachers working together more efficiently and effectively to plan their lessons to meet the needs and interests of their students;
- students learning one daily routine that increases their success; and
- teachers conferencing with students and teachers more efficiently to discuss the students' progress holistically.

Conversely, some of the disadvantages of team teaching include:

- students communicating more fully with one teacher than the other teacher(s);
- students cooperating more with one teacher than with the other teacher(s);

- students not completing homework equally for all teachers;
- students "playing" one teacher against another to get their way, just as children "play" their parents against each other;
- students who are "tracked" labeling themselves as more advanced or less advanced than those in the other tracks;
- one class elevating itself above the others as a teacher's favorite;
- students being challenged to stay organized and ready with materials, with materials tending to be left in lockers or other classrooms so students interrupt both the class they are in and the class where materials have been left when they have to retrieve their missing items;
- students being challenged to finish their homework—it is helpful to have one homework assignment sheet for students to record their assignments throughout the day to show their homeroom teacher at the start and end of each day and to share with parents at home at night; and
- teachers not liking the teaming assignments, the decision-making model, or some (or all) members of the team. Personality conflicts may arise within a team that can be detected by the faculty, students, and parents.

UNDERSTAND SCHOOL ORGANIZATIONAL PATTERNS

Most likely, your teaming configurations align with your school's organizational patterns. School schedules may be organized around various lengths of time such as the entire school year, two semesters, three trimesters, four quarters, or other time segments for year-round schools. Your science classes may be scheduled to meet every day at the same time for the same length of time.

Or your science classes may be scheduled in a block to meet every other day at the same time for a longer period of time. In this organizational pattern, students attend the same number of classes each day, but classes meet on alternating or scheduled days. Your team configuration may be limited to the same teachers who share the same daily schedules with you and your students.

You may be assigned to team with one or more other teachers with whom you share a block of time. For example, you and the language arts teacher may be assigned one hundred minutes and two groups of students. You and the language arts teacher must decide (a) how to divide the time, (b) how to divide the students, and (c) how to align your curriculum, instruction, and assessment. Look over the list of team-teaching configurations above; we think you will find an approach that fits your needs and interests.

MAKE THE MOST OF DEPARTMENTALIZATION

Many of you will work primarily with the teachers in your science department. Most often you will plan, teach, and evaluate with your grade level, and meet occasionally with other science teachers. For the most part, your courses will be taught independently of the other courses on your grade-level team, except for some culminating projects and shared school events. Here are some advantages or strengths related to departmentalization:

1. Students will be taught by teachers who specialize in their subject areas.

2. Teachers can focus and concentrate more on their own subject areas.

3. Teachers can develop overarching plans for only a few courses and can individualize instruction for students in various sections of the courses as needed.

4. Departments can identify major course outcomes and assign them, or aspects of them, to various teachers to assure coverage and sequence learning, and to avoid redundancy.

5. Departments can expand and enrich learning, or even provide multiple perspectives related to a select topic or issue; teachers can explore complex issues from conflicting points of view.

6. Teachers can organize and allocate time and energy for integrated culminating projects and schoolwide events.

7. Students experience unique yet coordinated learning styles and situations.

INTEGRATE SCIENCE ACROSS THE CURRICULUM

The study of acids and bases lends itself well to a geography lesson. It is interesting to compare the concentration of acid rain across the world. Included in this discussion is the effect of acid rain on depletion of fish stock in Norway, the recent increase in acid rain concentration in China that is due to rapid industrial growth, and how acid rain has been identified as a reason for the decline in North American songbirds in the northeastern United States. I have student groups choose a country, research the topic, and we create a bulletin board with a world map and short summaries of the problem.

—Tenth-grade chemistry teacher

The knowledge, skills, and dispositions of science play a huge role in relation to all other subject areas. Working with other subject areas to reinforce common academic vocabulary will support students' acquisition of new words and terms. The repetition will strengthen students' ownership as they see the relevance of this vocabulary across disciplines. Integration with other subject matter will help students see the connections between science, their lives, and society. Consider the ideas below.

• *Crucibles* (Chemistry, American Literature, and U.S. History, eleventh grade). Written by Arthur Miller in 1952, *The Crucible* describes events that occurred during the Salem Witch Trials. Miller used that event as an allegory for McCarthyism and the Red Scare, a period in the 1940s and 1950s in which Americans were in fear of communism and the government blacklisted accused communists. The relationship of this story to science is through the title's use of a piece of science equipment—the crucible— which is used to burn magnesium at a very high temperature.

• *Hiroshima* (Chemistry/Physics/Physical Science, World History, U.S. History, and Literature, eighth and eleventh grades). The bombing of Hiroshima and the nuclear age are critical topics of both world and U.S. history. Introducing nuclear chemistry from a historical perspective can add a real-world context to students' understanding of the atomic nucleus. For example, the neutron wasn't even discovered until 1932!

• *Plant Structure and Development* (Biology/Life Science and World History, seventh and tenth grades). When Christopher Columbus discovered America, the native populations of the area were conducting amazing scientific experiments with crops. Another set of topics within this intersection includes the historical and scientific understanding of race and how disease epidemics have impacted societies.

• *Metals and Gemstones* (Environmental/Earth Science and Economics/Government, twelfth grade). The intersection of environmental science, economics, and government is extensive, and includes how certain metals and gems came to be valued over others, how political decisions of one country impact the environment of another, the space race, global warming, and how weather patterns disrupt economies.

• *Marine Art and Poetry* (Life Science/Marine Biology, Art, and Literature/Poetry, seventh grade). Students can create two- and three-dimensional representations from simple drawings to more complex painting, *papier-mâché*, clay, or wire sculptures and digital drawings. Students may read excerpts from books and write *haiku* and other forms of poetry. One favorite poem about the beach is e.e. cummings's "millie, molly, maggie, and may."

The stronger the students' understanding, application, and appreciation of science becomes, the more successful the students will be at understanding math, social science, English, and their elective courses. Consequently, students will be more proficient, demonstrating mastery through papers, projects, and tests as well as in social settings, such as group work, academic clubs, and civic organizations involving critical thinking, problem solving, and decision making, both at school and in their everyday lives.

To integrate science effectively, lay out the standards and expectations for two or more subject areas. Connect the standards that fit together naturally. For example, using science and language arts as an example, you might use the language arts standards and expectations to guide your reading and writing responses to the science themes and topics. Students can collaboratively conduct a research study on a contemporary issue or become involved in a service-learning project.

Visiting a historic cemetery aligns with the National Science Education Standards, including science as inquiry. Specifically, it involves developing questions, forming an explanation, and then describing the results. This field trip may also align with specific content in physical science, life science, Earth science, science and technology, and science in personal and social perspective. In addition, cemeteries lend themselves to study from a variety of content areas. See Table 12.1 for ideas on an integrated unit on a historic cemetery that is appropriate for middle school students. Suggested activities include a variety of collaborative and individual research, art, and creative writing projects.

If you are a science teacher working with one other teacher, share your specific standards and resources to help everyone collaborate on some in-class activities and culminating projects. Students can develop a portfolio of outcomes informed and supported by standards from different subject areas to be shared at parent–teacher conferences.

TALK TO TECHNOLOGY SPECIALISTS

Teachers who are interested and advanced in technology, or who have become specialists, will be a great asset to you. They can help you design creative experiences for students, and keep you up to date on the latest technology developments. Ask them to model how they use tools, such as the graphing calculator (frequently available to science and math students), to represent numerical data from field investigations. Schools are also acquiring audience response systems, which not only engage students but also offer immediate feedback.

Many schools are now encouraging teachers to develop their own Web pages as resources for students and parents. You can post assignments and rubrics, homework help, reading schedules, information on special events, and test dates. Additionally, you can offer supplementary material and Web links for extended research. Once you have gained permission, you can display pictures of your classroom and special activities that take place there. Perhaps you'd like to create podcasts of lessons for students who are absent or for students to review before taking a test. You will need to contact your school/district information systems department for directions and guidance.

Table 12.1 Sample Integrated Unit: The Historic Cemetery

	The Historic Cemetery	
Content Area	Sample Content Standards (Grades 5–8, Louisiana)	Suggested Activities
Science **Life Science/Biology**	**Structure and Function in Living Systems:** Investigating human body systems and their functions (including circulatory, digestive, skeletal, respiratory)	Identify kinds of stone used (limestone, sandstone, wood, granite, slab, block and post). Which kind is prevalent in this cemetery? Which withstands weather the best?
	Populations and Ecosystems: Explaining the interaction and interdependence of nonliving and living components within ecosystems	Study the topography of the site. How have plants grown around tombstones and graves? Make a map of the cemetery, showing streets and memorable lots, bodies of water, landmarks. Determine why graves face the direction they do.
	Interdependence of Organisms: Exploring how humans have impacted ecosystems and the need for societies to plan for the future	Analyze the cemetery for erosion. Study animal life in the cemetery.
	Personal and Community Health: Researching technology used in prevention, diagnosis, and treatment of diseases/disorders	Compare the percentage of burials versus cremations. Look for changes in grave markers and draw connections between cemetery features and current technologies.

(Continued)

Table 12.1 (Continued)

Content Area	Sample Content Standards (Grades 5–8, Louisiana)	Suggested Activities
English/Language Arts **Reading and Responding**	**Reading and Responding:** Reading, comprehending, and responding to written, spoken, and visual texts in extended passages; using purposes for reading (e.g., enjoying, learning, researching, problem solving) to achieve a variety of objectives	Read poems and literature associated with death and dying, including: "A Begonia for Miss Applebaum" (Paul Zindel) "Death Be Not Proud" (John Gunther) "When I am Dead, My Dearest" (Christina Georgina Rossetti) "Because I Could Not Stop for Death" (Emily Dickenson) Complete a free write on death and these poets' ideas combined into a collective poem. Write three obituaries—one as if they were to die during this year, one as if they died twenty-five years from now, and one as if they died in fifty years. Bring in sample obituaries to show as models. Make tombstone rubbings or drawings of symbols and designs found on monuments. Determine what these symbols represent.
Mathematics **Data Analysis, Probability, and Discrete Mathematics**	**Data Analysis, Probability, and Discrete Mathematics:** Collecting, organizing, and describing data based on real-life situations; formulating and solving problems that involve the use of data: systematically collecting, organizing, describing, and displaying data in charts, tables, plots, graphs, and/or spreadsheets	Find the age at time of death, the oldest person, the oldest grave, the most recent grave, the number of years since someone has been buried in the cemetery, and the average age of people buried in a given year of a particular decade. Explore geometric shapes of stones— spheres, pyramids, rectangles, cylinders, cones, cubes, combinations of these.

Content Area	Sample Content Standards (Grades 5–8, Louisiana)	Suggested Activities
		Conduct a life span analysis.
		Tally and graph the most common names found in a local historic cemetery.
Social Studies **Geography: Physical and Cultural Systems**	**Places and Regions:** Explaining and analyzing both the physical and human phenomena associated with specific places, including precipitation and settlement patterns; describing and explaining how personal interests, culture, and technology affect people's perceptions and uses of places and regions	Explore the burial practices of the local area. Collect data on individuals and tombstones—birth and death dates, gender, and type of marker.
		Research famous individuals buried in the cemetery.
	Environment and Society: Explaining and giving examples of how characteristics of different physical environments affect human activities	Search for evidence of wars, catastrophes, and epidemics from inscriptions on the markers. Research both local and national history for reasons and details about these events.
Foreign Language **Cultural Practices**	**Cultural Practices:** Demonstrating an awareness of social customs related to religion, school, family life, folklore, and holidays; identifying and describing social, geographic, and historical factors that impact cultural practices;	Discover individuals of foreign origin. Gather evidence from inscriptions on stones as to reasons for immigration to your area. If no evidence is given, research the reasons.
		Compare modern and historical burial practices for different cultures, including Day of the Dead.

Additional Resources:
Easley, L. (2005). Cemeteries as Science Labs. *Science Scope, 29*(3), 28–32.
Lowry, P. & McCrary, J. (2005). Science and history come alive in the cemetery. *Science Scope, 29*(3), 33.
Historic Cemeteries: History Written in Stone: www.arkansasheritage.com/in_the_classroom/lesson_plans/ahpp/cemeterylessonplan.pdf

Classroom computers and/or videoconferencing systems will allow you to communicate with people outside the classroom. You can conduct interviews with resource people, job shadow professionals in the field, or collect survey information. As students receive information, they can create databases to record and organize their results. With the help of specialists, you will be able to provide a technology-rich classroom and stay abreast of legal and ethical issues.

> *Sometimes to prepare students for a complicated lab, or sometimes in lieu of a wet lab that doesn't often work well or requires special supplies, students will perform a virtual lab off a CD-ROM or the Internet. I use a laptop cart with wireless hub so each student or pair of students can use a laptop in class.*
>
> *—Twelfth-grade physics teacher*

TEAM UP WITH INSTRUCTIONAL AIDES TO SUPPORT STUDENTS

While all students differ in ways that require teachers to adapt their teaching methods, English learners, struggling readers, and students with special needs present a particular challenge. Most can learn the important concepts of science, but they need strategic support. For these special learners, you will need to provide optional avenues to high achievement, not a shortcut to lower standards. One way to do this is to make effective use of your instructional aides. Under your direction, instructional aides can model what students should do, help students form questions to ask the teacher, repeat explanations to help clarify information, provide important organization scaffolding, involve students in cooperative activities, monitor progress and provide feedback, and ultimately build student confidence in learning science.

Meet regularly with the teacher assistants or instructional aides who support your students, to identify the standards, objectives, activities, and assessments for each unit and your expectations for their roles in the classroom. Find out what their backgrounds are, what qualifications they possess, and what types of experiences they bring to the classroom.

CONTACT OTHER EMPLOYEES IN THE DISTRICT

There are likely several people at your school or in your district who will be able to make contributions to your curriculum. They can serve as guest speakers on a variety of topics for your students. The school resource officers or local police officers can come and speak about forensic science. Perhaps the school nurse will talk about human development or prevention of the transmission of germs for a biology class, or the effects of stress on the body for an anatomy and physiology class. School counselors might speak about careers in science.

With a little time, you will discover who has come to teaching as a second or third career following degrees in science. These individuals can provide your students with a personal look at the role of a laboratory technician, engineer, or other science-related professional. The teachers in your school are resources too; if you offer to take their classes for a day, they will be able to be a guest speaker for yours. Having guest speakers increases the sense of immediacy and personalizes the learning for your students.

SEE SCIENCE IN SOCIETY AND THE WORLD

Finally, help your students see science in society and the world by collaborating with students and teachers from other cities, states, and countries. Making global connections is a fabulous start for integrating the curriculum that you and your students will find captivating and rewarding. As we discussed in Chapter 10, you can use different ways to communicate and collaborate electronically. There are many ways to participate in science investigations and experiments with teachers and students in other cities, states, and countries.

Finally, you can join with others to celebrate International Youth Day, which promotes the ways in which young people contribute to their societies. The United Nations has established a different theme every year since 2000. You can have your students participate in discussions that focus on youth issues, or plan programs that showcase their achievements. See www.un.org/esa/socdev/unyin/iyouthday.htm for more information.

INTEGRATE SCIENCE NATURALLY . . .

When you integrate science with another subject area, across your team or throughout your school, you have achieved the ultimate goal. You want your students to experience science holistically, naturally, and authentically in their learning. They will connect the standards and outcomes with their everyday lives and future endeavors. In our last chapter, we will look at ways to reflect on your practice and offer ideas for further professional development.

Suggested Activities

1. Talk with an experienced science teacher about teaming pros and cons.

2. Work with a partner to plan an integrated unit. Decide what content you will incorporate. Identify the specific objectives to be covered and the assessments to be implemented.

3. Select a few local science-related current events and issues that will be a part of your students' daily lives in the near future as they begin to vote and pay taxes. Collaborate with a social studies teacher to find ways to incorporate these issues into your curriculum and instruction.

4. Identify the English learners and students with special needs in your classes, and meet with the English Language and/or special education teachers and instructional aides to plan how to coteach to support your students.

CHAPTER THIRTEEN

Reflect on Your Practice *to Fortify Your Future*

The best thing about the future is that it only comes one day at a time.

—Abraham Lincoln(1809–1865)

Y ou have your entire teaching career stretching out in front of you. Start by taking an honest inventory of your own knowledge, skills, and dispositions. Assess your competence, confidence, and readiness related to all of your responsibilities as well as your aspirations. Set some realistic goals and then take the essential steps to put your goals into motion. Enjoy the journey. And be sure to pace yourself: your goals may be ambitious and you don't want to burn out. The secret is to balance what you think you need to do with want you want to do. Our advice for you is exactly the advice you would give to your students.

LOOK BACK TO LOOK AHEAD

The first step in looking ahead requires you to look back and reflect upon your teaching (Schön, 1983). Take stock of what you know, do, and believe about science content and pedagogy. Consider what you value most as you establish your learning communities and identify the next steps that will benefit both you and your students (Van Manen, 1977). It is important to reflect upon what worked and what did not work when you were a learner in the very same grade level and/or classes where you are now the teacher. Then reflect upon what works and does not work now for your students in a contemporary context (Ziechner & Liston, 1987).

REFLECT ON LEARNING WITH PURPOSE

Becoming a reflective practitioner is vital to advancing your professionalism throughout your teaching career (Pultorak, 1993). Many teachers take time at the end of each day to mentally review the day. We encourage you to make some notes on your lesson plans or to keep a journal. It is helpful to talk with colleagues. Whatever format or combination you follow, we find adding structure will enhance your experience.

Hole and McEntee (1999) developed the Guided Reflection Protocol to help individual teachers improve their teaching by responding to four prompts. First the teacher describes an experience by writing about it in a concentrated manner. Writing helps to clarify and personalize one's ideas. Then the teacher seeks an explanation and adds that to the narrative. Next, an attempt is made to discover the significance, and finally the teacher determines future action in light of this analysis, extending the narrative with each additional insight. Here are the four prompts or questions found in the Guided Reflection Protocol:

1. What happened?

2. Why did it happen?

3. What might it mean?

4. What are the implications for my practice?

Jonson (2008) suggests that reflective thinking is most powerful when teachers talk to one another about their ideas. It is helpful to have an active listener respond to your description and share in your evaluation in a way that will promote your personal growth. Talking with a colleague can be very supportive.

Hole and McEntee (1999) also developed a structure to use with others in a group process experience. This is called the

Critical Incidents Protocol. Each teacher in the group takes time to write an account, then the members share their accounts. The group chooses one account on which to focus its conversation. The author reads what he or she has written and then answers "clarifying questions" posed by the group, such as:

1. What does this account mean within the larger context of your life?

2. In the account, what metaphors represent important themes to you?

3. What are some alternative endings for the account that you considered plausible?

4. What are some alternative endings for the account that you rejected?

5. What does this account reveal about your teaching that you value most?

Such questions lead to a deeper discussion of the issues raised in the account, not only for the author but also for the other members of the group. Participants then have the opportunity to personalize the themes and discuss the implications for their own practices, and the group debriefs the process.

Whether conducted individually, with a partner, or in a group, reflection gives you the opportunity to explore in detail the results of your decisions—what went well and why, as well as what needs improvement. Whether you take time daily, weekly, or biweekly, reflection allows you to analyze past events, acknowledging your accomplishments and supporting the development of your teaching skills and the successes of your students (Shermis, 1992). You also identify and learn from mistakes in order to change what you will do in the future. Perhaps you need to clarify directions, change the sequence of activities, or provide additional background for students in a unit of study. In talking with others, you may get new ideas of strategies and resources to try. You may choose to observe the way other master teachers address the same concept or skill, or decide to pursue some other form of professional development.

EVALUATE YOUR CURRICULUM

Beyond looking at lessons, effective teachers examine their curriculum as a whole. In Resource E at the end of this book you will find a tool for this type of analysis that looks at your teaching and the respective student learning in four categories. The topics are the extent to which authentic learning, academic focus, active learning, and articulated assessments take place in your science classroom.

As you determine what your needs are as a teacher, you will find many people and opportunities to promote your efforts to change your practice or do things differently in the future. We hope we have been helpful as we shared some of our experiences and observations throughout this book. While we have tried to provide a wide variety of ideas, our suggestions are by no means comprehensive, nor do we mean them to be prescriptive. We know you will continue to add to your repertoire as you personalize this book for your own use. Below, we look at the benefits of participating in school/district curriculum development projects, joining professional organizations, finding a mentor, participating in science research activities, and pursuing further education for your professional growth.

MAKE A DIFFERENCE AT THE SCHOOL OR DISTRICT LEVEL

There are many opportunities to make a difference at a school or district level. Most districts have an Assessment Committee, which is responsible for writing and revising districtwide quarterly and final examinations. Textbooks are adopted every five to seven years, and require Textbook Adoption Committees to review publisher texts and resources. Curriculum Development Committees write district-wide pacing guides, ensure all standards are covered in the curriculum guides, and align textbook resources with content standards.

You may participate in the school site council; parent, student, and teacher association; bilingual advisory council; or accreditation committee, among others. You may also have the opportunity to participate in special programs, such as AVID (Advancement via Individual Determination); Gifted and Talented Education, including Honors and AP classes; or a school-within-a-school, such as an academy program.

JOIN PROFESSIONAL ORGANIZATIONS

By joining professional organizations, you will be able to keep up with the latest developments in the field and to network with other teachers who share your interests. Your membership will provide you with journals publishing research and best practices along with other notices of conferences, meetings, and special events. Membership also entitles you to reduced rates to attend conferences and order educational materials. We strongly encourage you to join different professional organizations as a way to get involved and to stay informed.

The main organization related to science education is the National Science Teachers Association (NSTA), www.nsta.org. This organization comprises K−12 classroom teachers, department chairs, curriculum specialists, and university professors interested in and representing the associated groups of science education. Once you are a member, you will have access to the entire Web site.

Each state has a chapter of NSTA. Look on the NSTA Web site for links to your state. Most of the state chapters hold annual conferences and meetings in various locations around the state. Joining a state chapter of NSTA will enable you to network with other science professionals near you, and to find out more about the content resources in your state. Fortunately, most state chapters offer a comprehensive membership so you can join the national and state chapter all at once.

There are also organizations in all of the science-related academic disciplines, and some of them have active state and local chapters as well. Even if you cannot attend meetings or conferences, becoming a member will entitle you to receive their journals and/or newsletters with academic research and classroom practices; discounts on additional publications; announcements related to the subject area, such as newsworthy events and television specials and opportunities to apply for classroom grants; and a preview of future activities. Here are some science and science education organizations and their Web site addresses:

- **Geological Society of America:** www.geosociety.org
- **National Association of Geology Teachers:** www.nagt.org
- **American Chemical Society:** www.acs.org
- **American Institute of Biological Sciences:** www.aibs.org
- **National Association of Biology Teachers:** www.nabt.org
- **American Physics Society:** www.aps.org
- **American Association of Physics Teachers:** www.aapt.org

The National Association for Research in Science Teaching (NARST, www.narst.org) is a worldwide organization of professionals committed to the improvement of science teaching and learning through research. Since its inception in 1928,

NARST has promoted research in science education and the communication of knowledge generated by that research.

Finally, there are excellent organizations that address non-content-specific fields in education, such as the International Society of Technology Education (ISTE) (www.iste.org) and the Association of Supervision and Curriculum Development (ASCD, www.ascd.org).

ATTEND A SCIENCE EDUCATION CONFERENCE

You may discover that a conference will be held in or near your school that you can attend through advance arrangements with your department chair, principal, and/or district curriculum specialist. You may be able to receive financial assistance to attend the conference if you submit a proposal to present your own action research and/or teaching practices. Some districts may request you lead a workshop when you return, to share with other teachers what you learned at the conference. Making a presentation provides an excellent opportunity to collaborate with your colleagues too.

Attending a conference is a unique experience. Depending on where you live, science education–related conferences may be held independently or connected with general teacher education conferences. At the national, state, and local levels, you will be able to immerse yourself in science conversations, see the latest textbooks and newest supplementary materials, talk to resource professionals, gain knowledge of current pedagogy, and view the latest educational technologies.

The secret is to select wisely the sessions you attend, according to your needs and interests. Look for special-interest strands in the conference program, note the featured speakers in your subject area, and plan to spend time visiting exhibits. There will be opportunities for you to be a presenter and share your research and/or students' accomplishments too. You will meet new people, learn what other teachers are doing in their classrooms, and come home inspired.

FIND A MENTOR

All of us were new to our positions at one time, and we quickly appreciated the mentoring we received as preservice teachers from our cooperating/master teacher(s) and university supervisor(s). Hopefully, you have a mentor who is current in and enthusiastic about the research and practice of teaching as well as mentoring (Portner, 2008). If you have not been assigned to a mentor, you can either request one from your department chair or ask a school administrator to identify a person to fulfill that role for you. Or, informally, you can ask an experienced science colleague to serve as your mentor. Most experienced teachers will be honored to support you.

Many states have formal programs to ensure that new teachers and teachers new to their positions receive the assistance and guidance they need to be successful (Jonson, 2008). In fact, many school districts now have formalized induction programs that include orientations and programs for new teachers where mentors are assigned and time is allocated to delve into a variety of issues and concerns. Meetings are held on a regular basis (sometimes weekly, biweekly, or monthly) for new teachers to assemble to listen to a speaker address a timely topic or important issue, to interact with other new teachers, and to provide one another with much-needed support. These sessions are led by experienced teachers who have received professional development to provide support. They guide the sessions in positive and productive ways. Typical topics and issues include time management, classroom management, authentic assessments, standardized testing, teaching strategies, and lesson review. University credit may be available for participation in beginning-teacher and induction programs.

EARN A GRADUATE DEGREE OR ADDITIONAL CREDENTIAL

After you begin teaching, you will discover how much more you want to know and want to be able to do. Most universities offer programs of study designed to match your career goals and special interests. Why not take classes that you not only want to take, but will possibly open some future doors for you too? Look at the Web site for the university department where you are interested in taking classes, or contact the department chair to start your exploration.

When considering a graduate degree, you have several options. You may want to pursue a graduate degree in a pure science field, such as a Master of Arts in Biology or Environmental Science. Or, you may want to pursue a Master of Science in Education. Options in this field include curriculum and instruction, administration, reading, special education, or educational technology.

Some universities offer a MAT-S, or Master of Arts in Teaching Science. This degree usually combines units in science with units in education and science education.

Pursuing a doctorate is an even bigger step, but it can also be very rewarding. Again, there are at least three major options: a degree in the sciences, a degree in education, or a degree in science education. You may be able to create your own set of courses in a doctoral program, with a rich array of education coursework as well as history, philosophy, sociology, and even anthropology of science and science education courses.

The degree you decide to pursue will depend on your future goals. Do you want to stay in the classroom or shift roles to a school administrator or district curriculum specialist? Do you want to teach science or science education at the college or university level? Would you like to work with future teachers? Take plenty of time to decide and make a wise decision.

LOOK AT SCIENCE LITERATURE

There are several journals to support science teachers specifically, such as NSTA's *Science and Children* for elementary teachers, *Science Scope* for middle school teachers, and *The Science Teacher* for high school teachers. These peer-reviewed journals offer teacher-tested classroom lessons, current research developments in the field, links with literacy, and ideas for integrating the latest technology in the classroom. There are also publications in the specialized science education areas, including *Chem Matters* from the American Chemical Society, *American Biology Teacher* from the National Association of Biology Teachers, *The Physics Teacher* from the American Association of Physics Teachers, and the *Journal of Geoscience Education* from the National Association of Geology Teachers.

In both university and commercial bookstores, you will find books related to teaching strategies that will appeal to your students' interests. You may wish to look for materials earmarked as "elementary" or "secondary" education; many of those materials will fit your science classes quite well. You can consider adapting science strategies for one level to fit the other. And of course, you will also want to stay abreast of science news through books and magazines such as *Discover, National Geographic, Nature,* or *Science News.*

One last suggestion is the History of Science Society (www.hssonline.org), which is dedicated to understanding science, technology, medicine, and their interactions with society in a historical context. Among other resources, the society offers

Reading the History of Western Science: A List of Good Places to Start. Finally, there are many wonderful books on the history and musings of science. Here are a few of our favorites:

- Royston M. Roberts. (1989). *Serendipity: Accidental discoveries in science.* New York: John Wiley & Sons.
- Jack Weatherford. (1989). *Indian givers: How the Indians of the Americas transformed the world.* New York: Ballantine.
- Gene Dawkins. (1978). *The selfish gene.* London: Oxford University Press.

Take a look at Box 13.1 to explore the discovery of blood circulation.

BOX 13.1

History of Science

The Circulation of the Blood

We now accept that each person has a fixed amount of blood circulating throughout his or her system in one fixed direction. William Harvey, an English physician, is usually credited with explaining the circulation of the blood and the working of the heart. However, other scientists and doctors in other parts of the world came up with very similar explanations. Who should get the credit? We're going to let you decide.

Ancient Chinese. The ancient Chinese (second century BC) believed that blood was pumped by the heart, and flowed through the arteries, veins, and capillaries. Chinese doctors used a system of bellows and bamboo tubes to demonstrate to medical students how the heart and blood circulation worked.

Galen. With his dissections of animals, Galen, the famous ancient Greek doctor (AD 129), proved that arteries contained blood. However, he also incorrectly assumed that the system of arteries and veins were completely distinct, and that blood formed in the liver and became mixed with air in the heart. His ideas formed the core of the medical canon for centuries.

Ibn al-Nafis. In 1213, the Chief of Medicine at Al-Mansuri Hospital in Cairo challenged Galen's theories. Ibn al-Nafis theorized that blood must move from the right chamber to the left through the arteries via the lungs, where it was oxygenated. He maintained that the septum of the heart was not perforated and did not have either visible or invisible pores.

Michael Servetus. In 1553, Spanish physician and theologian Michael Servetus suggested that blood flowed from one side of the heart to the other via the lungs instead of through the wall between the ventricles. This

(Continued)

(Continued)

refuted Galen's theory; however, Servetus had more dangerous ideas and was ultimately burned at the stake as a heretic for denying the Trinity.

William Harvey. As the court doctor for British royalty in the early 1600s, Harvey conducted numerous experiments to challenge Galen's assumptions. His heart dissections demonstrated that valves in the heart allowed blood to flow in only one direction; observations of the heartbeat of living animals showed that the ventricles contracted together; and examination of beating hearts removed from a living animal demonstrated that the heart continued to beat, thus acting as a pump. Harvey also used mathematical data to prove that the blood was not being consumed, and theorized that arteries and veins were connected to each other by capillaries, which were later discovered by Marcello Malpighi.

So who should get the credit for the discovery of the circulation of the blood? It isn't an easy decision—and we've highlighted only five of the many contributors to this theory. Learn about others who played a role in the development of our understanding of blood and its circulation:

- **Circulation of the Blood:** www.timelinescience.org/resource/teachers/blood.htm. This site explores how the basic circulation of the heart was understood in China and the Arab world many centuries before the knowledge became available in Europe.
- **The Heart and the Circulatory System:** www.accessexcellence.org/AE/AEC/CC/heart_background.html. This display is part of the Access Excellence Classic Collection, which focuses on select individuals or events by putting them into historical context and relating them to current science. Included in each unit is a set of suggested references and classroom activities.
- **Red Gold: The Epic Story of Blood:** www.pbs.org/wnet/redgold/history/index.html. This PBS series examines the facts and myths of human blood and its impact on everything from religion and medicine to commerce and popular culture throughout history.

APPLY THE FINDINGS OF RESEARCH IN SCIENCE EDUCATION

There are many journals devoted to research in science education. The *Journal of Research in Teaching Science* is a publication of the National Association for Research in Teaching Science, which contains reports for science education researchers and practitioners on issues of science teaching and learning, and science education policy. *Science Education* is an independent journal that publishes articles on the latest issues and trends occurring internationally in science curriculum, instruction, learning, policy, and preparation of science teachers. This journal is divided into sections on learning, culture and comparative studies, science learning in everyday life, issues and trends, science teacher education, and book reviews. Both journals have Web-based databases of past issues, and you may request a free copy at their Web sites.

Research in science education has had a great impact on the teaching of science. Consider these important advances, identified as research and published by the *Journal of Research in Teaching Science*, felt to have had the most influence on science teaching (Holliday, 2003):

- *Four Stages of Cognitive Development.* Piaget (1964) applied his understanding of child development and learning psychology to science teaching. His four stages of cognitive development are still used today as a guide for determining grade-level appropriateness for science content and process skills.

- *Teacher Wait-Time.* Rowe (1974) conducted six years of investigations on the effect of teacher wait-time on development of language and logic of children in elementary science. Defining wait-time as the time between when the teacher stops speaking and when a student responds or the teacher speaks again, Rowe determined that a three- to five-second wait-time (the mean was one second) resulted in increases in length of student response, number of unsolicited but appropriate responses, and frequency of student questions.

- *Stages of Reasoning.* Karplus, Karplus, Formisano, and Paulsen (1977) suggested that Piaget's notions of child development had instructional utility, and maintained that children moved from concrete to formal operations based on four contributing factors: maturation, experience with physical environment, social transmission, and mental equilibration. He created the concept of the three stages of the learning cycle: (1) exploration, when students gain experience with environment and objects; (2) concept introduction, the process of social transmission; and (3) concept application, when students apply new concept to additional situations.

- *The Myth of Equality in Science Classrooms.* Drawing on data from 1976–77 NAEP surveys of students' attitudes toward science, Kahle and Lakes (1983) documented that as girls move from middle to high school, they report fewer classroom and extracurricular activities in science and increased negative attitudes toward science and science-related careers. This prompted changes in classroom instruction, including the introduction of female scientist role models and changes in teacher and parent expectations.

- *The Role of Target Students in the Science Classroom.* Tobin and Gallagher (1987) established that a few targeted students in classes asked most of the questions, were chosen by teachers to tackle sophisticated questions, and often received elaborate feedback from teachers compared with the vast majority of other students. They were also among the first in science education to employ naturalistic research using precise operational definitions and a mixture of qualitative and quantitative methods.

- *Physics Students' Epistemologies and Views About Knowing and Learning.* Roth and Roychoudhury (1994) asserted that students viewed science as having three aspects: a mathematical aspect and conceptual aspect, both transmitted by textbooks, and an experimental aspect rooted in everyday and laboratory experience. They maintained that students constructed personal knowledge about this world, and with it they constructed the intellectual worlds that they inhabited. Their work extended our understanding of the constructivist model of learning and how students' misconceptions must be addressed in the science classroom.

ENGAGE IN SCIENTIFIC RESEARCH

A Google search on summer science teacher research opportunities will yield many options. Summer institutes are very popular. They run from a few weeks to an entire summer, and are offered by a variety of discipline-based as well as education-related organizations. Check for the application deadlines, eligibility, and availability of fellowship programs and stipends. There may be university credit or professional development units from your school district available to teachers for their participation. Two examples of these programs are the Columbia University Summer Research Program for Science Teachers (www.scienceteacher program.org) and the Search for Extraterrestrial Intelligence (SETI) Astrobiology Summer Science Experience for Teachers (www.seti.org/epo/asset). Take pictures and share your research experiences with your students!

CONSIDER NATIONAL BOARD CERTIFICATION

The National Board for Professional Teaching Standards (NBPTS) Certification was started in 1987 as a way to assess and document experienced teachers. The creators of the National Board first drafted a set of core principles detailing what experienced and successful teachers should know and be able to do. These core principles are the foundation for the National Board Standards. The process of becoming a National Board–certified teacher requires teachers to submit four portfolio entries: three that are classroom-based, including written lesson plans, video recording of teaching, examples of student work, and extensive written reflections; and one that relates to accomplishments outside the classroom that have impacted student learning. In addition, teachers complete a timed written assessment aimed at evaluating content knowledge. You may learn more about this certification process at www.nbpts.org.

KEEP AN OPEN AND ACTIVE MIND

When you give your students ownership of their learning, you stay open and active yourself. New events and ideas are going to come along every day—that is the very nature of science. Science is contemporary and dynamic. The new events and ideas may confirm or conflict with your thoughts and beliefs or the accepted thoughts and beliefs in your geographic region. These insights and interactions also are essential aspects of science. We strongly encourage you to be alert to change and continue your own learning along with your students.

What and how you teach now will not be the same throughout your teaching career. New discoveries will be made, and new resources developed. With each new political administration, you can anticipate a change in focus that will become part of your state, school, and classroom. The changes will require time for implementation.

When you get involved at your school, in your school district, and at the state level of education, you become a part of the future of education. You will know that you have played a vital role in the future of education whether it is teaching in the classroom, voting on textbook adoptions, developing curriculum, refining academic standards, creating instructional materials, or participating in some other educational activity. Your contributions will be welcomed.

BECOME THE TEACHER YOU ALWAYS WANTED TO BE . . .

Deep inside you is the teacher you always wanted to be. Now is the time to fulfill those plans. There are many different kinds of teacher knowledge (Shulman, 1987) that you will develop throughout your career. We leave you with these final secrets to success:

Tell your personal history. Talk about your past experiences. Your students want to hear about you. Share the discoveries you've made that will help them to become inquisitive learners and solid citizens. Sharing about yourself will be inspiration to both your students and to you.

Take some risks. Act spontaneously and enhance your teaching. When you learn more about the world, you learn more about yourself and have more to offer your students. Teaching is both a journey *and* a destination.

Teach in the moment. Life *is* science so teach about it when it happens. Events may occur in the school or community, across the country, or around the world that you will want to bring into your classroom as they happen. Stay alert and try not to miss these teachable moments.

Take care of yourself. Pace yourself throughout the school year so you are competent, confident, and ready, both in and out of the classroom. You want to be healthy and hearty in mind, body, and spirit.

Think about your dreams and desires realistically. Set goals and identify the steps and resources you need and want to reach them. Dreams are fulfilled by chance and by choice. Celebrate successes along the way.

You *will* become the science teacher you always wanted to be. Best wishes for success in your classroom!

Resources

A. Science Safety Checklist

B. Science Textbook Evaluation Tool

C. Detailed Lesson Plan Guide

D. Abbreviated Lesson Plan Guide

E. Curriculum Evaluation Guide for Science

Resource A: Science Safety Checklist

Science Classroom Safety Checklist	
Upkeep of Laboratory and Equipment	• Conduct semester inspections of safety and first aid equipment and replace items as needed. • Do not use defective equipment.
Record Keeping	• Maintain records on teacher and staff safety training. • Maintain records of laboratory incidents.
Safety and Emergency Procedures	• At the beginning of each semester, orient students on the location and use of all safety and emergency equipment. Revisit applicable safety procedures and equipment prior to laboratory activities. • Post safety procedures to follow in the event of an emergency/accident. • Memorize and post the location of, and how to use, the cutoff switches and valves for the water, gas, and electricity in the laboratory. • Identify the location of all safety and emergency equipment, including the safety shower, eyewash, first-aid kit, fire blanket, fire extinguishers, and mercury spill kits. • Post emergency phone numbers near the phone and doorways. • Conduct appropriate safety and evacuation drills on a regular basis. • Explain in detail to students the consequences of violating safety rules and procedures.
Maintenance of Chemicals	• Conduct inspections of chemicals each semester. • Update and post the chemical inventory with each major purchase. • Provide a copy of the chemical inventory to the local emergency responders, such as the fire department or police. • Keep food and drink separate from all chemicals. • Store chemicals in their original containers in a locked facility with limited access. • Make sure all chemicals and reagents are labeled. • Do not store chemicals on the lab bench, on the floor, or in the laboratory chemical hood. • Consult the labels and the Material Safety Data Sheets for disposal information, and follow appropriate chemical disposal regulations.

Science Classroom Safety Checklist	
Preparing for Laboratory Activities	• Review potential hazards of the chemicals and reagents before using them in laboratory experiments. • Inspect all equipment/apparatus in the laboratory before use. • Review safety concerns and potential hazards related to the laboratory work that students will be performing before starting the work. Document in lesson plan book.
Ensuring Appropriate Laboratory Conduct	• Model good safety conduct for students. • Require students to wear appropriate personal protective equipment (i.e., chemical splash goggles, laboratory aprons or coats, and gloves). • Enforce all safety rules and procedures at all times. • Never leave students unsupervised in the laboratory. • Never allow unauthorized visitors to enter the laboratory. • Never allow students to take chemicals out of the laboratory. • Never permit smoking, food, beverages, or gum in the laboratory.

Source: Adapted from the National Institute for Occupational Safety and Health (2006).

Resource B: Science Textbook Evaluation Tool

Rate each item based on a score of "5" being high and "1" being low. Mark "0" for items not observed. Space is provided at the end for comments.

ITEM	RATING and COMMENT 5 high; 1 low; 0 not observed
Overall organization	
Coverage of state-specific standards	
Visually appealing layout	
Diversity of people's contributions	
Multiple perspectives on issues	
Diversity of people in photographs	
Connections to students' lives	
Science process skills	
Habits of mind	
Science themes	
Variety of activities	
Graphs, charts, and pictorial representations	
Chapter overview	
Headings to divide sections	
Variety of assessments	
Rich narrative	
Key terms highlighted	
Definitions or context cues for difficult words	
Controlled vocabulary	
Clear directions for lab activities	

ITEM	RATING and COMMENT 5 high; 1 low; 0 not observed
End-of-chapter summary	
Technology extensions	
Career connections	
History of science references	
Glossary	
Appendix features, such as classification, metric system, periodic table, using the microscope	
Index	
OVERALL RATING	

ADDITIONAL NOTES:

Resource C: Detailed Lesson Plan Guide

Lesson Plan Guide (Detailed)	
1. Title of Lesson	Catchy name that describes the desired knowledge, skills, and attitudes
2. Goal	General outcome that students will have at the end of the lesson, unit, and school year; frequently aligned with the unit theme and national and state standards
3. Objective(s)	Specific outcome(s) that students will demonstrate at the end of the lesson, usually stated as, "The learner will . . ."; these frequently align with the unit topic issues and district scope and sequence academic expectations
4. Inquiry Question	Prompt to help you set the tone and begin the learning; models an investigative approach that is curious and constructivist

5. Preparation	Detailed descriptions of:
	
	(1) Schema activation
	
	(2) Supplies and materials
	
	(3) Time and space
	
	(4) Anticipatory set and motivation
	
	(5) Accommodations and modifications for:
	
	    (a) English language learners
	    (b) gifted and talented students
	    (c) special education students
	    (d) individual instruction of any kind
	
	(6) Connections to life, living, and the community

6. Procedures	Steps for completing this lesson; usually these are stated as "The teacher will . . ." balanced with "The student will . . ." Be sure to include concrete examples, yet allow for individual expression regarding learning and outcomes.
7. Integration	Ideas for connecting this particular learning experience with language arts, math, social studies, health, technology, and fine arts
8. Vocabulary	Key words to emphasize during this learning experience
9. Guided Practice	Activities students complete in class with the guidance of the teacher so the teacher can ensure that all students understand expectations

Lesson Plan Guide (Detailed)	
10. Independent Practice	Activities students complete either independently in class or outside of class to practice and apply the new learning
11. Closure	Revisiting and recapping the highlights of the learning processes and lesson outcomes with students at the end of the lesson, followed by time for notes and announcements; do not let the ringing of a bell become closure!
12. Assessment	Entry-level, progress monitoring, and summative, emphasizing performance-based demonstrations showing the extent to which each student has acquired and mastered the objectives
13. Evaluation	Reflection upon the effectiveness of the overall learning experience, student engagement and outcomes, and teaching

Resource D: Abbreviated Lesson Plan Guide

Lesson Plan Guide (Abbreviated)	
1. Objectives	1. The learner will . . .
2. Standards	2. To fulfill . . .
3. Preparations	3. Using . . .
4. Introduction	4. By connecting with . . .
5. Body of lesson	5. Through the following activities . . .
6. Closure	6. Summarized by . . .
7. Assessment	7. Demonstrated by . . .
8. Evaluation and reflection	8. Next time, I will . . .

Resource E: Curriculum Evaluation Guide for Science

To what extent do you implement authentic learning, maintain an academic focus, involve students in active learning, and provide articulated assessment? Always? Sometimes? Not yet? For each of these categories, there are four questions for you to answer in this self-diagnostic tool.

AUTHENTIC LEARNING			
To what extent do teaching and learning . . .	**Always**	**Sometimes**	**Not Yet**
• emanate from a problem or question that has meaning to the learner and implications for humanity?			
• provide opportunities to create or produce a product or outcome that has personal and social value?			
• provide opportunities to integrate content, processes, and context while working within a variety of cooperative learning groups?			
• extend to a real audience and genuine effect?			
ACADEMIC FOCUS			
• guide learners in acquiring, applying, and appreciating one or more science disciplines or content areas?			
• model and reinforce understanding and developing skills using critical thinking, decision making, and problem solving?			
• support learners in establishing habits of mind as well as work required to complete complex tasks and to be resourceful?			
• challenge students to learn new concepts and practices with a variety of resources and technology?			

(Continued)

(Continued)

ACTIVE LEARNING			
To what extent do teaching and learning . . .	**Always**	**Sometimes**	**Not Yet**
• dedicate significant amounts of time to conduct field-based work to complete research?			
• challenge learners to build upon their individual learning styles and strengths while nurturing weaker areas?			
• include real investigations and use a variety of methods, media, and resources during experiments?			
• connect classroom experiences with the community in ways that are positive and useful?			
ARTICULATED ASSESSMENT			
• align assessments with educational objectives?			
• include entry-level, progress monitoring, and summative assessments?			
• provide rubrics and scoring guides to orient the learner?			
• involve participation by both teacher and learner in setting the criteria related to the processes, products, and outcomes?			
• expect reflection by both teacher and learner relative to the processes, products, and outcomes?			
• provide for learners to demonstrate their achievement in a variety of ways?			

Identify the areas you feel need strengthening. Reflect on your own or with others to develop an action plan that identifies specific objectives, resources, and a time line.

Readings and References

Abramson, L. (2007). *Sputnik left legacy for U.S. Science Education.* National Public Radio (NPR). Retrieved November 11, 2008, from http://www.npr.org/templates/story/story.php?storyId=14829195.

Aikenhead, G. (1994). What is STS science teaching? In J. Solomon & G. Aikenhead (Eds.), *STS education: International perspectives in reform.* New York: Teacher's College Press.

Aikenhead, G. (1996). Science education: Border crossing into the subculture of science. *Studies in Science Education, 27,* 1–52.

Aikenhead, G. (2001). Students' ease in crossing cultural borders into school science. *Science Education, 85*(2), 180–188.

Ainsworth, L. (2003). *Power standards: Identifying the standards that matter most.* Englewood, CO: Advanced Learning Press.

Alleman, J., & Brophy, J. (1993). Is curriculum integration a boon or a threat to social studies? *Social Education, 57*(6), 287–291.

American Association for the Advancement of Science (AAAS). (1990). *Science for All Americans Online.* Retrieved November 1, 2008, from http://www.project2061.org/publications/sfaa/default.htm.

American Association for the Advancement of Science (AAAS). (1993, 2008). Benchmarks [Online]. Retrieved November 1, 2008, from http://www.project2061.org/publications/bsl/default.htm.

Armstrong, T. (1994). *Multiple intelligences in the classroom.* Alexandria, VA: Association for Supervision and Curriculum Development.

Ausubel, D. P. (1963). *The psychology of meaningful learning.* New York: Grune & Stratton.

Banister, S., Ross, C., & Vannatta, R. (2008). The impact of Web 2.0 tools in the reading classroom. In C. Crawford et al. (Eds.), *Proceedings of Society for Information Technology and Teacher Education International Conference 2008* (pp. 3617–3621). Chesapeake, VA: AACE.

Beyer, B. K. (1995). *Critical thinking.* Bloomington, IN: Phi Delta Kappan Educational Foundation.

Bloom, B. (1984). *Taxonomy of educational objectives, book 1.* White Plains, NY: Longman.

Bol, L., & Strange, A. (1996). The contradiction between teachers' instructional goals and their assessment practices in high school biology courses. *Science Education, 80*(2), 145–163.

Bonnstetter, R. (1998). Inquiry: Learning from the past with an eye on the future. *Electronic Journal of Science Education, 3,* 1.

Borich, G. D., & Tombari, M. L. (2004). *Educational assessment for the elementary and middle school classroom* (2nd ed.). Upper Saddle River, NJ: Pearson Education.

Brogan, B. R., & Brogan, W. A. (1995). The Socratic questioner: Teaching and learning in a dialogical classroom. *Educational Forum, 59*(3), 288–296.

Brunner, J. (1959). *The process of education.* Cambridge, MA: Harvard University Press.

Butin, D. (2000). *Science facilities.* Washington, DC: National Clearinghouse for Educational Facilities (NCEF). Retrieved November 11, 2008, from http://www.edfacilities.org/pubs/pubs_html.cfm?abstract=science.

Bybee, R., & Fuchs, B. (2006). Preparing the 21st century workforce: A new reform in science and technology education. *Journal of Research in Science Teaching, 43*(4), 349–352.

Callahan, J. F., Clark, L. H., & Kellough, R. D. (1998). *Teaching in the middle and secondary schools* (6th ed.). Upper Saddle River, NJ: Prentice Hall.

Carmine, L., & Carmine, D. (2004). The interaction of reading skills and science content knowledge when teaching struggling secondary students. *Reading & Writing Quarterly, 20*(2), 203–218.

Cattani, D. H. (2002). *A classroom of her own: How new teachers develop instructional, professional, and cultural competence.* Thousand Oaks, CA: Corwin Press.

Cavanaugh, C., & Cavanaugh, T. W. (2004). *Teach science with science fiction films: A guide for teachers and media specialists.* Columbus, OH: Linworth.

Chiappetta, E., & Fillman, D. (2007). Analysis of five high school biology textbooks used in the United States for inclusion of the nature of science. *International Journal of Science Education, 29*(15), 1847–1868.

Colwell, R. (2008). Silent Sputnik. *BioScience, 58*(1), 3.

Costa, A. (1991). The inquiry strategy. In A. Costa (Ed.), *Developing minds: A resource book for teaching* (pp. 302–303). Alexandria, VA: Association for Supervision and Curriculum Development.

Costa, V. (1993a). School science as a rite of passage: A new frame for familiar problems. *Journal of Research in Science Teaching, 30*(7), 649–668.

Costa, V. (1993b). The use of a course question to facilitate learning: How does chemistry impact my personal life and society? *Journal of College Science Teaching, XXIII*(1), 49–53.

Costa, V. (1995). When science is "another world": Relationships between worlds of family, friends, school, and science. *Science Education, 79*(3), 313–333.

Costa, A., & Kallick, B. (2000). *Discovering and exploring habits of mind* (book 1 of 4). Alexandria, VA: Association for Supervision and Curriculum Development.

Crick, F. (1988). *What mad pursuit: A personal view of scientific discovery.* New York: Basic Books.

Crouch, C. H., & Mazur, E. (2001). Peer instruction: Ten years of experience and results. *The Physics Teacher, 69*(9), 970–977.

Curie, M. (1921). *The discovery of radium, address by Madame M. Curie at Vassar College, May 14, 1921,* Ellen S. Richards Monographs No. 2, Poughkeepsie, NY: Vassar College.

Danielson, C. (1996). *Enhancing professional practice: A framework for teaching.* Alexandria, VA: Association for Supervision and Curriculum Development.

Dils, L. (1997). Science fiction and the future. In *Yale-New Haven Teachers Institute, Volume II.* www.yale.edu/ynhti/curriculum/guides/1987/2/87.02.04.x.html.

Dong, Y. R. (2004/2005). Getting at the content. *Educational Leadership, 62*(4), 14–19.

Dubeck, L. W., Moshier, S. E., & Boss, J. F. (2003). *Fantastic voyages: Learning science through science fiction films.* New York: Springer-Verlag.

Echevarria, J., Vogt, M., & Short, D. J. (2005). *Making content comprehensible for English learners: The SIOP model* (2nd ed.). Boston: Pearson Allyn and Bacon.

Epstein, J. (1997). *School, family, and community partnerships: Your handbook for action.* Thousand Oaks, CA: Corwin Press.

Evans, R., Newmann, F., & Saxe, D. (1996). Defining issues-centered education. In R. Evans & D. Saxe (Eds.), *Handbook on teaching social issues,* NCSS bulletin 93 (pp. 1–5). Washington, DC: National Council for the Social Studies.

Fensham, P. J., & Kass, H. (1988). Inconsistent or discrepant events in science instruction. *Studies in Science Education, 15*(1), 1–16.

Fine, M. (1995). *Habits of mind: Struggling over values in America's classrooms*. San Francisco: Jossey-Bass.

Firooznia, F. (2006). Giant ants and walking plants. *Journal of College Science Teaching, 35*(5), 26–31.

Flick, L., & Lederman, N. (2004). *Scientific inquiry and nature of science: Implications for teaching learning, and teacher education*. New York: Springer.

Framework for 21st Century Learning. (2004). Tucson, AZ: Partnership for 21st Century Skills.

Gallagher, S. (1995). Implementing problem-based learning in science classrooms. *School Science and Mathematics, 95*(3), 136–146.

Gallavan, N. P. (1997). Achieving civic competence through a DRAFT writing process. *Social Studies and the Young Learner, 10*(2), 14–16.

Gallavan, N. P. (in press). *Strengthening social studies education: Purposes, concepts, and strategies for middle school teachers and students*. Columbus, OH: Prentice Hall.

Gardner, H. (1983). *Frames of mind*. New York: Basic Books.

Garfield, E. (1980). *Essays of an information scientist, Vol. 4*, 488–493. Retrieved October 31, 2008, from http://www.garfield.library.upenn.edu/essays.html.

Grahame, K. (1992 [1913]). *Wind in the Willows*. New York: Viking.

Greenwald, N. L. (2000). Learning from problems. *The Science Teacher, 67*(4), 28–32.

Hawkins, D. (1974). *The informed vision: Essays on learning and human nature*. New York: Agathon.

Hazen, R. (2002). Why should you be scientifically literate? *American Institute of Biological Sciences*. Retrieved November 11, 2008, from http://www.actionbioscience.org/newfrontiers/hazen.html.

Hess, D. (2005). How do teachers' political views influence teaching about controversial issues? *Social Education, 69*(1), 47–48.

Hinrichsen, J., & Jarrett, G. (1999). *Science inquiry for the classroom: A literature review*. Portland, OR: Northwest Regional Educational Laboratory.

Hoge, J. D., Field, S. L., Foster, S. J., & Nickell, P. (2004). *Real-world investigations for studies: Inquiries for middle and high school students based on the ten NCSS standards*. Upper Saddle River, NJ: Prentice Hall.

Hole, S., & McEntee, G. H. (1999). Reflection is at the heart of practice. *Educational Leadership, 56*(8), 34–37.

Holliday, W. (2003). Influential research in science teaching: 1963–present. *Journal of Research in Teaching Science, 40*(S1), v–x.

Howe, N., & Strauss, W. (2000). *Millennials rising: The next great generation*. New York: Vintage.

Independent Scientific Contributions. (2007). Institute for Neurological Research. Retrieved November 11, 2008, from http://www.nrimed.com/scientists.html.

Johnson, D. W., & Johnson, R. T. (1989). *Cooperation and competition: Theory and research*. Edina, MN: Interaction Book Company.

Jonson, K. (2008). *Being an effective mentor: How to help beginning teachers succeed* (2nd ed.). Thousand Oaks, CA: Corwin Press.

Joyce, B., & Weil, M. (2003). *Model of teachings* (7th ed.). Boston: Allyn & Bacon.

Karplus, R., Karplus, E., Formisano, M., & Paulsen, A. (1977). A survey of proportional reasoning and control of variables in seven countries. *Journal of Research in Science Teaching, 14*(5), 411–417.

Kahle, J., & Lakes, M. (1983). The myth of equality in science classrooms. *Journal of Research in Science Teaching, 40*(S1), 58–67.

Kesson, K. (2004). Doing "Good Science": On the virtues of simply messing about. *Paths of Learning, 20*, 14–19.

Kottler, E., & Gallavan, N. P. (2007). *Secrets to success for beginning elementary school teachers*. Thousand Oaks, CA: Corwin Press.

Kottler, E., Kottler, J. A., & Kottler, C. J. (2004). *Secrets for secondary school teachers; How to succeed in your first year* (2nd ed.). Thousand Oaks, CA: Corwin Press.

Kottler, E., Kottler, J. A., & Street, C. (2008). *English language learners in your classroom: Strategies that work.* Thousand Oaks, CA: Corwin Press.

Krashen, S. (1996). *The natural approach: Language acquisition in the classroom* (Rev. Ed.). Englewood Cliffs, NJ: Prentice Hall.

Learning for the 21st century: A report and mile guide for 21st century skills. (2003). Tucson, AZ: Partnership for 21st Century Skills.

Manning, M., Manning, G., & Long, R. (1994). *Theme immersion: Inquiry-based curriculum in elementary and middle schools.* Portsmouth, NH: Heinemann.

Manzo, A., & Manzo, U. (1990). *Content area reading: A heuristic approach.* New York: Merrill.

Manzo, A., Manzo, U., & Estes, T. (2001). *Content area literacy: Interactive teaching for active learning* (3rd ed.). New York: Wiley.

Marx, R., & Harris, C. (2006). No Child Left Behind and science education: Opportunities, challenges, and risks. *The Elementary School Journal, 106*(5), 455–466.

Marzano, R. J., Marzano, J. S., & Pickering, D. J. (2003). *Classroom management that works: Research-based strategies for every teacher.* Alexandria, VA: Association for Supervision and Curriculum Development.

Marzano, R., Pickering, D. J., & Pollock, J. E. (2001). *Classroom instruction that works: Research-based strategies for increasing student achievement.* Alexandria, VA: Association for Supervision and Curriculum Development.

McCarthy, B. (1997). *4MAT course book* (Vol.1, p. 61). Barrington, IL: EXCEL Inc.

Molebash, P., & Dodge, B. (2003). Kickstarting inquiry with Webquests and Web inquiry projects. *Social Education, 67*(3), 158–161.

A nation at risk: The imperative for educational reform. (1983). Washington, DC: National Commission on Educational Excellence (NCEE). Retrieved November 11, 2008, from http://www.ed.gov/pubs/NatAtRisk/title.html.

The National Academies. (2005, August 9). US high school science lab experiences often poor, but research points way to improvements. *Science Daily.* Retrieved October 21, 2007, from http://www.sciencedaily.com/releases/2005/08/050809065445.htm.

National Research Council (2000). *Inquiry and the National Science Education Standards: A guide for teaching and learning.* Washington, DC: National Academy Press.

National Educational Technology Standards for Students (NETS-S). (2007). Washington, DC: International Society of Technology Education.

National Educational Technology Standards for Teachers (NETS-T). (2008). Washington, DC: International Society of Technology Education.

National Science Education Standards (NSES). (1995). Washington, DC: National Academy of Sciences. Retrieved November 11, 2008, from http://www.nap.edu/readingroom/books/nses.

National Science Teachers Association (NSTA). (1990). *Science/technology/society: A new effort for providing appropriate science for all.* NSTA position statement. Retrieved November 11, 2008, from http://www.nsta.org/about/positions/sts.aspx.

National Science Teachers Association (NSTA). (1999a). *Science competitions.* NSTA position statement. Retrieved November 11, 2008, from http://www.nsta.org/about/positions/competitions.aspx.

National Science Teachers Association (NSTA). (1999b). *The use of computers in science education.* NSTA position statement. Retrieved November 11, 2008, from http://www.nsta.org/about/positions/computers.aspx.

National Science Teachers Association (NSTA). (2003). *Beyond 2000—teachers of science speak out.* NSTA position statement. Retrieved November 11, 2008, from http://www.nsta.org/about/positions/beyond2000.aspx.

National Science Teachers Association (NSTA). (2007). *The integral role of laboratory investigations in science instruction.* NSTA position statement. Retrieved November 11, 2008, from http://www.nsta.org/about/positions/laboratory.aspx.

National Science Teachers Association (NSTA). (2008). *Responsible use of live animals and dissection in the science classroom.* NSTA position statement. Retrieved November 11, 2008, from http://www.nsta.org/about/positions/animals.aspx.

Newmann, F. M. (1990). Higher order thinking in teaching social studies: A rationale for the assessment of classroom thoughtfulness. *Journal of Curriculum Studies, 22*, 41–56.

125 questions: What don't we know. (2005, July). *Science,* Special Issue. Retrieved November 11, 2008, from http://www.sciencemag.org/sciext/125th.

Parker, W. C. (2005). *Social studies in elementary education.* Upper Saddle River, NJ: Prentice Hall.

Philosophical Transactions of the Royal Society. (1671, February 19). Volume 80, 3075–3087.

Piaget, J. (1964). Part I: Cognitive development in children: Piaget development and learning. *Journal of Research in Science Teaching, 2*(3), 176–186.

Pimentel, G., & Coonrod, J. (1987). *Opportunities in chemistry: Today and tomorrow.* Washington, DC: National Academies Press.

Portner, H. (2008). *Mentoring new teachers* (3rd ed.). Thousand Oaks, CA: Corwin Press.

Prensky, M. (2001a). Digital natives, digital immigrants. *On the Horizon, 9*(5), 1–6.

Prensky, M. (2001b). Digital natives, digital immigrants, part 2: Do they really think differently? *On the Horizon, 9*(6), 1–6.

Pultorak, E. G. (1993). Facilitating reflective thought in novice teachers. *Journal of Teacher Education, 44*(4), 288–295.

Readence, J. E., Bean, T. W., & Baldwin, R. S. (1998). Prereading strategies—anticipation guides. In J. E. Readence, T. W. Bean, & R. S. Baldwin, *Content area literacy: An integrated approach* (6th ed., pp. 159–161). Dubuque, IA: Kendall/Hunt.

Rising above the gathering storm: Energizing and employing America for a brighter economic future. (2007). Washington, DC: Committee on Science, Engineering, and Public Policy (COSEPUP).

Roth, W.-M., & Roychoudhury, A. (1994). Physics students' epistemologies and views about knowing and learning. *Journal of Research in Science Teaching, 31*(1), 5–30.

Rowe, M. (1974). Reflections on wait-time: Some methodological questions. *Journal of Research in Science Teaching, 11*(3), 263–279.

Salpeter, J. (2003). 21st century skills: Will our students be prepared? *Technology and Learning, 24*(3). Retrieved November 11, 2008, from http://www.techlearning.com/showArticle.php?articleID=15202090.

Sayer, A. (1975). *Rosalind Franklin and DNA.* New York: Norton.

Schacter, J. (1999). *The impact of education technology on student achievement: What the most current research has to say.* Santa Monica, CA: Milken Exchange on Education Technology.

Schmoker, M. (2006). *Results now.* Alexandria, VA: Association for Supervision and Curriculum Development.

Schön, D. A. (1983). *The reflective practitioner: How professionals think in action.* New York: Basic Books.

School Chemistry Laboratory Safety Guide. (2006). Washington, DC: National Institute for Occupational Safety and Health. Retrieved November 11, 2008, from http://www.cdc.gov/niosh/docs/2007-107/pdfs/2007-107.pdf.

Scieska, J. (2004). *Science verse.* New York: Viking Juvenile.

Science Framework for California Public Schools, Kindergarten through Grade 12. (2004). Sacramento, CA: California Department of Education. May also be accessed at http://www.cde.ca.gov/re/pn/fd/documents/science-framework-pt1.

The Science of Star Trek. (1995). Television Documentary. A & E Television Network.

Sheltered Instruction Observation Protocol. (2005). The SIOP Institute. Retrieved June 28, 2006, from http://www.siopinstitute.net.

Shermis, S. S. (1992). *Critical thinking: Helping students learn reflectively.* Bloomington, IN: ERIC Clearinghouse of Reading and Communication Skills.

Short, D., & Echevarria, J. (2004/2005). Teaching skills to support English language learners. *Educational Leadership, 62*(4), 9–13.

Shulman, L. S. (1987). Knowledge and teaching: Foundations of the new reform. *Harvard Educational Review, 57*, 1–22.

Siegfried, T. (2005). In praise of hard questions. *Science, 309*(5731), 76–77.

Singleton, R. L. (2006). Preparing teachers to use simulations. *Trainers Times, 10*(1), 3–4.

Slavin, R. (1995). *Cooperative learning: Research, theory, and practice* (2nd ed.). Boston: Allyn & Bacon.

Stiggins, R. (2005). *Student-involved assessment FOR learning* (4th ed.). Upper Saddle River, NJ: Merrill Prentice Hall.

Street, C. (2002). The P.O.W.E.R. of process writing in content area classrooms. *Journal of Content Area Reading, 1*, 43–54.

Strong, W. (2006). *Write for insight: Empowering content area learning, Grades 6–12.* Boston: Pearson Education.

Taba, H. (1962). *Curriculum development: Theory and practice.* New York: Harcourt Brace.

Thompson, F., & Logue, S. (2006). An exploration of common student misconceptions in science. *International Education Journal, 7*(4), 553–559.

Tobias, S. (1990). *They're not dumb, they're different.* Tucson, AZ: Research Corporation.

Tobin, K., & Gallagher, J. (1987). The role of target students in the science classroom. *Journal of Research in Science Teaching, 24*(1), 61–75.

Tomlinson, C. (1999). *The differentiated classroom: Responding to the needs of all learners.* Alexandria, VA: Association for Supervision and Curriculum Development.

Tomlinson, C. A., & McTighe, J. (2006). *Integrating differentiated instruction and understanding by design: Connecting content and kids.* Alexandria, VA: Association for Supervision and Curriculum Development.

Van Manen, M. (1977). Linking ways of knowing with ways of being practical. *Curriculum Inquiry, 6*, 205–228.

Wallis, C., & Steptoe, S. (2006, December 18). How to bring our schools out of the 20th century. *Time*, 50–56.

Watson, J. (1968). *The double helix: A personal account of the discovery of the structure of DNA.* New York: Atheneum.

Wiggins, G., & McTighe, J. (1998). *Understanding by design.* Alexandria, VA: Association for Supervision and Curriculum Development.

Wiggins, G., & McTighe, J. (2005). *Understanding by design* (expanded 2nd ed.). Upper Saddle River, NJ: Pearson Education.

Wright, B. (1994). *The real Mother Goose.* New York: Cartwheel.

Yeager, R. (1996). *Science/technology/society as reform in science education.* New York: SUNY Press.

Yildirim, A. (2003). Instructional planning in a centralized school system: Lessons of a study among primary school teachers in Turkey. *International Review of Education, 49*(5), 525–543.

Ziechner, M. K., & Liston, D. P. (1987). Teaching student teachers to reflect. *Harvard Educational Review, 57*(1), 23–48.

Zinsser, W. (1988). *Writing to learn.* New York: Harper & Row.

Index

CORWIN

A SAGE Company

The Corwin logo—a raven striding across an open book—represents the union of courage and learning. Corwin is committed to improving education for all learners by publishing books and other professional development resources for those serving the field of PreK–12 education. By providing practical, hands-on materials, Corwin continues to carry out the promise of its motto: **"Helping Educators Do Their Work Better."**